SAFARI JEMA

*A Journey of Love and Adventure from Casablanca
to Cape Town*

TERESA O'KANE

ISBN: 1463741790
ISBN 13: 9781463741792

Haraka-haraka, haina Baraka
Hurry-hurry has no blessings.

DEDICATION

For Scott, of course. Without his enthusiasm and infectious sense of adventure, I would never have given Africa a second chance.

For Martha O'Kane who taught me all the important things I needed to know.

For Cyndy who said, "Tell me a story about Africa!"

And for my brother Mike who would have liked this.

Table of Contents

A NOTE

Just after my twenty-third birthday, my husband and I enrolled in a Mediterranean studies program offered through Eastern Michigan University. We had on-site lectures at historic locations all around the Mediterranean: at the Roman coliseum in the ancient city of Carthage, outside the Temple of Karnak in Luxor, among the ruins of the Acropolis in Athens, at the Oracle of Delphi, atop Masada in Israel, and literally in the shadow of a pyramid in Egypt. In Tunisia, we bumped across the desert for eight tortuous hours in a rusty Land Rover. I remember it even today as one of the hottest and most painful experiences of my life. In Egypt I was briefly held captive by a horseman, incapacitated by food poisoning, and again, nearly taken down by the heat. Several years later my husband suggested we return to Africa. Recalling my impressions of Tunisia and Egypt and thinking that all of Africa would be the same, I said, "No thank you! No more sand and tummy rumbles for me!"

It took fourteen years before he finally convinced me that the rest of Africa was nothing like the north of Africa. We loaded our backpacks, leased out our house, and spent four months in East, Central, and Southern Africa. I cried when we had to leave. Not because of sand and heat exhaustion but because Africa had filled my heart. I was surprised how often I was brought to tears by scenes of struggle and hardship, and even more so by those of joy and hope. I thought about all the things I had taken for granted at home—things such as education, and nourishment, and success, and knew that if ever I wanted more of those things all I had to do was work harder.

Such is not the case in much of Africa. Returns on hard work are sometimes completely erased by drought, disease, famine, war, over-population, politics, or corruption. Cause and effect are rapid. Locust invasion equals drought and famine. War equals displacement. Much of the time disease results in death. These destroyers of security and comfort occur with such regularity in sub-Saharan Africa, it's as if they have their own season.

On a particularly dreadful day in West Africa after witnessing massive crop destruction caused by a swarm of locusts, I wrote to my mom, "It seems Africa cannot get a break." Though my mom wasn't raised in Africa, she understood hardship. Born on a farm in rural Kansas, she and six sisters worked alongside her father and three brothers in the fields. Before dawn each morning she milked the cows and separated the cream before walking several miles to a one-room schoolhouse. The family shared one book, a German Bible. They made their own clothes and canned their own food. Mom said, "We girls had to work like men in the fields. We not only had to do all the jobs that the boys did, we also did all the cooking, cleaning, canning, and sewing too." After the harvest it was Mom's job to drive the horses, wagon piled high with grain, to the train depot. Disease and illness weren't uncommon. One brother died from scarlet fever. Another had polio. Mom sometimes told my brothers and me her stories of growing up on the farm in Kansas as we stood on chairs rinsing and drying dishes after dinner in the kitchen of our modest home in Northern California. The night she taught us "Button, button! Who has the button?" where one person hides a button and everyone else looks for it was the night we learned she grew up without toys. Her dolls were barn cats that she attired in handmade outfits. "Getting them dressed was always the hardest part!" she said emphatically. For recreation they played Kick the Can or "ran and jumped."

In a moment of nine-year-old innocence or idiocy, I said to my mom one evening, "You were so lucky to live in Kansas! I would love to live on a farm with lots of animals and nothing but fields surrounding me."

With a look of sudden exhaustion or incredulity Mom said, "Oh honey, you don't know what you are saying! It was just hard work on top of hard work. It was always one step forward and two steps back. My mother worked herself into an early grave. My father worried himself sick. It was windy, and dusty, and just *hard*. We spent a lot of our time hoping and praying it would get easier." After a pause she added, "But it was a good life, a good upbringing." Huh? How could it be hard *and* good? I didn't get it.

Years later, after spending a total of over two years in Africa, I understood what my mom meant. All over Africa I encountered men and women who felt blessed by life despite how hard it was and I learned that hope is possibly the most powerful of all human emotions. I was glad that my mom and I could share the understanding that hardship needn't always displace contentment. In one phone call home I described how African women gathered together after hours of backbreaking work revived and nourished in community and friendship and knew that Mom could empathize. "I never experienced poverty such as you describe in Africa, but the day to day life, and the hope for a better one, I can relate to that," she said.

So if Africa is so hard why am I drawn to her? Because it is so *real*. Expressions of joy, adversity, love, exhaustion, anticipation, curiosity, hope—every emotion imaginable is transparent and undeniable. There is no pretense. Asking someone, "How are you?" is rarely necessary. The answer is boldly written in body language and on faces: I am glad, I am tired, I am sick, I am full of hope, I am so joyful I have to sing and dance about it.

More than thirty years ago my husband and I chose to live a life of adventure and discovery. Learning something new each time I travel makes me feel like a kid again. Seeing the great migration for the first time in the Masai Mara National Reserve, walking with lions,

watching baby elephants romp at a water hole, canoeing amongst hippos on the Zambezi River, flying over Victoria Falls, drifting through
the Okavango Delta in a dugout canoe, and getting a chance to be
close to nature are reasons enough to make me want to return to Africa
again and again. That I get to do this with my best friend is the icing
on the cake. But the reason I most love Africa is because of my mom.
Most Africans have the same character traits of hard work, hope, grace,
and genuineness that emanated from my mom. When I am in Africa,
I feel at home.

PART 1
THE DREAM

MEAT IS MEAT

Victoria Falls roared nearby while Scott watched a tourist leap from the bridge between Zimbabwe and Zambia and disappear into the abyss over the Zambezi River. He couldn't bring himself to actually lean over the railing because he has a fear of heights. Just standing on the bridge was enough to make his knees buckle. While he waited for the next bungee jumper to vanish from sight, he became an instant trillionaire when he bought a stack of Zimbabwean one hundred billion dollar notes from a man on the bridge. A trillion Zimbabwe dollars didn't buy much. Inflation had topped 500 million percent and a single one-hundred-billion dollar note would buy little more than a loaf of bread or a few eggs. But the billion-dollar notes had become a commodity. While President Mugabe continued to ruin an entire country, he had inadvertently created a market for Zimbabwe dollars on eBay.

Unfortunately many months later, in Thailand, our backpack was relieved of eight hundred billion dollars along with our beloved Swiss Army Knife. The knife wasn't your run-of-the-mill gadget with a blade and screwdriver. It was one I had purchased direct from the source in Switzerland. It was called The Superchamp and it had *dozens* of tools encased within its only-available-in-Switzerland black body. Not only that, engraved on its side was a personalized mushy dedication to Scott. More than a portable toolbox, its knife and corkscrew alone represented romantic picnics in the Alps and glasses of Riesling along the Seine. Somehow I think I would have mourned the loss a little less if the Superchamp were being put to use building a bridge in Africa instead of opening a can of beans in some communal kitchen of a backpacker hostel in Thailand.

Billion dollar notes aside, it was tragic what was going on in Zimbabwe. People desperately waited for something to change. There were fuel shortages, grocery store shelves were empty, and farms sat derelict. Those who were able would cross the border into Zambia each day to work—or to sell stacks of Zimbabwe dollars to travelers—before returning at night to a ruined Zimbabwe. Most Zimbabweans seemed to accept their lot with something closer to pragmatism than bitterness. We asked a taxi driver waiting for fares near the bridge how he felt about what was happening in his country and if he thought Mugabe should step down or be thrown out. He answered with a resigned shrug, "It's better to have the devil we know than one we don't."

It wasn't always like that in Zimbabwe. Until recently it was our favorite African nation. It is a physically beautiful country and we had always admired the resourcefulness of her people. As recently as 1999, Zimbabwe was still considered a breadbasket of Africa, the economy was relatively healthy, and inflation was not yet a major headline. On two previous visits we had been able to travel anywhere in the country in relative comfort and security.

During one such trip we noticed a billboard advertising "Business Days, Zimbabwe Trade Zone," from our seats on a crowded long-distance bus. As we entered the colonial city of Bulawayo, we decided it might be interesting to see how a trade show in Zimbabwe might differ from one in Silicon Valley and we made a plan to attend.

I am sure we were the only tourists there. When we arrived at the entrance they couldn't decide under what category to admit us. Finally someone handed us badges that read, "Foreign Guest," and we entered the trade show floor. Salesmen hawked furniture, crafts, and import-export opportunities from within hundreds of tents and booths. In lesser number were agents representing safari and game lodges. One lodge, located in Hwange National Park, offered trade show attendees a full board package including game drives at a place called Ganda Lodge for a price almost too good to believe. Scott gave me a look that said, "What have we got to lose?" We purchased two nights and received an official-looking voucher.

The next day we took another bus to Hwange National Park where we met Happiness, Cuthbert, Fortunate, and Boniface, all part of the Ganda Lodge staff. I wondered who they thought we were because we received the royal treatment. Soon we learned we were the first guests they had had in weeks and that we would have Ganda Lodge to ourselves. After a welcome drink of something orange and cool, we were shown a selection of two-story cottages to pick from. We quickly chose one fronting both the water hole and the swimming pool. This in turn overlooked a grassy savannah shaded by acacia and mahogany trees. In a branch of a thorn tree overhanging a second-story viewing platform, a lilac-breasted roller came to rest not two feet from where we sat. The spectacularly colored bird preened its feathers like an actress preparing for a close-up. It was the dry season at Hwange and most of the water in the holes had evaporated. Fortunately there was still water in the pond near our cottage and that was what brought thirsty animals practically to our front door.

After we settled in, the head ranger David took us on a game drive. We stopped briefly to watch zebra and giraffe grazing near the lodge, and then headed out into the bush. One hour into the game drive we stopped near a herd of some two hundred elephants. One juvenile elephant immediately performed an impressive mock charge, running at our vehicle with his ears flared out and his little trunk flailing wildly. Then while I held my breath, another young female elephant walked directly over to where I sat in the backseat of our open-topped Land Cruiser and calmly draped her trunk over my shoulder. My heart was beating so hard I thought it would leap from my chest. I sat like a statue even though my insides tingled with excitement. There was nothing I could do to stop the happy tears that ran down my cheeks.

After a few minutes of close-encounter bliss, we continued through the game park stopping again to watch a group of slow-moving impala and giraffe. The air was so hot and parched that the grasses crackled under the hooves of the animals. I felt nearly on the verge of heatstroke. I've never been one to handle the heat well anyway, and the temperature out on the savannah was pushing me to my limit. Evidently it showed because David glanced at my clammy, flushed face and asked, "Would you like to go back now?" As much as I wanted to have another close encounter with an elephant, I knew that driving around in one-hundred-degree heat in an open-top vehicle might do me in. Reluctantly I nodded at David and said, "Yes, please."

Back at the lodge we changed into swimsuits and chilled down in the icy cold pool. As we hung on to the pool's edge feeling our body temperature return to normal, we watched zebra come to the water hole and drink. Boniface brought us cold beers. It was heaven. Though attending a trade show is not something most travelers usually do, it paid off big for us. The price for the all-inclusive stay at Ganda Lodge was only fourteen dollars per person, per night. Total. For everything.

At lunch a tall and dapper African named Cuthbert whose every move conveyed style and grace served us a plentiful meal and more cold drinks on a covered terrace. Watching Cuthbert move around the terrace, I couldn't help but be reminded of the elegant giraffe we had encountered during our game drive that morning. When we finished eating, he cleared the table so effortlessly that it was as if he had just waved his hand over it and made the dishes disappear. He smiled at us more like we were guests in his home than visitors to a game lodge. "Which meat would like to have for dinner?" he asked.

"You mean we get to pick?" I asked. "What are our choices?"

"Chicken, or beef, or pork," replied Cuthbert.

"Well, chicken sounds good. We'll have the chicken," Scott answered for both of us. Cuthbert seemed a little disappointed at our choice.

After lunch David drove us back to a water hole located about forty minutes from the lodge. During our game drive we had noticed a ladder leading to an enclosed platform in a tall tree near the water and asked if we could spend the afternoon alone there.

David parked the vehicle directly under the tree so that we could safely and quickly climb to the platform. Before leaving, he handed us a small box of cold drinks and said, "Be careful, and try not to become overheated." We climbed the ladder and spent the next three hours well hidden in the leafy tree spying on elephant and antelope as they came to the water to drink.

Game viewing that afternoon was a vastly more rewarding experience because the animals were completely unaware of our presence. Perhaps they were under the influence of the heat as well, but I have never seen African animals so relaxed. Some even napped. Without half a dozen safari vehicles filled with excited tourists destroying the calmness of nature ("Marge! Did you see that? Look over there. No, over *there!* Oh, you missed it! He's gone now."), we were able to see antelope just being antelope. It was just Scott, the African bush, and me. Because it was so hot and dry at Hwange, animals naturally gravitated to the water hole so it bustled with activity. Some animals drank from the water's edge then rested in shade nearby before returning for another drink. Adult elephants stood in the pool and cooled their bodies with showers of water from their trunks while baby elephants rolled in the mud or playfully charged one another. The one behavior all the animals had in common was that they seemed reluctant to leave. So were we. When Happiness and Fortunate arrived to take us back to the lodge, it struck me that their names expressed our emotions of the day perfectly.

We were called to dinner at 7:00 p.m. Again it was a buffet with copious amounts of food, way too much for just the two of us. And there was plenty of chicken. I said to Cuthbert, "There's so much food!" and he responded, "If you eat more, you worry less." It didn't take too long for us to realize that the staff of Ganda Lodge and their families would be eating what we couldn't finish. We also understood that when there are no guests at the lodge, there are no leftovers to eat. We took small but sufficient portions of food to our table and ate while the staff watched at a distance.

From the terrace we could see impala, warthog, and giraffe come to drink. Gesturing towards the animals at the water hole, I remarked to Cuthbert, "It's so beautiful! It would be wonderful to have a meal closer to the water hole."

From the comfort of our bed the next morning, we watched more than eight hundred buffalo cross the savannah before we headed to the terrace for breakfast. Cuthbert met us at the step and swept his arm around until it pointed down to the water hole. There on the bank was a table for two beautifully set with white linen, china, and a small vase of wildflowers. "Today, you will eat breakfast at the water hole."

I burst into tears. To this day it is the most spectacular place I have ever dined.

As we finished our eggs, Cuthbert came to our table and asked, "Which meat would you like for lunch today?"

"Which meat do you recommend, Cuthbert?" Scott asked.

"Well," he said slowly. "Meat is meat." He shrugged as if it did not matter which meat was chosen. "But," he added quickly, "I don't think you care much for the chicken. I think you prefer the beef."

Scott looked over at me and smiled. "I think we prefer the beef too," he said to Cuthbert.

And that is what we all had for lunch that afternoon. There was enough beef on the luncheon buffet table to feed twenty.

After lunch Cuthbert again approached us with, "Which meat would you like for dinner?"

We smiled at him and asked, "Do we still like the beef?"

Cuthbert smiled back. "Yes, I think you like the beef most of all."

Two days later when we left Hwange, we stopped back in Bulawayo and traded facemasks and snorkels (I honestly can't remember why in the world we had facemasks and snorkels with us) and a little money for a graceful wooden giraffe. Almost six feet tall and hand carved by the seller, I named him Cuthbert.

Planning a Trip to Africa during Commercial Breaks of Jeopardy!

"What is, 'The Amazon'?" My question was directed not to my husband but to the TV screen. As *Jeopardy!* went to commercial break I mused aloud, "I wonder if we will ever travel again."

Scott looked at me but said nothing. When I saw a smile begin to creep across his face I knew he was imagining us on a beach in Thailand or trekking in Nepal. We continued to stare at each other through several commercials until I noticed Alex Trebek back on the screen. "Quick, de-mute!"

Most nights when Scott and I watch *Jeopardy!*, we compete along with the contestants and with each other. But that night, we watched the Double Jeopardy round in silence. As the returning champion waged a true daily double, I thought about the mutual passion for travel and adventure we discovered on our first date at a college dance more than thirty years prior. As our peers partied on the dance floor, we spent the evening outside by the hotel pool talking. We had the usual first date conversation: Where were you born? How many siblings do you have? etc. But we also talked about travel and exotic places we each wanted to see. He: "I want to sail around the world." Me: "I want to be independently wealthy and see every country in the world. And Disneyland!" We talked about the future and how we wanted to live our lives. Big picture things that I had never discussed on a first date.

The next morning my mom asked, "Did you have a nice time?"

"It was fun. Well, interesting." I struggled while trying to think of the words to describe Scott. "He's different. We talked about philosophy of life stuff, hopes and dreams and such. We even talked about religion." I smiled at the memory. "He said he was a Frisbiterian. He believes when he dies his soul will go up on the roof and he won't be able to get it down."

"So, he's not Catholic?" Mom said with some disappointment.

"No. He's witty!"

"Does he golf?" Dad asked hopefully, looking up from his newspaper. Dad would have approved of any beau if he knew his way around the links, Catholic or not.

"Sorry, Dad. I don't think he knows a driver from a putter."

But he was smart and handsome and wanted to see the world just like I did, so we began dating regularly despite the fact he never was an altar boy.

A few months later I became impatient to get going on the "independently wealthy" part of my dream. I left university and took a job four hundred miles away (near Disneyland!) saying to Scott as I left, "I hope I meet you again when I'm thirty because I really like you."

The next weekend, even before I was completely settled in my new digs in Los Angeles, there was a knock at my door and there, standing on the stoop, was Scott. "I thought I would come down to see you," he said with a confident smile.

"How in the world did you get here?" I asked while giving him a hug. I knew he was a starving student, and while he owned something that resembled a vehicle, it wasn't running ("at the moment," he always said). He grinned while explaining, "I made a deal with my fraternity brother that if he drove me down in his car, I would write an outline for his history paper. Guaranteed him a B," he finished proudly with a look that said, "Aren't I clever?" and "I really like you, too."

There are many examples of Scott's out-of-the-box creativity, but this was the one that made him the most irresistible.

And so it went with long-distance drives and phone calls so we could be together in any way possible and we began to talk about spending the rest of our lives together. I guess I was an unusual girl. While growing up I never fantasized about a big wedding or walking down an aisle in a white dress. I had attended some big to-do weddings and even as a kid came away thinking no more of the events than that they were expensive, stressful, and predictable and I wanted none of that for myself. So after a year, two months shy of my twentieth birthday, Scott and I eloped with our parents' blessings. A month later we started our own business, a fitness center for women. While I hired staff and ran the first one, Scott built another. Within two years we had five locations. The business was a success, but we worked six days a week and could never go anywhere. That certainly wasn't what we had in mind when we talked about seeing the world on our first date. We suddenly had the financial means to travel the world, but not the time to do it. We knew if we continued to be obligated to a business with fifty employees, we were going to have to resign ourselves to a one-week vacation once a year when what we really wanted was to be travelers who explored the world for months on end. We were earning a good living. We owned a sports car, and a Mercedes, and probably seemed successful in the eyes of our family and friends, but we were becoming shackled to a life we didn't want. Were we actually going to give up our dream just so we could appear successful to others and acquire fancy cars and more *stuff*?

We sold the business. It wasn't even an agonizing decision. It sold quickly and boy, we thought we were financially set for life. (At the age of twenty-two it doesn't take much to make you feel like you have all the money anyone would ever need.) We both returned to college, lived by the beach in Capitola, California, left college, bought a boat, sailed to Hawaii on our 40' catamaran named Different Drummer, lived for several years in a cozy rented studio over a garage near the University of Hawaii, and eventually received our degrees—Scott's in history, mine in economics. With just a semester to go before graduating, we did the responsible thing and took a good look at our balance sheet in order to make a plan for the future. Not only were we *not* set for life, we were almost back to square one. We had to do something and quick. But this time we wanted to own our livelihood not let it own us. We tried to come up with the perfect business that would allow us time off to travel. We thought about what we had learned in our first business venture and knew what we *didn't* want. We didn't want to have a business that needed permanent employees or one that required us to be there one hundred percent of the time. It had to be something project-oriented that would earn us enough money to build a nest egg and see the world.

Through sheer serendipity an opportunity presented itself in Hawaii. Scott was working as a researcher for the Pacific Island Development Program at the East-West Center adjacent to the University of Hawaii. A colleague who was a pilot occasionally offered to take us flying, as long as we paid for the fuel. On the next cloudless Saturday afternoon he took us flying over Oahu. As we rounded a point on the rural North Shore, we spied below us the most perfect bay we had ever seen. It was dotted with a few simple bungalows and palm trees on an unspoiled white sand beach. We tried to memorize the landscape so that we could find the bay by car or on foot the next time we were on the North Shore.

A few weeks later we drove around the island to the area where we thought we might find the bay. The vegetation was so thick along the road we practically had to hack our way through the brush to the ocean. Suddenly there it was, as perfect on land as it was from the air.

Scott looked at me with a huge smile. "This is the Hawaii of my mind's eye. This is the real Hawaii."

We spent an hour on the quiet beach and left saying, "It would be like living in paradise to live here."

A week later, still dreaming about the morsel of "Real Hawaii" we had seen on the North Shore, we met a friend for lunch at his office in downtown Honolulu. He waved us in and continued a conversation he was having on speakerphone. It turned out that the person on the other end of the phone call was selling a piece of land on the North Shore of Oahu and wanted to know if our friend was interested in buying. When the man began to describe the oceanfront lot and how close it was to "the most perfect bay on Oahu," I looked at Scott with wide eyes and held my breath. It couldn't be.

Our friend brought his conversation to an end saying that he wasn't in the market for a real estate project and hung up. He rose from behind the desk and asked, "Ready for lunch?"

Project? Near the most perfect bay on Oahu? Scott asked, "If you aren't going to pursue buying that lot, do you mind if we do?"

"No, not at all," he said. "Now can we go to lunch?"

We purchased the lot and moved two old plantation houses from one side of the island to the other, placing them side-by-side on new foundations facing the beach. Over twelve months we plumbed, roofed, wired, caulked, and painted one of them into something nice enough for a Hollywood actor to buy. For the remainder of our time in Hawaii we lived in the other house and walked to that perfect bay to swim whenever we wanted.

That's how we became home renovators and builders. Not because real estate development turned us on particularly, but because it was something project-oriented and had no permanent employees. If we stayed focused and were lucky enough, we could successfully complete a project and have the freedom to travel.

After three years we moved back to California where there were endless fixer-upper projects from which to choose. We worked hard then took a trip. Lather rinse repeat. But there was always another project waiting for us upon our return, so the longest we were ever away was a month. A long holiday to be sure, but we still yearned to take a journey not a vacation.

Since our first date we had talked about backpacking around the world. Year after year we tossed ideas and articles clipped from newspapers and magazines into a box labeled, "World Trip." We could have labeled it "Complete Fulfillment," or "Utter Happiness," or "Lifelong Dream" because that's what the box represented to us. Whenever we needed encouragement, we attended lectures given by others who traveled the world and our hearts would ache to do the same. Our bookshelves became filled with travel essays, historic fiction set in foreign lands, and guidebooks to exotic destinations. We had the dream so clearly in our sights. We just needed to pull the trigger.

In 1995, after we had been married nearly seventeen years, I was running out of space for all our travel books and was about to buy another bookcase. I suddenly realized that I was tired of storing our dreams. I wanted to live them. I turned to Scott and said, "This independently wealthy thing. I think it was only possible before the government enacted income tax. Let's travel anyway." We finished one last project, bought new backpacks, leased out our house, and took off around the world. We were finally living the dream we had talked about on our first date.

After eighteen contented months traveling the globe, we checked the balance sheet again and realized that even though we had become expert at traveling on a shoestring, exploration was eating into our capital. We needed to earn a living, be productive, save up for our old age, and do all the other things society tells us we should do while we are young. Once again we took on project after project. Our occupation as home renovators soon took over our lives. Before we knew it, days and years turned into a decade and we were in a comfortable rut. We were living our lives, but not living the life of our dreams. As we watched *Jeopardy!* that night, I could tell that Scott was thinking along similar lines. Rather, I could *feel* him thinking about it.

As Alex Trebek congratulated the returning champion in Final Jeopardy, my husband interrupted my daydream. "To afford it, we would have to do it on a budget and lease out our house again."

"You took the words right out of my head!" I replied. "And since when have we not traveled on a budget?" I added. My motto has always been: *If you travel for less, you can travel for longer.*

So that's how during one *Jeopardy!* show, in fifty spoken words or less, we decided to pick up the thread of our dream to see the world. I should mention that we married when I was nineteen and we have remained married for nearly thirty-four years. We have probably had every debate possible in a relationship, which is why we can come to a consensus on any issue without too much noise. Anyway, as Scott switched the channel to a *Seinfeld* episode, I went upstairs to our computer and composed an ad on Craigslist to lease our house out for a year:

Perhaps you are on sabbatical or rebuilding your home and need a comfortable place to live while you build or work in the Bay Area. We will be out of the country for one year and are looking for an executive, professor, or family to rent our fully furnished home while we are gone.

Within half an hour, I received a response from a professor in the neighborhood who was about to remodel his house. I began to pack.

LAB RATS

In just under a week the details of renting the house were complete and a lease was signed. Now there was the actual trip planning to do. By the second *Jeopardy!* show after our commitment to dig our backpacks out of storage, we were still deciding where in the world we would go. We finally narrowed it down to Sri Lanka or Africa. I think it was because of the Final Jeopardy category one night, "African Capitals," that we decided on a destination that took up the most space in our travel box: Africa—specifically an overland transit of the African continent, top to bottom, from Casablanca to Cape Town. We booked a one-way flight to Casablanca leaving six weeks later (when our tenants would move in), and we began researching and planning a potential itinerary. We knew we wanted to visit countries in Africa we hadn't been to before including Madagascar and Ethiopia, we wanted to do the trip overland as much as possible, and we wanted to climb Mount Kilimanjaro. Not a very detailed plan, more a concept that we would build upon. But that is how we have always done things.

"This sounds do-able!" I said aloud. Not all our conversations are silent.

One challenge was going to be transport, especially through Western Sahara and Mauritania. We'd been to East Africa before and knew that it would be possible to get from Kenya to points south and west with relative ease. But transiting across the Sahara along the west coast as we hoped could be tricky. Soft sand, rising sea tides, and land mines left over from a long running conflict over Western Sahara between Morocco and Mauritania could catch a traveler off guard. We needed to find a way to get from Casablanca to at least as far as Ghana with as much predictability and safety as possible. We tracked down a few overland companies who were poised to transit West Africa, but their trips would not begin before completion of a much-anticipated paved road through the desert. We didn't want to wait a year.

Scott spent hours on the Web searching for transport through West Africa before coming upon "a unique offering." An Australian mechanic building an overland truck in England intended to drive it from London, England, to Cape Town, South Africa, and was seeking "adventurous people to share the experience and expense." His Web site had a link to a radio interview he had done in England about the journey. We listened in. His enthusiasm was infectious. Though the quintessential trans-Africa route is from Cairo to Cape Town along the east coast of Africa, the Mechanic wanted to be part of a select few to do a trans-Africa entirely down the west coast before the paved road was finished. He had previously driven for an overland company in East Africa, but West Africa would be completely new territory.

His plan was to build the truck and stock it with truck parts in high demand in East Africa. He would sell the parts and the truck in South Africa or Nairobi and recoup what he had spent to build the truck, and he would finance the expedition itself by selling seats on the truck. That's where we came in.

We weighed the pros and cons. We had traveled in Africa with a group of strangers on an overland truck before and while it was fun and safe, it was far less independent than we wanted to go now. But this sounded a little different. This would be a group of people who (said the Web site), after engaging in respectful discussion much like a family, would together decide the route and how to run the trip.

Also, having a qualified mechanic along on a transit through Africa is never a bad thing. The best part was that we would be allowed to get on and off the truck as often as we liked along the way, which appealed to our sense of independence. The Mechanic's plan sounded reasonable and we admired him undertaking such a challenging venture at considerable personal financial risk. Some of our friends had thought Scott and I were crazy to move two plantation houses across an island in Hawaii when we had never done anything like that before, so we could relate to someone taking risks and doing something no one else was doing at the time. Joining the Mechanic on his home-built truck and driving across Africa sounded like an interesting experiment. Filled with enthusiasm at taking any step that would get us started on our dream, I turned to my husband and said, "I have always wondered what it would be like to be a lab rat. Let's do it!"

The Mechanic was asking a fairly reasonable investment from each participant, so Scott and I agreed that even if we stayed aboard only as far as Ghana (around seven to eight weeks), it would be worth the money. If we decided to stay on the truck all the way to Cape Town, the entire journey would take around six to seven months, or even longer. It all depended on the condition of the roads, whether the vehicle broke down, and how often we would be delayed by the coming monsoon, political coups, or civil wars.

"How bad could it be?" I mused as we folded up our map of the continent of Africa and dialed the number of the Mechanic in England.

A few weeks later, in December 2004, the house was tidied, our personal things were in storage, keys were delivered to our tenants, and we were on our way to Casablanca.

PART 2
THIS ISN'T A BLOODY HOLIDAY!

Madam, You Must Take Care

As we made our way to the immigration counter in Casablanca, Morocco, we were reminded of the differences in personal space parameters between the Western world and the rest of the world. Men and women clad in heavy robes pushed past us as we tried to maintain a semblance of a line. After receiving an elbow in the ribs, I went into what I call "Toto mode" as in, "Toto, we're not in Kansas anymore." Surroundings and cultural mores are different so you have to be different. Hold your ground. Look like you have been around the world dozens of times and that you carry multiple passports. Scowl. For God's sake, don't behave as we did on our first trip to sub-Saharan Africa ten years earlier.

It was 1995 and Kenya was the first stop on our long-anticipated trip around the world. Despite decades of yearning, we had never been to Kenya and we were filled with nervous excitement. At the Nairobi airport, in the city our guidebook called "Nairobbery" in reference to all the thefts that occur there, we waited in the crowded open-air baggage claim for the two small backpacks that contained said guidebook plus everything else that would get us around the world for the next year and a half. We placed our two green packs onto a small flatbed trolley and proceeded out of the airport. We were indescribably happy to be finally on the continent we had dreamed of and read about for years. I'm sure we looked like a couple of delirious fools as we pushed the trolley through the baggage claim lounge and out the exit, taking in Africa's brilliant blue sky with anticipation and awe. We grinned at one another, misty-eyed and giddy with excitement. Several minutes went by. Then there was a light tap on my shoulder.

"Madam," said a Kenyan man with a look that was an odd blend of both pity and regret. "You must take care," he said while indicating back into the airport towards baggage claim. Our backpacks had tumbled off our cart only seconds after we had plucked them from the conveyer belt and lay where they had fallen, just a few feet from the baggage carousel. We decided to take it as a good omen. In this city of "Nairobbery" our bags were still there and our first Kenyan contact was an act of kindness.

Ten years later as we began our overland transit of Africa, we were a lot more savvy but not any less sappy.

We wanted our first night on the continent to be special. Any hopeless romantic or movie buff would know exactly where to go to dinner in Casablanca—Rick's. After quick showers to wash off the airplane funk, we took a taxi to Rick's Café in the heart of the city. We met the owner, a kindred spirit, who had done a good job of replicating the café made famous by Humphrey Bogart in the movie *Casablanca*. We stood around the piano while "Sam" played it again and toasted the beginning of our African adventure with champagne.

Jet lag always knocks us both for a wallop. Our physician had given us a prescription for ten Ambien, a sleep aid that helps with jet lag, but when my husband went to the pharmacy to have it filled before our trip, he almost had an infarction over the ten-dollar per pill price tag. Instead of getting all ten tablets, he bought only two. We each took a pill during the flight to Morocco and slept like babies. But even the late night at Rick's did little to conquer our jet lag and we were a rummy wreck for the first two days in Casablanca. We needed more Ambien.

Scott is a paper packrat. He always has bits of paper on or around him: in his trousers, on the fireplace mantel, pretty much all over the house are small bits of paper and ads torn from newspapers and magazines. Fortunately, because it qualified as a small bit of paper, he had not only saved the Ambien prescription from our doctor, he'd brought it along to Morocco.

"Let's see if a drug store here will accept this," he said between yawns, and we presented the prescription at a pharmacy near our hotel. Since our French was minimal and our Arabic was nonexistent, we pantomimed epic fatigue. I played a sleepy Ingrid Bergman, my husband a droopy-eyed Peter Lorre. We received sympathetic nods and twenty-eight Ambien tablets for only eight dollars.

The next morning we overslept. Hampered by an Ambien hangover and having no time to shower, we quickly pulled on T-shirts and jeans, zipped our backpacks, and ran to the station. We took a train, a bus, and a taxi to meet our overland truck as it disembarked in the port city of Cueta at the northernmost tip of Africa.

The Mechanic made a good first impression. He was attractive, around thirty-five-years-old, and had a shirt on. Forever after, a shirt would be a rarity. The truck that the Mechanic built also initially impressed me. It was roomy and had that new truck smell and fresh paint. The interior design was clever and well thought out. The Mechanic had installed a row of seats along each side of the truck's interior. Under each passenger's seat (which he had scavenged from a long distance bus in England) was a roomy compartment for personal gear. We simply removed the seat bottom to get at whatever we needed underneath. This eliminated the need to stop the truck in order to get into a cumbersome locker accessible only from the outside, as is often the case on commercial overland vehicles. Stored under plain plywood flooring between the two bench seats were tents, sleeping mats, camp chairs, and scads of non-perishable food items. At the back of the passenger area was a prolific library containing fiction and non-fiction books stocked by fellow passengers. Most ingenious, but apparently not legally imported, the Mechanic had an entire backup engine, two radiators, two sets of springs, an extra fuel tank, and lots of other marketable spare parts stored under a raised compartment at the front of the passenger area of the truck. These were the spare parts he planned on selling in East Africa. The compartment was covered with a thin mattress and blankets to disguise it as a double bed for the driver. No border inspector ever gave it a second glance. There were only two design flaws to the truck. One was that the cab and hence driver were completely independent from the passenger section. To get the attention of the Mechanic we had to pull up some of the clear plastic vinyl (which made up the sides of the truck) and stick an arm or, more commonly, roll of toilet paper out the gap until he noticed that we needed to stop. The other flaw was that since the seats were not actually attached to anything, whenever we hit a bump, the seat bottoms and everything on them, including us, would go flying.

After a quick introduction to the truck, it was time to meet our fellow expedition members. They had transited down from London with the Mechanic and so had already been on the truck together for a week. Our ten travel mates ranged in age from twenty to forty-eight and were from all over the world. Everyone made us feel welcome and seemed eager that we have a favorable impression of the truck and the group. After the briefest get-to-know-you session in my life, we drove a short distance to a grocery store so that we could stock up on whatever we might be lacking in the way of developed-world needs or wants before leaving Cueta.

As Scott and I sat in the cab talking with the Mechanic and paying him the balance we owed, Mike, a British man in his thirties, popped his head through the window and said with a big smile, "Six of us are thinking of doing a beer kitty. Do you want in on it?"

"Sure! Let's make it eight," said Scott while reaching for his wallet. "How much do you want?" He handed Mike the required amount to be part of the kitty and off Mike went to buy the beer with a skip in his step. Scott looked at me with a happy grin. "Everyone is so friendly. I think it's going to be a good trip!"

A kitty for alcohol can be a fun and efficient thing. Participants pool funds and buy enough beer so that each person can enjoy a few sundowners every evening over several weeks. There isn't a lot of room for personal belongings on an overland truck and group purchases are allowed to be stored with community supplies where there is more available space. We knew that some people might abuse the system and take more than their share on a night or two, but for the most part beer kitties work out well. In this case it only took a day to realize that the beer kitty was heavily subsidizing Mike's drinking habit.

We drove until dusk and parked along a beach that was still within city limits. To keep a low profile, we wouldn't be allowed to set up tents. We would have to sleep in the truck. With only ten passengers there was plenty of room for everyone, but I was glad this wasn't to be the norm. A Welshman, Bill, and his lover Maggie, both in their late forties, were at the stage in their relationship that involved plenty of heavy petting and tongue swabbing. And that was during the daylight hours. At night it was much worse. Sleeping with them in the truck was like being *in* the kind of movie you watched as a kid where you wanted to cover your eyes during the gross parts. Besides Scott and I, and Bill and Maggie, there was one other couple on board. Beautiful, six-foot-tall, one blue eye and one brown eye Petra from England, and Sam the Hilarious and Hairy from Australia, both in their early twenties. They were the youngest, funniest, most adorable, and most enthusiastic passengers on the truck. They slept through the night like good babies, usually on the double bed over the contraband truck parts. I actually wouldn't have minded sleeping with them on the truck every night, if I absolutely had to.

I didn't think anyone would sleep very well that night in Cueta. After more than a few beers Mike was on an idealistic soapbox. Though he was a well-read intellectual who spoke four or five languages, the dent Mike put in the beer kitty brought out the uncompromising and verbose socialist in him.

Finally everyone was safely tucked in his or her sleeping bag and all was quiet. After a few minutes we sensed movement from the cab where the Mechanic shared a mattress with his girlfriend Jackie. Jackie had impulsively quit her job and joined the expedition the day it left England. She was still clad in her bank clerk work clothes. Jewelry, heels, the whole nine yards. Originally planning to stay on board only as far as Spain, she decided to "see Africa for a week or two before going back to England" and had crossed the Straight of Gibraltar with the truck.

We could hear the Mechanic and Jackie as they adjusted around the steering wheel and gearshift. A brief silence was followed by a string of six rapid squeaks. Then it was over. That was it. The Mechanic was a six-squeak lover and everyone on the truck knew it. Some overland truck drivers consider trysts with consenting single passengers an occupational perk. He had just dimmed his chances of scoring with any of the single women on board once his girlfriend left the trip. For a few minutes no one in the truck said anything. Then the truck exploded in laughter. We had bonded over six short squeaks.

The next morning Scott and I rose quietly and took a walk. We were anxious to discuss our impressions of the last sixteen hours in private. Turned out we both had a bit of a sinking feeling. Aside from our unhappiness at sleeping where we could still see the ambient light of a big city on our first night of an African expedition, something didn't feel right about the group. There was palpable tension between the Mechanic and some of the passengers. And man! Someone on the truck sure needed a shower. Halfway down the beach we turned around to see Petra and Sam watching us. When we got back to the truck Sam asked, "Everything OK?"

"Sure. Why do you ask?"

"Oh nothing. Just want to make sure you are OK!" he said with a big smile. Then Luis, a longhaired, striking, twenty-two-year-old Spaniard, who looked like Jesus Christ and sounded like Antonio

Banderas, walked up and said, "I am very glad to have left Spain. I hated living like a homeless person in my own country."

"What do you mean?" I asked. Then because it was so obvious I blurted, "Luis, did anyone ever tell you that you look like Jesus Christ? I mean, the version Italian painters used during the Renaissance?"

"Me? Like Jesus? No. But until six months ago I wore thick glasses and had short hair. No one ever noticed me. After I grew my hair and got contact lenses, I got a lot more attention but I didn't know it was because I looked more…holy. So, thanks! I guess. Anyway," he said, getting back to why he was glad that Spain was behind him, "we drove pretty much non-stop through France and Spain only pulling over late at night to sleep. None of us have had a shower in a week." Frowning, he added, "I've never done anything like this in my life. This is my first time traveling outside of my country. I don't know if I am going to like this," he said gesturing towards the truck. "And I miss my girl-friend. She is the first girlfriend I've ever had!" He paused, and then explained further, "You see, I had ice cream for the first time in my life two weeks ago. Now that I know what ice cream tastes like, I miss it," Luis added in a charming way of telling us that two weeks ago, he was a virgin.

"Do you mean to say you have been sleeping on the truck for a week?" I asked.

"Yes," he said, obviously disheartened.

"In *Europe*?" I was bewildered since I knew that campgrounds in Europe are abundant and cheap. Luis nodded.

"That's completely unnecessary. We shouldn't have to live like that." I found the Mechanic and we had our first of many "family" discussions. I reminded him that Scott and I had been on an overland truck for two and a half months in Africa before and there was no rea-son people should be going without showers for an entire week, espe-cially in Europe. I told him that while we expected and looked forward to bush camping most of the time through Africa, we should try to use organized camps when available. I reminded him that camping fees, in addition to fuel and provisions, was part of what our investment was supposed to cover. We got out the guidebook and maps and together chose such a campsite in Chefchaouen, Morocco, for the evening.

That night when we arrived in camp, Luis, in an effort to gain control of the beer kitty, stated, "Tonight, each person in the kitty gets two beers."

After everyone had nice long hot showers, we cooked dinner over a wood fire and watched Mike finish off all the beer in the kitty. He had help from the two bubbly Australian women on board, Patty and Suzanne. The three of them sat around the campfire smoking cigarettes, drinking, philosophizing, and giggling. Patty had the most lyrical laugh I have ever heard and Suzanne was a smart young woman of Portuguese descent who could hold her own against Mike in a debate. Mike was just finishing a story about how he had once been stabbed by a girlfriend when the Mechanic announced we would camp there for at least three nights. "I need to finish work on the bloody truck," he said. He seemed very stressed out. It was the first of many times we would hear, "This isn't a bloody holiday, you know!"

While it was early in the trip for us (only the second day!) it seemed everyone, especially the Mechanic, needed a break from driving. Scott and I wanted the Mechanic to do whatever he thought he needed to do on the truck so that he too, could relax and enjoy the adventure.

The campsite at Chefchaouen was a good place to take R & R. It was on a hill overlooking the cobbled streets of a medieval village located at the base of the Rif Mountains. There were steep hills nearby to explore and plenty for us to do in the village below over the next few days. The Mechanic would have many uninterrupted hours to work on the truck. Bill was an enormous help. He knew about trucks and what made them go. Whenever Bill wasn't making out with Maggie, he could be found under the truck helping the Mechanic.

On the way to our tent the first night, I saw Luis standing over a sink basin near the showers. He was a picture of confusion and disillusionment. Mostly confusion.

"Hey, Luis, everything all right?" I asked as I came up next to him.

"Yes, Tris." Only with his beautiful Antonio Banderas accent he trilled, "Trriiis." I loved the way Luis said my name. I was dying to ask him to read a bedtime story to me.

Luis stared down at a bundle of his T-shirts and trousers in the sink as if they were objects unfamiliar to him. "But," he said looking up at me, "how do I do this?"

"Do what?"

"How do I wash these clothes? I have never done laundry before in my life."

I smiled. "I'll make you a deal. If you keep saying my name the way you do for the rest of the trip, I'll teach you how to do laundry in a sink."

When we had finished the lesson, Sam walked up with Carl, an affable blond-haired, brown-eyed, twenty-three-year-old perpetual student from Canada. Carl and Sam had the most extensive travel experience after Scott and me, and both had seemed anxious to talk since we met.

"How ya goin'?" asked Sam with his ever-present jovial smile.

"Good! Luis and I have just bonded over laundry soap and a universal sink plug," I answered.

Sam stuck his hands in his trouser pockets and blurted out, "What do you think of the trip so far?"

I hesitated a beat before answering him honestly. "Well, I have to say, Scott and I notice some tension in the group."

"Yeah," he said, obviously relieved that I was willing to talk about it. "Petra and I were afraid you and Scott were going to leave this morning because of the friction. The Mechanic is furious with a few of us who came down with him from England. He feels we pressured him to leave England before he had finished everything on the truck. But we really felt we needed to leave by a certain date to avoid the rainy season and getting stuck in the mud in Cameroon or in the Congo. The Mechanic kept pushing the departure time back and we were all anxious to get going. Also," he added quietly, "the Mechanic didn't sell as many seats as he wanted to and the trip really needs your contribution, both financially and physically, to even have a chance of succeeding. That's why we were worried that you would leave."

I immediately felt both relief and anxiety. At least now I knew the source of the unease present in the group. "Thanks for telling me. Scott and I definitely felt a weird vibe and it helps to know what's going on."

Carl nodded his head in agreement but still had a deer-in-the-headlights look about him. "I don't know what is going to happen," he said. "I have to leave the trip in a few weeks when we get to Senegal so I can get back to Canada in time for my final semester of college. The Mechanic has always known that I have to leave the trip early, but he keeps bringing it up and is not very happy about it. I feel bad, but I have to finish school this year or my parents will disown me."

"You shouldn't feel guilty about having to leave in Senegal! It's not as if the Mechanic wasn't aware that you signed on for only a few weeks of the trip. I don't think anyone else on the trip is going to hold it against you. At least Scott and I won't." Looking back at Sam I could see that he needed further reassurance so I continued. "The good news is that we all have the same objective. We all want to reach Cape Town and we want to have a good experience while getting there. I think everyone wants this trip to be a success, and Scott and I plan on doing whatever we can to help the Mechanic so we can all achieve our dream. We've flown a long way for this journey and we are fairly determined people, so I don't think you need to worry about us bailing."

"You don't know how good it makes me feel to hear you say that," said Sam with relief. "Well, I think I'll turn in. See you in the morning!"

A few minutes later, as I curled up next to Scott in our tent I said, "I just taught Jesus how to do laundry." I pulled the sleeping bag up around my neck and reached for my earplugs. Over Suzanne and Patty's campfire giggles, I could just make out the Mechanic cursing at Sam.

"Holy smokes. I think this experience is going to be like a season of *Survivor.*"

"What do you mean?" Scott asked sleepily.

"Well, it's like there are two tribes. The Mechanic is on one tribe and everyone else is on the other. Because we joined the trip later than the others we're somewhere in the middle. The Mechanic is perturbed with the group that started with him in England because, according to Sam, they pressured him to start the trip before he was ready. Hopefully there will be a merger of tribes sooner rather than later, and we can all get on with the business of getting to Cape Town."

Back on the road after our respite in Chefchaouen, I sat up front with the Mechanic while he drove. The days spent at the campsite had been fruitful. The Mechanic had finished some work on the truck and seemed happier, more positive. So positive that he had found someone in the campground to tattoo the name of the expedition across his torso, prompting Scott to offer the Mechanic some unsolicited feedback, "*That* can't be a good idea." The Mechanic also seemed upbeat because he was now a free agent. His girlfriend had decided she had had enough (or not enough) and was making her way back to England.

As I sat next to the Mechanic I learned that what Sam had told me was true. The Mechanic blamed those who had joined the truck in England, but mostly Sam, for his anxiety about not completing the truck to his satisfaction and for feeling like he started the expedition before he was ready. He revealed that he was flat broke and had only the money we all had contributed to run the trip. "I put everything into building this truck," he said. I quickly did the math and realized that if we didn't sell more seats, we probably wouldn't make it to Cape Town. Either that or we would all have to increase our contribution.

That worried me, but what bothered me more was how much he detested Sam. The Mechanic felt that Sam should act more like a partner in the expedition and, in the Mechanic's eyes, Sam acted like he had paid for the trip and it was now up to the Mechanic to get him to Cape Town. Sam was such a happy-go-lucky person that he didn't realize how much his attitude affected the Mechanic. Sam was oblivious that anyone wouldn't like him. Though we often disagreed on how the trip should run, the Mechanic and I got along and spoke to one another as siblings might, so I spoke freely. "You need to let your anger at Sam go. It's unproductive. Why not focus on getting to Cape Town instead of stewing about Sam? You should be enjoying this adventure as much as the rest of us. It was your dream to begin with!"

The next day I again sat up front with the Mechanic. One never knew what kind of mood he would be in and few wanted to subject themselves to the Mechanic's steady litany of regrets and blame, so it was usually just Scott, me, or Luis who sat up front. The three of us seemed to most regularly take on the role of trying to keep the Mechanic focused and on track, encouraging him to see things in a more positive light. Bill and Maggie were usually busy necking, and the rest had little patience or empathy for the Mechanic's frustrations. His rants didn't bother me enough to keep me out of the cab because I loved seeing Africa head-on through the large windscreen, and I usually tried to get the Mechanic to talk about something else to get his mind off the stress of running the trip. "Tell me about your life in Australia," I said, hoping he would welcome a change of subject. Besides, I was truly interested. For all his foibles the Mechanic had led an adventurous life.

He had spent his youth in boarding schools and later worked on cattle stations to earn a living. He had a tough childhood. He was in the midst of telling me about his uneasy relationship with his father when he surprised us both by saying, "And well, actually, I'm married." Then he went on to say that his wife had been trying to track him down for two years to get him to sign divorce papers. "She sure has problems," he added.

I felt for the Mechanic. He was a hard-working man built as solid and tough as his stubborn nature. He could be very charming, but when things went wrong it was always someone else's fault. Over the next few weeks I learned a great deal about him. He shared that he had never been able to execute a satisfying life for himself. He admitted he was forever "searching" and had just spent considerable time before the trip "getting his head together" at an ashram in Australia. He also had several different personalities (most of them quite pleasant) and loved talking about himself. Fortunately, all his personalities knew how to fix a truck and he (they) really was (were) a fine mechanic.

The expedition fell into a regular routine. We drove all day with a brief stop to prepare a roadside lunch of canned tuna, or corned beef, or cabbage salad before making camp around sundown. The days went smoothly but some nights while we sat around the campfire, tensions would begin to build. At the end of the second week I again rode in the cab with the Mechanic. He started in on Sam almost immediately, "If I could just kick Sam off the truck, everything would be better."

I tried to get him to stay focused and be rational, but his constant negativity was starting to become draining. "Then Petra will leave," I said with exasperation. "And others may too. You know you need every last one of us to have a chance of reaching Cape Town. Don't forget, we are all in this to fulfill a dream of transiting Africa, but we are also helping *you* achieve *your* dreams."

For a few minutes he was silent. Then he shared more of himself than he should have when he said to me, "I've never finished anything in my life. Never bloody ever."

I knew then that the expedition would probably never reach Cape Town. I could see that it wouldn't matter what anyone said or didn't say, did or didn't do. The Mechanic didn't have it in him to do whatever it would take to reach his goal, and I wasn't willing to continue to cheer someone on who refused to even suit up for the game.

I violated the Mechanic/lab rat privilege and shared with Scott what the Mechanic had said. As bad as it made us feel, we decided to put back on the table our option of remaining on the expedition only through the Sahara to Ghana. We hoped that the expedition would even make it to Ghana.

TEXTURE AND TAGINE

In contrast to the sobering angst present on the truck, sites like Chefchaouen or Fez in Morocco provided such endorphin pumping positive vibes for the group that I thought if we could take the journey in little bites, from ancient desert outpost to capital city, and ignore the day-to-day animosity between the Mechanic and everyone else, we just might make it all the way to Cape Town. Like children with a sudden attack of attention deficit disorder, we all seemed to need something bigger than personalities and peeves to focus on in order to remind us that we were here to fulfill a dream. Morocco, and Fez in particular, provided just the right dose of distraction.

Morocco is all about shape, texture, and color. Everything looks and tastes hi-def and 3-D. It all starts with the national dish, tagine. First of all, you eat tagine out of a tagine. Tagine is the only meal that has the same name as the pot it comes in. The tagine pot with its Mount Fuji-shaped lid is the color of a golden leaf in autumn and the tagine meal inside is thick and creamy. It was so delicious and the weather so cold in Morocco that we never tired of eating the hot spicy dish. With it we drank glass after glass of hot sweet tea filled to the brim with bright green mint leaves. The entire town of Chefchaouen was painted sky blue—except for the doors, which were trimmed in vibrant turquoise. Almost all the door fronts were decorated with rows of shiny bumps that looked like flattened conquistador hats. In place of knobs were enormous brass rings. Everything—spice, fabric, carpets, and lamps, even tiled Mosques — was vividly colored. It was as if a paint store exploded over the entire country. The air smelled of earth and spice. Except in Fez that is, where the air smelled like vomit.

The ancient city of Fez is home to an enormous grid of leather dying vats swarming with barelegged men and wet animal skins. The pungent throat-tightening stench of fermenting hides unique only to Fez was so pervasive that we could smell the vats long before we could see them. It's an olfactory experience somewhat like a combination of fish sauce and Scott's gym socks, only more humid. Apparently the hides are soaked in watery pigeon poo because something in the poo concoction makes the leather soft and supple. I know I'd go all floppy if you smeared pigeon poo on me too.

Aside from the odiferous funk that is Fez, it was there we felt most like time travelers. We visited the University of Al-Karaouine, which was founded in 859 CE. It is the oldest continuously operating university in the world and it looks it. Later, as we walked through the ancient souk (marketplace), we again felt as if we had stepped back in time. Until we were brought back to the present by a laugh track as we passed a café where djellaba-clad men inside were watching an American sitcom. "Hey! *Seinfeld* is on!" Scott exclaimed. We looked up to see thousands of satellite dishes competing for space on rooftops all over Fez. I watched the men inside sipping tea while intent on the TV screen and wondered if they had already seen "The Puffy Shirt" episode and what they would think of "The Contest."

We sat down in the café to ponder the abundance of satellite dishes in Fez and ordered our second tagine meal of the day. "I can't wait to get to the *real* Africa," I said. Despite all the rich colors and aromas that surrounded us, I was anxious to get to the real Africa, the one without satellite dishes. I wanted to get to the Africa of my mind's eye and Morocco was feeling just a bit too European. Soon I got my wish. In the coming weeks we would see parts of Africa so real I was sorry I wished for it.

Can Riding Camels Cause Hemorrhoids?

Over the next week the atmosphere on the truck reached a sort of equilibrium. Everyone accepted that we probably wouldn't beat the monsoon, and the Mechanic obsessed openly that he was unhappy about starting the trip before he was ready and that his expedition was not going to turn out as profitably as he had hoped. Everyone decided to make the best of it. For Scott and me it wasn't hard to do. We liked everyone on the truck, including the Mechanic, who was the classic tragic figure in our overland opera. Scott and I were seeing Africa slowly, the way we wanted. Once we accepted that we would probably soon be transiting the rest of Africa on our own, we began to really enjoy each day to the fullest. Besides, it was almost Christmas and that put everyone in a good mood.

Outside of Merzouga in Morocco, the ten of us took a multi-day camel trek into the desert. We would finish the trek in time to celebrate Christmas together back in Merzouga. The Mechanic and the truck stayed behind at the guesthouse in the dunes. He said he needed another break and that it would relax him if he could "get some things done on the bloody truck without interruption!" The truck always seemed to perform well, so I was beginning to wonder if this was merely a convenient excuse or if there was actually something wrong with the truck. African roads aren't kind to any type of vehicle, and I knew it required hours of maintenance after driving over dusty deserts or rough terrain. The Mechanic wanted the truck to stay in tiptop shape for re-sale, so he constantly tinkered with it and tried to make it look and run better. He even asked Petra to use her artistic talents to paint the expedition logo along the sides of

41

the truck, prompting Scott to say again, "Now *that* can't be a good idea." Not because Petra couldn't handle the job, but because it was the same red, yellow, and brown logo that the Mechanic had tattooed across his torso in Chefchaouen. Whatever the case, the Mechanic was always in a more relaxed mood after working on the truck, so no one tried to persuade him to join us for the camel safari. Or maybe he was more relaxed because of all the local dope he smoked while we were gone. Scott, I, and a few others had insisted we wanted no part of an expedition that transported illegal drugs across borders, but somehow the Mechanic always seemed to have ready supply of the stuff. That he smoked it with the locals bothered us even more because it made him, thus our belongings on the truck, vulnerable. We all made sure our valuables were safely locked away before heading off into the desert for the camel safari.

It was a crisp Saharan morning when a Bedouin led a troop of camels out of the dunes to our guesthouse. I tried to pick the one that growled with the least enthusiasm and only spit on occasion.

The first hour on the camel was novel. It was fun to be so high up on a living hump, looking out over endless hills of tawny-colored sand. Our heads and faces were swathed in headscarves, which turned out to be good protectors not only from sun and wind but also kept camel spit out of our hair. We felt a bit romantic, and even noble in the *Lawrence of Arabia* sense. (You may have guessed by now that we are both overly influenced by the movies we saw growing up.) Anyway, the first hour on the camel was wonderful. The next seventeen were sheer agony. My rear end hurt, my back hurt, I had chaffing in a delicate region, and from the look on Scott's face, he and his family jewels were not enjoying the ride much either. By the time we arrived at the first set of Bedouin tents, our accommodation for the night, Scott was walking like Tex Ritter, and I had major turban hair. I soon gave up on the Peter O'Toole fantasy and worried about whether riding a camel for too long could cause hemorrhoids.

The gait of a camel is very plodding and jarring. It's a rhythmic pain. I felt like I was being dropped repeatedly on what my wonderful and genteel

Aunt Martha referred to as the "middle hip." Aunt Martha believed "pelvis" wasn't a word one should say in polite company, so the year she broke her pelvis she claimed that she had broken a hip. When I asked her which hip, she replied, "Well, Honey, the middle one." Aunt Martha had other unique expressions for body parts. Her expression for rear end was "horse's patootie." Oddly this was also her term of endearment for me.

After the first day, Scott walked his camel through the desert, holding it by the lead while staying projectile-loogie distance away. I remained on Torture, which was what I named my camel because being on him was. "Waaaait uuuup!" I shouted as I bumped zigzag across the desert trying my best to keep up with Scott. Even on foot, he and his camel had a comfortable lead on Torture and me.

The second night, we stayed at an "oasis" that consisted of three tall bushes, endless sand, and one broken-down five-foot by seven-foot surf shack. The shack was covered in ads ending in exclamation marks (Have fun here!!) as if they were competing with a row of surf shacks out in the desert. Snowboards or skis were available to rent for sliding out of control down an enormous sand dune. We thought that sounded like fun!

No two skis matched and most of the bindings were missing from the snowboards, so we rode down the high, steep dunes in a sitting position, our rear ends hanging over the edges of snowboards, while we clutched bits of binding in one hand ala cowboys riding bucking broncos.

"Yeeeeeeehaaa!" I said in my best Howard Dean scream as I sped down the dune. I couldn't believe how fast we could go. Or how loud I could shriek. Or how good my Howard Dean impersonation was.

The next morning I took a solitary walk towards the rising sun. Our cud-chewing camels watched me as I trudged up and ran down dune after dune. The sand and the air around me felt soft. The post-dawn light made the dunes look as if a spray on tan had been lightly applied over the surface, which seemed to soften them even further. The landscape around us absorbed all ambient sound. My shouts of exhilaration and the growls of the camels sank and disappeared somewhere deep below the surface. There was only occasional spitting in my direction, and I was able to pee in private, something that is not that easy to do when there is nothing but a camel to pee behind as far as the eye can see. I was contented and at peace. Yet I couldn't resist looking for signs of life at the surf shack. Nothing beats the E ticket exhilaration of speeding down an enormous sand dune on a snowboard, and I was hoping to get one more ride in before we had to leave the oasis. That afternoon I reprised my Howard Dean impression for an audience of ten camels.

After three days we returned to our desert lodging and bid a-not-so-fond farewell to Torture and the other disagreeable camels. That evening after we celebrated Christmas with copious toasts and a gift exchange, Scott and I decided to phone home. Just before we lost the sporadic connection, Scott's mom informed us that there had been an earthquake that day in the Indian Ocean. A powerful tsunami had struck Sri Lanka, Indonesia, and Thailand and was heading for the east coast of Africa. It sobered us up immediately. We returned to our group, who were by now extremely drunk and trying to do the limbo beneath a nomad's walking stick. We told them what we had heard, but they were either too far-gone, or couldn't conceive of what we had told them, or both. It was a week before we could get to an Internet café to confirm the news. The devastation was real.

In addition to feeling saddened by the loss of so many lives, we felt a mixture of other emotions. Khao Lak was one of our favorite places in Thailand. The beach bungalow we stayed at and the people who ran it were no more. Sri Lanka lost more than thirty-one thousand lives.

Just a few weeks earlier, we had been sitting in our living room deciding where we would travel. We couldn't help but wonder, what if we had chosen Sri Lanka over Africa?

DEAD GOAT WATER

When we are traveling, we always try to stay somewhere unique during the holidays to help distract us from longing for friends and family back home, so we felt grateful that we would be spending New Year's Eve in the main square in Marrakech. Few places on earth are more distracting than Marrakech, at least the Marrakech from my memory.

We had been to Marrakech once before, twenty years prior when it was still "far out man!" Back then, boisterous men selling dubious food and funky souvenirs set up tents willy-nilly in the dust. The scent of marijuana drifted thickly across the square, and snake charmers diverted your attention while someone else picked your pocket. I loved it! Now it seemed sterile, organized, and far from far out. The tea sellers looked like they'd come off a set at Disney's Epcot, or central casting in Hollywood.

These days, at 4:00 p.m. sharp, identical carts are wheeled onto an expansive concrete plaza and set up in the exact spot they had been the night before. All the vendors are anonymous and monotonous in their matching white aprons. There is one section in the square for fruit, one for nuts, one for calamari. Every cart in each section is identical. The night market in Marrakech had become more of a passive experience. It was as if we were watching a show rather than participating in the possibilities of a Marrakech night of yore when you didn't know what would happen next. I had been looking forward to spending New Years Eve in *Marrakech, man!*

The food in the stalls was still good, and the hookah pipes were still there. But it wasn't the wild New Year's Eve I had anticipated in the Marrakech of my mind's eye. I can only imagine what it was like in the 1960s when it was on the hippie backpacker circuit. Far, far out, I bet.

It was just as well that Marrakech was a bust. We didn't even stay until midnight. By 11:00 p.m. everyone's tummy (except mine) had begun to rumble in unison. It was the kind of Third World tummy rumble that strikes fear in travelers. You just know it's going to be a long night spent either doubled over puking your guts out, or in a squatted position over a porcelain hole in the ground. We quickly left the square and made our way back to the campground located just outside the city. For the rest of the night everyone, including the Mechanic, was violently ill "from both ends" as they say.

What caused everyone but me to get sick? Dead goat water. Or rather the stream from which the Mechanic insisted we fill the jerry cans as we made our way into Marrakech that day. The Mechanic excelled at finding free sources of drinking water, and as we drove through the Atlas Mountains, he chose one such source, a stream close to the road.

"I want you blokes to get every empty container and fill it up with water!" he commanded while striding down the slope to the stream. Hesitant but wanting to be a team player, I began handing the metal cans down to waiting arms until I noticed that upstream and not far from where the Mechanic was getting water was a dead goat. A very dead goat.

"Uh, maybe we should get water in the next town. There's a dead goat there," I said pointing towards the bloated remains in the river.

"Blood-y hell!" said the Mechanic along with a few other choice words as he continued to fill the cans. "I worked on a cattle station in Australia, and I can tell you that this water is perfectly safe!" He liked to reference his time on a cattle station to counter almost anything he and the rest of us disagreed on. When we said we needed to increase our daily mileage or we would be caught by the rains in Central Africa and risk getting stuck in the mud he'd say, "I can tell you based on my time on a cattle station, we will not get bogged! This isn't a bloody holiday, you know!" as if that made perfect sense.

So fill the jerry cans we did, and when we arrived at the campground I bought five liters of bottled water. Scott scoffed at me before taking a mouthful of dead goat water. "Tris, you can't rely on being able to buy bottled water all over Africa. You're going to have to build up your immunities sooner or later," he said shaking his head and taking another big swallow.

"Maybe so, but I'm not going to drink that dead goat water, that's for sure."

The only disadvantage of me being the only one well that New Year's Eve was that I was up most of the night too, taking my storebought bottled water tent to tent to re-hydrate some of the sickies.

On the bright side, the Mechanic was more diligent about finding good and frequent sources of water after our experience with dead goat water. Water was to become the critical focus on the next leg of the journey as we made our way into the Sahara Desert.

For as far as the eye can see, the Western Sahara and the Mauritanian desert are as flat, gray, and drab as a winter sky in New Hampshire. There is an occasional shrub, but it is usually only a few inches high and must have come to be there by accident.

It was the Mechanic's first time driving in any desert much less the Sahara, and he had shared with us his anxiety about crossing it, especially his concern that we would run out of water if the truck broke down. He gave the truck a more thorough inspection than usual. He went over the body and the engine like a pilot about to embark on a flight across the Pacific Ocean. Though the truck had a built-in water tank that we had filled to the brim, we bought a second enormous plastic cask and filled it too with water.

We became stuck in the sand several times over the next few days. Each time we did, I felt more vulnerable. It wasn't as if there were other vehicles around to help us if we needed a tow out of the sand. "This is why it is called an expedition, not a bloody holiday!" reminded the Mechanic as we stepped off the truck into deep sand to prepare the sand mats. The blistering heat should have made our task more difficult, but we were primed with adrenaline. We dug in silence around all the tires and used sand mats as traction to free the truck. Twice, while we ran alongside, the truck hit another wall of sand, and we again began digging. Everyone became slightly dehydrated. We didn't drink as much as we should have because we wanted to be sure there was enough water for an emergency, and we couldn't predict how many more times we would get stuck. Except for Sam, who was a relentlessly optimistic person, no one was light-hearted. I don't recall much conversation. We were so focused on getting through the desert in Western Sahara and Mauritania that for three days it seemed we held our breath.

When we arrived at a short stretch of brand new tarmac, instead of staying on the truck to experience what would probably be the smoothest ride of the entire trip, we walked the flat new road for a few miles simply for the joy of feeling an even surface under our feet again. It was like being on land again after months at sea.

Anxiety may have reigned the day, but gratitude ruled the nights. The vast dark desert around us with only the moon and billions of stars providing ambient light made us feel privileged that we had it all to ourselves. There was renewed hope that if we could conquer the desert, we could reach South Africa. Even Mike, who automatically resented Scott and I because we were American "and therefore capitalists," was nice to us for once though it might not have been sincere. On the second night in the desert, everyone ran out of libations except for Scott who had a half-empty bottle of whiskey he had acquired in Casablanca. Mike put his anti-American angst aside for once and was all smiles when Scott brought it out to share, "Here, comrade. Drink up!" he said to Mike.

Despite Mike's socialistic diatribes, we appreciated him. He was the only one on the truck who was fluent in French, and that made him very useful at borders. I found him especially heroic the day the Mechanic suddenly and forcefully changed shirts with a border official. I'm sure it was because Mike was able to explain in perfect French something to the effect of, "This man is crazy. Please pay no attention to him. Stamp our passports so that we can take him to the nearest mental hospital in the next country," that we were able to drive away from that border post without having to pay a huge bribe. I think it bothered Mike that he was communicating in the language of a former colonial power because sometimes he refused to translate. But when his beer, or his beer money, was at risk of confiscation, he never hesitated to get involved with the officials at border crossings.

In addition to diffusing potentially explosive situations at border posts, Mike was a very good cook. Scott and I love spicy food. Especially five-alarm curries that make our eyes water. To our gastronomical delight, Mike used every hot spice and chili available from the on-board pantry in his meals. Suzanne, who didn't appreciate pepper of any sort in her food, complained the most when Mike cooked. "I can't taste the food," she said. "It just tastes of hot!" She seemed to resent the rest of us for encouraging Mike's adventurous cooking.

After a particularly good sinus-clearing meal in the desert, I noticed that Suzanne began delaying our departure time in the mornings. After we had packed up our tents and the kitchen crew had finished putting away the dishes, the Mechanic would start the truck, signaling it was time to leave. Once everyone was seated, Suzanne would often reach for her cigarettes or a roll of toilet paper and say, "Hang on, back in a sec," and she would make her way slowly across the desert a sufficient distance away from the truck to enjoy a leisurely smoke or poo. This drove the Mechanic crazy. Suzanne's sudden urges didn't outwardly bother Mike one bit, but his meals became progressively more ear-tingling and snot-producing.

In Western Sahara, we forgot all about petty disagreements when we saw the aftermath of the plague that I had described to my mom as a plague of biblical proportions. Ever-increasing mounds of dead locusts rearranged the landscape, providing eerie geographic relief to the monotonous desert. Millions of crisp-winged carcasses lined the route as if a giant's broom had swept them there. We learned these were the locusts that had earlier decimated the entire southern edge of the Sahara. During their brief lifespan they traveled across Africa with the prevailing winds, eating everything in their path. The same wind that pushed them along as they obliterated crop after crop blew their dry remains toward the sea. Months later this plague would contribute to a devastating famine, especially in Niger, thousands of miles east of Mauritania at the heart of the Sahara Desert.

There are few things more real than famine. Even before we crossed the southern Moroccan border, locals suggested that we bring canned food for the people of Mauritania. Because of the locust (and drought) there was sure to be a dire food shortage. When we reached Mauritania, the border officials explained that warnings of famine usually fall on deaf ears saying, "If aid comes at all, it comes too late."

Africa is teeming with non-governmental aid organizations. They see firsthand the warning signs of future famine, but sometimes even their pleas for help go unheeded. The aid that finally came during the African famine of 2005 was too little too late. The price of delay is enormous. According to a July 25, 2005 article in *New Scientist Magazine*, "In the days of the first appeal, just $1 per day per individual could have offset the crisis. But now it will take $80 to save each starving person."

We were all relieved when the desert was behind us. The Mechanic called a well-deserved two-day rest at the well-established Zebra Camp located near the Mauritania border in Senegal. European motorists participating in the Plymouth to Banjul Race (the little brother to the Plymouth to Dakar Challenge) often use the camp as a stopover, so it is always well stocked with food and drink. There were enormous plastic bins to wash clothes in, hot showers to wash bodies, and cold beer and hot sun to restore us as we lay in hammocks slung between palm trees. Zebra Camp had everything overlanders required. But the best part of Zebra Camp was its proximity to a nearby village, which is were Scott and I headed the next day.

In a scene that would become familiar to us in villages all over Africa, we watched women draw water from the town well and walk home balancing full buckets on their heads. Others collected bags of rice, bought and sold fruits and vegetables, and greeted friends at the open-air market. Nearly one hundred children walked by after the morning school session ended. Several little girls stopped to shake my hand as I sat on a bench under a shady tree. They said, "Bonjour!" and I replied, "Hello!" But mostly it was just a smile and two quick pumps of the hand.

While I greeted the school children, two women sitting next to me watched with amusement as Scott tried to arrange transport to St. Louis, a town twenty-five kilometers away.

Formerly the French colonial capital of Senegal, St. Louis sits pictuesquely at the mouth of the Senegal River. After gaining independence from France in 1960, the capital was moved to Dakar and St. Louis became less vibrant, but no less picturesque. Today it is a World Heritage site, the second of several (the Medina in Fez was the first) we would see during our journey through Africa. We wanted to take a day trip to St. Louis to see some of the old colonial buildings and take in the sunset, which was reputed to be spectacular.

As I sat shaking hands with the school children, I wasn't sure we were ever going to get to St. Louis that day. Scott had already spent nearly an hour trying to find someone to take us. Based on all the gesturing, discussion, and laughter of the women next to me, I could tell they were critiquing Scott's fruitless attempts to find transport. Finally, tired of watching a play with no ending, one of the women stood up, walked slowly to the center of the dirt road, and thrust her right arm high up in the air. Seconds later, a vehicle pulled up beside her. She had a few words with the driver, then, with a big grin, she motioned us over to the vehicle. As soon as we got in, she and five others climbed in behind us. They all had suddenly decided to go to St. Louis, or in the direction of St. Louis, for the day, too. Africans are smart and they don't often miss an opportunity if it's presented to them.

When we stopped to let people out and take in a few more along the way, the woman who had hailed the taxi cheerfully explained to the other passengers that there was no need to pay because we were footing the bill. I could tell this because after getting situated, the new passengers all smiled at us and exclaimed, "Merci!" We didn't mind. The fare was not unreasonable, and if it weren't for the women on the bench, we probably never would have made it to St. Louis.

I spent a hot hour squished between Scott and a broken door handle that was jammed in my side. We had to stop a few times to add water to the radiator and avoiding the many goats along the way was tricky. But we were happy. This was why we came to Africa. In America the act of hailing a taxi is mundane and gets us just that, into a taxi. In Africa, it lets us into her people. The colonial buildings and sunset were as spectacular as promised, but what I remember most about that day in St. Louis is how we got there.

LIFE ON THE TRUCK

People often ask, "Weren't you ever bored during the long drives in the truck?" Never! For the first weeks we spent the days getting to know one another. There is something about overland travel with a group of strangers. You sometimes end up knowing more about each other than your friends or family back home do. This was why I found out that Luis missed ice cream, and that Bill was married to someone other than Maggie.

For reasons still unknown to me, my father began calling me Tris when I was a little girl, and the nickname stuck. Everyone on the truck called me Tris too, except for Bill who was noticeably uncomfortable when addressing me by name. He would say things like, "Scott, please ask your wife to pass the salt," or, "You there, are you finished with that book?" He certainly was friendly enough towards me, so I knew that it wasn't because he disliked me that he wouldn't use my name. Finally one day he sat down next to me on the truck and said, "Do you mind if I call you *Tess* instead of *Tris*? You see, Tris sounds too much like my wife's name."

"Call me whatever you want," I said agreeably. "Just don't call me late for dinner!" They must not have that joke in Wales because he just stared at me and repeated, "So, is it OK if I call you Tess?"

There is an odd security in telling your innermost thoughts and secrets to someone who you most likely will never see again, though sometimes people on overland trucks become lifelong friends despite learning everything there is to know about one another. Also, on an expedition there is this feeling of "We're in this together" and you want to know whom you can count on in challenging situations. This encouraged a lot of "get to know you" discussion. Carl, the perpetual student, shared the least about himself because he was usually curled up in his sleeping bag asleep. When he wasn't sleeping, he was reading. I think he read every book in the library. When he wasn't sleeping or reading, he stared at Patty. Patty may have been twice his age but she was what all young men hope for when they go for a cougar experience. She had long, dark brown hair, a youthful body, and enjoyed having fun. All Carl's sleeping and reading must have been somehow appealing because he eventually got Patty into his tent. No one was supposed to know. But when we heard slow dance music coming from an iPod inside Carl's tent, we guessed. When Suzanne teased her about it the next day, Patty said with a sheepish grin, "It was sweet that he felt he had to romance me with make-out music from the eighties," then she giggled her fabulous giggle and added, "but it was totally unnecessary!"

Aside from getting to know one another, we also occupied our time researching countries along the route to South Africa from the well-stocked library of books and maps at the back of the truck. Sam was the one most conscious of time and weather constraints. Almost every day he would open the map of Africa and start pointing to countries farther down in the loose itinerary. "If we don't get *here* by *then*, we're screwed. We'll be stuck in the mud in Cameroon or Angola." As much as it upset the Mechanic, Sam was right. We needed to keep moving to avoid the worst of the rainy season. The last thing we all wanted was to be bogged down and vulnerable on a muddy track for days on end. This put further pressure on the Mechanic, which gave him more reasons to hate Sam. The Mechanic also increased his resentment of Suzanne, mostly because she had made it clear she thought of him as a misogynist. Actually his infamous six squeaks hadn't helped his relationships with any of the single women on board anyway.

Almost every day we took turns shopping for food or cooking for the group. Bargaining with street vendors over bananas, tomatoes, or carrots along a crowded dusty road in Africa involves tact, courtesy, and patience. For some reason there is a great deal of laughter. I quickly got over any discomfort or hesitation and began to enjoy being part of the show. My downfall was that I always tried to buy from the oldest woman in a long row of women selling the same item. She knew she had me when I started respectfully with, "Hello, mother." I was lousy at bargaining and usually overpaid, so before too long I was asked to help guard the truck around markets instead of shop. That was OK with me since the truck often drew a crowd of happy children who wanted to play. They rarely asked for anything but attention.

Then there were the hours and hours spent watching Africa pass by. What are people wearing here? What do their homes look like? What vegetables do they eat here? What language do they speak? What is their word for corn? For carrot? Are they farmers or do they own cattle? Which tribe is that? How many children are able to go to school in this village? How many goats will I see today?

There was much to see that was new and stimulating. But there were two constants. One thing I could always count on was the presence of children in Africa. Children are everywhere. Outside of the larger cities, when children spy foreigners in a vehicle, they run towards it smiling, laughing, waving, and shouting. "How arrrre you?" they say with an impressive roll of the *r*. They inquire hopefully, "Bon-bon?" or "Cadeaux?" if it is a former French colony and, "Where are you from?" or "Give me pen!" if it is a former British colony.

The other constant is the industrious African woman. I can count on one hand the women I saw idle in all the time I have spent in Africa. The African woman travels long distances each day with a heavy collection of wood, food, or water on her head. She prepares the meals. She builds the hut, tends the fields, and takes the produce to market. She celebrates milestones with her friends. If she sees a foreigner passing by, she often pauses to wave and smile. Her face is often a study in joy or fatigue. She does it all with a baby tied to her back.

How could I possibly get bored with so much to learn, to look at, to absorb, to laugh at, or to weep about?

TABASKI

HOW TEN FOREIGNERS IN A BIG YELLOW TRUCK WERE INVITED TO A MUSLIM CELEBRATION

During a stop in Mauritania in the small desert town of Nouadibou, we met a local man who had been working as a guide for a German team in a car race from Plymouth, England, to Banjul in The Gambia. The Banjul Rally is kind of a Monty Python version of the more famous Paris to Dakar Challenge. The Plymouth to Banjul version has a few simple rules: The vehicle—often referred to as a banger—must cost no more than one hundred British pounds (around US$150) and no more than fifteen pounds can be spent on preparation. Once (if) the cars arrive in Banjul, they are donated or auctioned off to benefit local Gambian charities. During the race, days are spent driving as fast as possible from England to the ferry that takes them to Africa. Upon reaching the continent, the drivers spend most of their time maneuvering through the desert and digging out of the sand. Nights are spent in intoxicated laughter at campgrounds or wherever the car decides to rest for the night.

After the German's car went kaput near the town of Nouadibou (far short of the finish line) the team made their way back to Europe and the Mechanic offered their guide, Abda, a lift to his hometown in Senegal.

Scott and the Mechanic had met Abda in Nouadibou outside a guesthouse/barbershop where Abda was getting a trim. Normally Scott sports a beautiful thick head of blond hair, but once we entered the desert, he could think of little else but getting a haircut. Only, instead of a haircut, he was sheared. Yes, like a sheep. Not surprising, since the Australian who shaved his head used electric sheep shears. In the end Scott was left with a uniform, low-nap, blond-colored carpet sticking up an eighth of an inch all over his head. I had my very own blue-eyed Chia Pet. And he *was* fun to pet! When I ran my palm over the top, it felt like I was stroking the micro fibers of a fancy sofa or, more appropriately, the skin of a newly shorn sheep. He said he felt much cooler but complained that his head itched like crazy. "Perhaps you need a spritz of sheep dip," I teased.

When we arrived in the sprawling capital city of Dakar, Carl flew back to Canada as planned, and Abda invited us to stay at his family home. We slept on straw mats in a small courtyard situated between two wings of the house. The Mechanic slept in the truck, which was parked in the dirt road in front. The truck caused considerable excitement in the neighborhood. It wasn't long before a posse of kids surrounded the truck waiting to see if something interesting would happen. And it did. Sitting in plastic chairs in the road near the truck, Petra and Luis were proud recipients of cornrows neatly woven by Abda's nieces. On Petra it was fine. She ended up looking like Bo Derek in the movie *Ten*. But cornrows were made for tall blondes and African women, not for already fabulous looking Spaniards. After Luis's shoulder-length black tresses were constrained in fifty or more tight pigtails, my image of him was shattered. I mean, come on, Antonio Banderas in cornrows? From then on I had to close my eyes for Luis's "Trriiis" to have the same effect on me.

As if staying at Abda's home and getting new dos weren't enough, we were fortunate to arrive in Dakar during one of the most important feast days in Muslim Africa. Tabaski is a festival that commemorates the sacrifice Abraham was asked to make. In the days and weeks leading up to Tabaski, tens of thousands of sheep are transported through the streets, from city to city, village to village, on top of buses, trucks, and cars, or grouped together for sale at dusty intersections. On the feast day, the male head of the family digs a deep hole somewhere on his property or in the dirt in front of the house or hut. He gives a sheep or a ram a bath, turns its face towards Mecca, slits its throat, and says a prayer while the blood runs into the hole. Then everyone puts on new clothes and goes to mosque. When they come back, they butcher the ram, cook the meat, and then share it with friends and neighbors for at least three days.

We participated in the entire Tabaski ceremony (except for attending mosque) and helped prepare the food. Knowing that I was not going to be any help cutting up the ram since I had just been petting him that morning, I helped Maggie and Petra peel and slice potatoes into strips, which we then fried in a pot of hot oil. The Mechanic was in his element. He knew his way around a butcher knife (no doubt from working on a cattle station), and he sprang to his feet when it was time to butcher and barbeque the meat. When the men came back from mosque, we all sat on the floor around heaping platters of cooked ram and salty French fries. Both before and after the meal, our host poured water from a small pot over our hands to cleanse them.

For three days we ate various forms of ram: barbeque ram, ram stew, ram over spaghetti, and ram every morning for breakfast. I offered to do the dishes and washed them in the African fashion, bent over a bucket that sat on the ground, so they gave me an African name, a Senegalese dress, and called me their sister. Their family name is Kane, a prestigious name in Senegal. Since my last name is O'Kane, I guess they felt a connection. The fact that I'm Irish, with dark blond hair and green eyes (and a rather pale complexion), didn't stand in the way of me becoming a member of the family. It is a Muslim custom to treat guests as if they are a blessing from God. The Kanes couldn't have been more generous or hospitable or treated us more like family.

It wasn't the first time in our travels that we were the recipients of Muslim generosity and warmth. During a trip to Quetta, Pakistan, in 1995, we learned that hospitality is an essential part of what it is to be a Muslim. Extending hospitality and having it openly received is a matter of honor and is an essential part of how Muslims judge themselves as good people.

Quetta is a very traditional city in the Islamic sense, including manner of dress. Even though I was covered head to toe in a loose fitting dress, leggings, long-sleeved shirt, and scarf for my head, as I crossed the street the day we arrived, men stared at or circled me on their bicycles. The next day, we decided to purchase a traditional shalwar kameez so I would be attired in the same fashion as the women of Pakistan in baggy pants, loose-fitting blouse that fell to my ankles, and a headscarf.

As we walked through the town, we noticed there were hardly any women in the streets and none working in the shops. The few women we saw were escorted by a male family member who assisted with the shopping and carried the purchases. It turned out I had a difficult time shopping alone. It wasn't that I wasn't allowed to walk into shops and *try* to purchase something. But when I did, I wouldn't get any service. It was as if I were invisible. I went into one store to buy sandals, but the proprietor would not speak or look at me. He wasn't rude or snooty the way a salesman at an exclusive store in America might be. He simply didn't know what to do with me. Where was my escort? I returned with Scott who did all the talking.

The shalwar kameez I picked out was enormous. They all were. The pants looked like they were made for a Sumo wrestler. The proprietor handed Scott an elastic band and said, "For tailoring." I had to pull the elastic through the waist and cinch it up under the very blousy blouse to keep the trousers from falling off.

I quickly took to Pakistani clothing because it was so sensible. More dust jacket than fashion statement, I simply shook it out at the end of each trip into town. All of my Western clothing underneath stayed as clean as a whistle. I understood the practicality of the clothes but I was irritated that it was somehow inappropriate for me to wander around by myself. It was an inconvenience to us both that Scott had to do everything for me. "Why don't the women rise up so they can work, shop, and eat where they want?" I said to him as we walked around town.

We rarely saw women in the restaurants. We soon realized that rooms in the cafés were segregated by gender; the men were in the front and the women were in a separate room in the back. Some restaurants had a "family room" where families could eat together.

Later that week, fully covered in the local attire, I stood by my husband as he got a shave in a barber chair under a tree. The barber, after barely a glance at me, said to Scott, "It is very good that your wife dresses this way," he paused before adding, "because in Pakistan, all eyes are hungry."

He articulated perfectly what I had seen that morning when I entered the hotel café seeking a cup of tea. The café had been transformed into an intimate movie theater. The dimly lit room was filled with Pakistani men intently watching an episode of *Bay Watch*. It wasn't only their eyes that were hungry. The room was humid with desire.

Back in our hotel room I switched on the TV and was surprised to find a show coming in crisp and clear starring unfamiliar American actors. The program was horrible. All the stereotypes that Muslims find offensive about American culture played out on the screen. Scantily dressed teenagers called their parents stupid before slamming the door on their way to the mall. Spouses communicated with one another in disrespectful one-liners, then retired to the bedroom. The entire display of hedonism and sleaze was overlaid by a loud laugh track. It made me angry. Where did this come from? Who produced it? Why would Pakistani TV buy it? What did Pakistanis think of Americans when they saw it? Did this show exist for propaganda purposes? If so, it was working! If this is their only view of America, no wonder some Muslims think our culture is degenerate.

Despite the broad misconceptions many Pakistanis may have of Americans, the people of Quetta consistently treated us with generosity and kindness. They always seemed to end up giving us more than we asked for, be it a meal or a service. And every conversation, transaction, or visit to a shop always came with a cup of tea.

We walked the streets of Quetta for a week becoming more comfortable each day. This was before September 11, so most of our prior knowledge of Muslim culture had come from a World's Religions class in college and a few public television specials, not CNN news. Still, being there and experiencing Islamic culture firsthand was nothing like what we had read or heard.

Pakistan is dry, and by that I don't mean arid. Muslims are not allowed to drink alcohol. In Quetta maybe all eyes are hungry, but we were thirsty! As hard as we tried to respect the customs of the Muslim culture, we really missed happy hour. We hadn't had a beer in two weeks and, while we aren't heavy drinkers, it is a tradition of ours to toast the end of a travel day with a sundowner of some sort.

Acquiring alcohol in Pakistan is not an easy task, but it is not impossible. First, we would have to go to an office and apply for a "permit as a non-Muslim," which we would then present at a building where we could purchase a case of beer. That didn't seem too difficult and since traditions must be honored, my husband turned to me one morning and said, "I'm going to get one of those beer drinking permits. Be back in an hour!"

An hour went by, then two, then four, and I was more than a little worried about what might have happened. I started thinking things like, "If he gets back alive, I'm going to kill him!" as people do when they are worried about a loved one.

At dusk he returned. Here's the story he told after I demanded, "What took you so long?" and "Did you at least get some beer?"

"Why do you look so angry?" he replied managing to actually look puzzled as to why I would be upset that he went missing in a city where almost all the men walk around carrying guns. "OK. So you saw me drive off in the auto rickshaw, right? Well the driver didn't know the exact office to go to get the permit, so we had to pick up a friend of his who said he knew where the office was located. The driver and his friend took me to the place where I would ultimately get to buy some beer if I was able to get a permit, but I was told I had to go to the police station first. Then the beer agent invited me to have some tea, so we all sat, and had tea, and talked. We eventually got to the police station, and I was invited to have tea with the police officers while we waited for a man who supposedly knew about beer permits. He had stepped out to pray. After tea and the usual questions—where are you from, how many children do you have—the man who knew about non-Muslim beer drinking licenses arrived and told me that the police station wasn't the place to get a permit, but he knew where to go. After more tea, he led the way in an army vehicle, which for some reason made my rickshaw driver very nervous, and we drove in convoy to an office where, lo and behold, a *woman* was working behind a desk! She looked at me with curiosity as the police officer, the auto rickshaw driver, his friend, and I sat down to have tea with the other men in the office. Then the woman at the desk began speaking to me in Urdu. One of the men translated. 'She wants to know how many children you have.' I told her none, but I took out your passport, which I had with me and showed her your picture for, you know, potential. Pointing at your picture, and at me, she asked through the translator if we would do her the honor of coming to her home for tea! I didn't know what to make of the whole thing, but she wrote a bunch of stuff down in Urdu, which turns out to be directions to her home, and here it is!" Scott finished his story and proudly produced what looked to be a jumble of squiggles.

I looked down at the scrap of paper saying, "So it wasn't your fault you were gone all day. It was the tea."

"Exactly! Anyway, what do you think about going to this lady's house?" he asked excitedly. I took his extreme, definitely not Scott-like animation to be due to his excessive caffeine consumption that day.

"You're Red Bulling on me. Calm down." I said taking the scrap of paper from him. I couldn't tell if I was holding it right side up. "What does it say?"

"I *told* you. It's her address, and all we have to do is hand it to an auto rickshaw driver and *he* will be able to read it and will know where to take us. We are invited there for tea!" He jabbed his finger at the Urdu written on the paper for emphasis.

"How do we know this doesn't say, 'Take these two infidels up to the hills and sacrifice them to Allah?'"

"C'mon, Tris. It's *tea.*"

"Well, did you at least get some beer?" I asked, softening some.

"Of course! After the woman gave me her address, the paperwork was a slam dunk. We all drove back to the beer vendor in the unmarked building, and the rickshaw driver, his friend, the police officer, and I were given cups of tea and I was presented with a whole case of warm beer. Want one?"

The next afternoon we handed the scrap of paper to an auto rickshaw driver and saw places in Quetta we never would have if my husband had not been thirsty for a beer the day before.

The driver spoke a little English. He told us that written on the note were two things—a street name and "The House of Muhammad." After many wrong turns and stops to ask for directions, we finally arrived at Muhammad's house.

The eldest son, also named Muhammad, greeted us at the door and invited us in. His English was excellent, which was a good thing because I was wondering how we were going to be able to communicate. Muhammad introduced his father, his two brothers, his sister, and the woman my husband had met in the office. Muhammad was the only one who spoke any English.

In the sparsely furnished but tidy house, there was a sewing machine, a dowry trunk, a few pillows on a silk area rug on the floor, and some photographs of ancestors hanging on the wall. A one-burner stove with neatly stacked pots and dishes sat on a tiled area in a small courtyard at the front of the house. In the largest room, we were offered pillows to sit on and the family sat around us on the carpet in a semi-circle. Rather, everyone in the family but the twelve-year-old girl who sat apart behind the family. Tea and several plates of pretty cakes and sweets were set down in front of us. It must have cost a small fortune.

Scott commented to Muhammad how surprised he had been to see his mother behind the desk the day before. The son explained that the family was not happy that his mother had to work. Several years prior, his father had become very ill, making it impossible for him to work. As I looked at the father I could see that something had affected his motor skills.

"The most my father can do now is sweep floors at a clinic," said Muhammad. "So my mother had to go to work to support our family." He paused. "I am anxious for the day when I can do my duty so that my mother will not have to work."

"How did your mother and father meet?" I asked. Muhammad's mother told the story to us in Urdu, and the son translated.

She began, "It was very long ago! My parents and the parents of a distant cousin arranged our marriage while I was outside playing. I was five years old." She spoke with excitement and had a smile in her voice. When she got to the part about playing in the street, she threw back her veil to take us back to the time when she was just a girl and not yet covered. She had a beautiful face, and it struck me that she and I were about the same age. She continued, "When I came in from outside, I met the little boy who was to become my husband."

Despite not having many choices in her life, she seemed to be a very happy woman. I desperately wished I could talk to her in her own language. As she adjusted her veil, I asked Muhammad, "What is the role of Muslim women in Pakistani society?"

I could tell that he knew what he wanted to say but was struggling with how to make it understandable to us. Finally he said, "Are you familiar with computers and how they operate?"

Though we come from the capital of Silicon Valley, we answered honestly, "A little."

"Well," he continued with sincerity, "here women are like the motherboard on a computer. They are so important! Without them, nothing works. Nothing succeeds. Women are what give order to our world." He paused then added, "They are also the moral backbone of society."

It was a pivotal moment for me. I had been walking around Quetta not getting it. At the same time they may have been held back from participating in society fully, women were held high up, on a pedestal.

As we sat talking with Muhammad Jr., I tried to bring his young sister into the circle and in on the conversation. "Your sister is very quiet. Won't she sit next to me?" I said indicating a space to my right.

Muhammad looked a little annoyed and didn't answer.

"Her clothes are very beautiful," I said, still feeling that she was being excluded.

"She makes all the clothes for the family," he replied dismissively.

"Wow! They are very lovely and very well made. When she is older will she open a shop and sell the clothes she makes?" I asked naively. Men were the tailors, not women. And she would certainly never receive encouragement from her brother, or her religion, to work outside of the home.

Tiring of me talking about something as unimportant as his sister, Muhammad said with finality, "When she is fourteen she will be married and that is all."

It would have been beyond rudeness for me to say it, but I couldn't help but think that respect for women must only start when their backbone is fully formed—at marriage.

We had brought with us photos of our families to share. My husband and I with our mothers, a Christmas celebration, all twenty-three of us playing charades together as we often did. Muhammad spoke to his family in Urdu, translating my descriptions of the images. As they looked at the pictures, I could see they were puzzled about something. Muhammad finally turned to us saying, "Your family seems very close. We thought that American families do not spend time together and that children rarely even speak to their parents."

I flashed on the absurd TV shows I had seen at the hotel and hoped I could dispel some misconceptions.

"I think my family is a pretty typical American family," I replied. "We get together often, and we respect our parents very much. We have a lot of fun together."

Muhammad translated what I had said and there was more discussion. Muhammad's mother looked through the photos once more, then lifted her veil and gave me a smile of understanding. I was stunned. *Was this really the first time they were presented a different way to view the American family?* From the looks on their faces, it was.

We left The House of Muhammad that evening with a little more knowledge of Muslim culture and the place of women in it. Muhammad's mother gave me a headscarf, which she took from her daughter's dowry trunk and carefully arranged it on my head. I was moved to tears by her gift. Muhammad told us that we were the only foreigners who had ever crossed their threshold.

As we rode back to our guesthouse, I said to Scott, "Who would have thought that your desire for a beer yesterday would have turned into this wonderful experience today?"

The next day we scoured the few shops in Quetta. We wanted to buy something to give to the family in return for their generosity and hospitality. Nothing was suitable. If there was a gift shop, we never found it. Shops in Quetta only seemed to carry things like flour, or inner tubes, or trousers, and none of those seemed sufficient. We decided to give Muhammad Jr. a brand new well-designed school backpack that we had brought with us from California. He was so pleased with it! He stressed that it would always remain in the family and that after he was finished with his schooling it would be passed down to his brother and that his brother would pass it on to the next.

The following morning Muhammad Jr. brought us a special gift, a meal. He said his mother had stayed up all night preparing it and that it was a meal prepared once a year to honor their ancestors. What a gesture! My heart was so full it ached. It was as if she had cooked an entire Thanksgiving dinner just for us.

That afternoon, we tried to find someone to reinforce some stitching on my tired old backpack. We had it repaired at a tailor on the main road, but instead of receiving a bill for service, we were given tea. When we insisted on paying, the proprietor excused himself and came back with a gift for us.

Whenever we went to a bank to cash traveler's checks in Pakistan, we were always immediately taken to the office of the bank manager and given tea and engaged in conversation. It seemed impossible to give without getting something in return. We learned from a shopkeeper that the Urdu word for "guest" means blessing from God.

Ten years later in Dakar, Senegal, the Muslim Kane family was also treating us as if we were a blessing from God. They couldn't do enough for us and they expected nothing in return.

As we prepared to say our good-byes to the Kane family, I thought about Muslim women in Iraq and Afghanistan struggling for their right to work, vote, and attend school. Maybe someday soon a young girl in Pakistan will be able to design and sell the clothes she makes and not be married off at age fourteen. But change will not come easy. Shortly after first meeting her, a Muslim woman who immigrated to our city from Bosnia more than fifteen years ago was having trouble recalling my name at a neighborhood function. She finally exclaimed, "Oh yes! Now I remember. You are the woman of Scott."

My Gambian Husband

After Tabeski, we all left the truck and the Mechanic for a week. We all wanted to see The Gambia but the Mechanic refused to drive us there. He claimed that the roads in Gambia were notoriously rough and that he wasn't in the mood to subject himself or the truck to the stress. It didn't matter. I was glad for a chance to see Gambia and leave group dynamics behind for a while. We waved goodbye to the truck, the Kane family, and the Mechanic, and crossed the river to Gambia.

The Republic of The Gambia, at fifty kilometers wide and five hundred kilometers long, is the skinniest and smallest country in Africa. So small that when looking for it on a map, it looks like nothing more than a finger jabbing into the side of Senegal. Imagine Senegal as a hotdog bun and The Gambia as a cheese weenie. The Gambia River, which runs the length of Gambia, is the cheese in the weenie. Verdant brush defines the river course like one continuous untrimmed unibrow. It was such a welcome change after the drab desert scenery we had been traveling through since Morocco. We had spent so much time in the beige world I had almost forgotten what green looked like. I remember exclaiming to Scott, "I smell vegetation!" Unfortunately, while the river was navigable, no one seemed to use it for transportation. There were rumors that the one and only passenger boat had sunk, so we would have to rely solely on bush taxi to get around the country.

The Mechanic was right about the roads. I'm sure a few of my internal organs were rearranged after a week in bush taxis—at least it felt that way. Drivers entirely abandoned the heavily potted road and drove along the side of what remained of it, in the area usually reserved for a ravine. This too was rutted and canted at such a steep angle that after ten minutes everyone in the vehicle ended up perched on one butt cheek. By the completion of the journey, the child who had originally been placed on the lap of the person next to me ended up teetering on my hip like a loose hood ornament. What got us through the long, hot, rough, dusty days in bush taxis were peanuts, the national snack food of The Gambia. Peanuts are the main crop, and locals find many innovative ways of introducing peanuts into almost every meal. To our digestive regret there was always somebody ready to whip up a batch of thick peanut stew for us to eat.

I was enjoying a small bag of peanuts in the city of Bakau one day when a nice looking, very fit young Gambian man approached me. "Do you have a Gambian husband?" he asked.

"No," I answered. "My husband is from California." He shrugged and began talking to me in a way that made me feel uncomfortable. I finally had to be rude. "I have to go now to meet my non-Gambian husband who is very big and strong!" Then I made a Mr. Universe pose, arms inverse akimbo with fists in the air to demonstrate the mighty muscles of my husband.

Despite the fact that I had just looked like a lunatic, another young man approached me with an unmistakable leer and asked, "Do you have a Gambian husband yet?"

I was beginning to get perturbed by all this attention. "No, my husband is *not* Gambian. Why do you ask?" wondering what he meant by "yet." He too shrugged and walked a little closer to me until I gave him the strong man pose. Immediately after he left, a third attractive young man sidled up to me. "I do not have a Gambian husband, and you are standing way to close to me, Buster!" I said in a culturally sensitive way. I felt like there was a one-act play going on all over town, but no one had bothered to give me a script.

I cut short my confusing walk and headed to the beach where I had agreed to meet Scott. I wanted to share my encounters with him and show off my strong man pose. While I waited for my husband, I watched a group of young men playing volleyball. I noticed that all the Gambian men were good-looking and very fit. Then as I scanned the rest of the beach I saw several European women strolling arm in arm with very attractive African men. But the women were all older, *much* older than the men.

I had seen older North American or European men with young woman in Thailand, but I had never heard of the older woman, younger man arrangement that seemed to be the main event in Gambia. We had arrived in Cougar Country. Apparently one can have a Gambian husband for an hour, a day, a week, a month, or a lifetime—whatever the two parties arrange.

Men and women are different. Mars, Venus, I think we all agree. Lonely men may go to Thailand for sex. But women go to Gambia for a *relationship*. I watched one such couple at the local store in Bakau, the aged European woman standing next to her young Gambian husband as she browsed the cereal aisle. "Do you think we should get Corn Flakes or Mueslix?" she asked while her "husband" feigned interest and said, "Whatever you would like," with a look on his face that said with frustration, "Why can't she just use me for sex? Why do we have to have discussions about cereal? Or discussions at all?"

European women who are into Gambian husbands seem to go to The Gambia to play house for a while. I suppose some of them might even be married to average guys back home and just want to know what it would be like to go grocery shopping with a stud. Some of the women end up marrying the young men and take them home to Europe where I suppose they live out their days happily browsing the cereal aisles at Sainsbury's or Safeway.

We spent two days observing this phenomenon. It must have been low season for the paramour business because there was a glut of handsome bucks and an undersupply of old European women. So while I was getting quite a lot of attention, it was fatiguing to constantly glower at beautiful men while doing my strong man pose. We decided it was time to make our way farther up country. I donned my tightest clothing in an effort to keep my organs in place for the bush taxi rides ahead of us.

Bribery stations—I mean random checkpoints—were much more prevalent along the roads in Gambia than in Senegal. One day we made the mistake of choosing a bush taxi near a Gambian police outpost. An official sauntered over and peered in over the baskets and bundles and Gambians until his eyes came to rest on ours. He asked to see our passports and added, "Are you enjoying your stay in our country?" Without waiting for a reply he put his hands on his hips, leaned back and said at great volume, "*What* do you have for the Gambian Police?"

Confused, we looked to our driver for a clue as to how we should respond. He sat with both hands on the wheel staring straight ahead and pretended he was invisible. No one else in the taxi moved a muscle.

Looking back at the policeman I said, "We don't understand."

"*What* do you have for the Gambian *Police?*" he repeated. He arched back even further so that he looked at us over the very tip of his nose.

We looked at one another unsure what to do or say. We had to do something quick before the policeman ended up falling over. Finally Scott reached into our daypack and pulled out a bottle of rotgut whiskey we had taken one sip of three days earlier before gagging. We had hung on to it only because it might come in handy if we wanted to start a campfire or blind someone.

"Well," Scott said with hesitation while holding out the bottle, "we have this." We held our breath not sure at all if this would please him or make him angry.

"*That* would be *fine!*" he said stowing the bottle in his jacket pocket and returning to a full and upright position before waving the driver on.

A week later, after more bruising bush taxi rides and propositions than I could count, it was time to leave The Gambia and rejoin the Mechanic in Senegal. Getting out of The Gambia turned out to be more of a challenge than we thought and reminded me what it is about Africa that makes me cry, laugh, despair, and hope. We waited hours at a main crossroad, asked many drivers, even bribed another official but could not get a ride into Senegal. Finally a man transporting hundreds of pounds of potatoes to market in Senegal let us pay him a considerable sum to ride amongst his cargo.

In a vehicle that was once a small truck but was now a collection of jiggled off parts of other vehicles, he crammed all his potatoes and sixteen people. Like sardines. The vehicle looked like a bloated zit about to pop. Scott lay on his back atop a mountain of potatoes like an upside-down crab, his knees to his chest and his arms bent at a forty-five-degree angle, giving the illusion that he was holding up the potato laden roof that sagged only inches above him. Another man, thinking he had found the sweet spot on top, bounced off and the roof suddenly bowed a bit less. I sat in the center of the front seat, my arms across the shoulders and out the windows of the driver and the passenger next to me. My job was to hold both doors shut for the four-hour journey. The man next to me taught me a few words of Wolof, and I taught him some words in English, such as "spuds" and "overcapacity" and "unsafe." There was no reverse gear, so when we had to turn around (to pick up the man who had fallen off) we all had to de wedge ourselves from the truck and help push the vehicle around. And we must have entered Senegal by the back entrance. We never did see a border post.

Police checkpoints, rough roads, and potato trucks aside—bush taxis in The Gambia were my favorite. There was always so much going on. During a journey from Serekunda to Georgetown, a cute little boy, Sisi, sat next to me on his mother's lap. He stared at me, and I smiled at him. "He is very handsome," I said to his mother. After she translated what I had said, he suddenly became very shy. He whispered something to his mother that made her burst out laughing. "He says he loves you!" She placed Sisi on my lap and said, "Here! Now you have a Gambian husband!"

Sisi used my lap as a platform for pits he discarded as he ate a fruit the size of a small cherry, spitting out each pit with a wet "ptui" while gazing at me with the love only a Gambian husband can give. I was completely smitten.

"What kind of cereal do you like?" I asked.

Timbuktu, So You Think You're Funny

When I was little, Mom often said, "If you kids don't behave, I'm going to pack my bags and go to Timbuktu!"

Mom never actually made it to Timbuktu, but I did.

Timbuktu is not easy to get to. On the way there we had one flat tire, one broken spring, and one broken radiator, not to mention getting stuck in silt for a few hours while driving off the Niger River ferry.

In addition to all the mechanical issues involved in getting to Timbuktu, a desperate nomadic family waved us down and pleaded for medicine for their sick baby. We could see them coming towards us from far across the desert for some time. At first they looked like nothing more than a mirage or a speck in motion as they made their way on foot with purpose across the sand to intercept the truck. Eventually the speck and the truck converged. The French-speaking patriarch spoke for the family of three adults and six children, one an infant. He looked distraught as he gestured towards the baby.

"Mike, what is he saying?" we all asked at once when the man had finished speaking.

"The baby is very sick and they want us to give them some medicine."

"I have some Paracetemol," offered Suzanne immediately as she stood up to retrieve her first aid kit.

The Mechanic frowned. "Wait," he said to Suzanne. "Mike, tell them they can all come on board and we will drive them to the very next village that has a doctor."

Mike translated the nomad's response. "He says they don't want to go to the village. They just want us to give them some medicine."

"Bloody hell!" swore the Mechanic with exasperation. "That's the problem!" He began to pace beside the truck. "They have seen or heard about the curative powers of Western medicine so they think this child's life can be saved with a pill we give her. We can't possibly know what illness she has. We only know she is very sick. She could have malaria, or typhoid, or countless other serious diseases. She needs tests and proper treatment! If we give this man medicine, he'll go away thinking she's cured and then be surprised and angry when she dies. The Mechanic kicked the sand with frustration. "Tell him he must take the baby to a clinic."

Mike tried to persuade the family to get on the truck while the rest of us debated what would be best for the baby. We were faced with a moral dilemma, but for once we were all in agreement. It was agonizing to watch the baby suffer but the Mechanic was right. If we gave the family medicine, something they thought of as a cure, we might be doing more harm than good. For reasons clear only to him, the patriarch refused to let us take him and the baby to the next village. It was incredibly frustrating. In the end we gave the man a tiny segment of a baby aspirin. It was barely a crumb but maybe it was enough to give the baby some temporary relief.

As the Mechanic climbed into the cab, he cursed again and asked Mike to stress that it wouldn't cure her. Mike reiterated one last time that the patriarch should come with us and take the baby to a doctor for proper treatment and that we would pay the clinic fees, but the man refused. The Mechanic drove away slowly. We were heartbroken and uneasy knowing that the next foreigner to come along might give the man some magic out of a pill bottle and that the baby would never make it to a doctor in time.

Hours later, we were still thinking about the nomads and their way of life when the president of Mali and his motorcade of five Hummers blocked our route in what looked like a reelection campaign tour. Quite the Sunday drive. As he drove across his country taking the pulse of his constituents, he smiled and waved from his Humvee and periodically stopped to press the flesh of village elders along the way. In every town we drove through, people lined the road, cheering and dancing while they waited hours in the hot sun for the president to pass.

At one roadblock, we climbed up on the roof of our vehicle and had a bird's eye view of the dignitaries as they left their Humvees to visit the home of a village chief. As he returned to his vehicle, the president of Mali removed his golf cap and gave us a happy wave before speeding away in a cloud of Hummer dust. I wanted to tell him about the family who needed help a few hours away in the desert but what good would that do? The president would no doubt give me a look that said, "And your point is?" I don't think the family would have listened to their president—a man they'd never heard of—any more than they would have heeded our advice anyway.

A few hours and four more pit stops later, we finally came to the Niger River and the ferry that would take us across and start us on our final push to Timbuktu. While waiting for the ferry, we all climbed up on the roof of the truck and watched dusk settle over the river. For once, everyone was quiet. It was another moment when we were all grateful to be exactly where we wanted to be, doing exactly what we wanted to do. Despite the fact that he had already been forced to use most of the spare parts he had intended to sell in South Africa, even the Mechanic seemed momentarily at peace.

Finally. Timbuktu. The scenery—buildings covered with sand and people shrouded in fabric to protect them from the sand—looked so otherworldly that I could see why Mom wanted to go there. Either that or she wanted to get as far away from us as possible because it really is in the middle of nowhere.

"There's nothing here, just sand!" Scott said while squinting into the sun and dust and nothingness.

"Exactly! That's what makes it so great!" I said with a smile. "You have to admit, the sunset over the Niger was one of the best ever."

Flushing grit from his eyes with his water bottle, Scott grumbled, "The sunset is all orangey beautiful because even the *air* is saturated with sand!"

"Sheesh. I can't believe you are complaining. We're in Timbuktu man. TIMBUKTU!"

Ideas differ on how Timbuktu got its name. One is that it was taken from a Berber word meaning *far away*. Even today, Timbuktu retains its mystique as a place unreachable and exotic. For centuries non-Muslim foreigners were made to feel unwelcome, usually by being killed. In 1824 the French Geographic Society offered a large reward to any non-Muslim who could reach Timbuktu and return with a report about her people and customs. The first attempts did not end well. It wasn't until 1828 when a Frenchman disguised himself as a Muslim to gain access to Timbuktu (is that fair?) that the award was claimed.

In those days Timbuktu sat on the edge of the Sahara. But as the desert expanded, her border kept shifting south. Timbuktu is directly in the path of desertification. Photos taken from the air show it completely surrounded by sand. Another World Heritage site, Timbuktu was put on the endangered list in 1990. After significant restoration projects were completed, Timbuktu was removed from the list in 2005. But its unique location in the desert on the cross-Saharan trade route is what continues to make preservation a challenge today. No one can stop the shifting sand in its determination to eat Timbuktu.

It took several days to get the sand out of my eyes, ears, hair, and bra strap, but the discomfort didn't lessen the sense of accomplishment I felt to be in the proverbial boondocks known as Timbuktu. I'm glad I didn't wait too long to go. An account from 1700 speaks of "large forests at the eastern border of the city." Today there is barely a tree, much less a forest, in sight. It looks as though the Sahara will be covering the entire city completely someday soon. But visiting a city in the middle of nowhere before it disappears isn't the only reason to visit Timbuktu. Its origins are fascinating.

Timbuktu started out as a Taureg trading post serving nomadic Berber and Arabic merchants from the north. Soon it became a trading center for gold, rock salt, and slaves. Traders and Islamic scholars from the north came in droves. Three universities—one of which is said to be the first in the world—were founded, and hundreds of thousands of manuscripts were written there. Timbuktu became an important hub not only for trade but also for education, inspiring the Islamic proverb, "Salt comes from the north, gold from the south, but the word of God and the treasures of wisdom come from Timbuktu." Though much smaller than it was during it's golden age, Timbuktu still serves as an important stopover for traders, nomads, and overland adventurers.

All travelers have their personal list of places to see before they die, and Timbuktu was one for me. After all, I grew up hearing about Timbuktu almost every day in my childhood. Though Mom often seemed anxious to go to Timbuktu, my brothers and I didn't see how our behavior had anything to do with it, so her oft-repeated warning had little effect on us. Until one day. The ultimate Timbuktu moment for me as a kid, the day I really thought Mom was serious about packing her bags and going, occurred the day my brother Sean and I found a couple of big, fat, red, swollen with ink permanent markers. Markers in hand, we did the obvious. We removed the caps and used them like swords on each other. My brother Sean was and is much taller than me, so I had to leap and slash, and jump and thrust, to try to "stab" him. I bounced up and down like a lunatic on a pogo stick while he stood over me poking red dots all over my face.

"Arrr! I have you now!" I said with a final vigorous lunge. I sprang at him, flinging my sword upward and side to side with wild force, my crazy floundering making my brother laugh as I thrust my marker with even more gusto. On the duel and the laughter went—until I caught a glimpse of the ceiling. We both stopped and stared in silent horror at what I had done. I had missed my intended target entirely. Instead, each and every fling of my marker resulted in countless bright red splatters all over the eight-foot high ceiling.

When my mom finally noticed her new polka dotted ceiling (we didn't feel it necessary to bring it to her attention), she said, "So you think you're funny! If you kids can't behave, I'm going to pack my bags and go to Timbuktu!" Then, "Ach du lieber Gott! Klein scheisse!" When Mom was really exasperated she would revert to swearing at us in the language of her youth. For years I actually thought these were terms of endearment. It wasn't until my brother Joe studied German in high school that we learned she had been calling us little turds all those years.

Splattering her ceiling made her threaten *in German* (which for some reason made her sound a lot more resolute) to leave us little turds and go to Timbuktu.

The red splotches from our sword fight remained on the living room ceiling for a few years—until my parents threw an engagement party for my sister who was sixteen years older than me. She had her wedding gifts on display in the living room (they did weird things like that in those days), so new living room furniture was purchased and the ceiling was given a fresh coat of paint. Until they were painted over, those red spots were a daily reminder to Sean and me of the time we almost pushed our mom to the limit, to Timbuktu.

Our group had planned to stay in Timbuktu for one or two days, but it took five to replace the springs (the last set) and radiator (the last one), which had been damaged during the journey. We passed the days helping the Mechanic repair the truck while he carried on about how "no one ever bloody helps fix the bloody truck." When we weren't helping or being berated for not helping enough, we ate tasty fish called capitan caught fresh from the Niger River.

My favorite thing to do in Timbuktu was to walk a kilometer out of town over the carpet of soft sand that passed as a road, sit quietly and wait for a blue ghost on a camel to pass by. Due to the constant fine, gritty sand that passes for air in Timbuktu, the Taureg nomads cover everything but their eyes in vivid blue cloth fashioned into flowing robes and bright blue turbans. There I was in the hot desert, nowhere in the middle of nowhere, and off in the distance what looked like a shimmering blue ghost, sometimes on a camel, slowly undulated towards me over the waves of heat. Temperatures were over a hundred degrees, but the sight always gave me a chill.

We tried hard to find postcards to send home to our loved ones proving that we had been to this land known as far away. Finding none, I finally had to telephone my mom to say, "I packed my bags, and I'm in Timbuktu!"

There was a lot of static, but I could just make out her reply: "So you think you're funny…"

THE MOSQUE THAT GETS A FACELIFT

Mali is home to the oldest and largest mud structure in the world, the Mosque of D'jenné. We couldn't have timed our arrival better because we arrived on market day when the vibrant primary colors of fruits, vegetables, and clothing against the backdrop of the magnificent tawny-colored mosque shows D'jenné at her very best.

A building made out of mud requires a lot of maintenance. But government officials based in Bamako aren't likely to travel long distances to maintain a building regularly, even if it *is* a World Heritage site. In D'jenné, villagers take matters into their own hands. While they are at it, they turn building maintenance into a festival. Each year, people from surrounding villages come together to resurface the entire mosque. For several days, volunteers collect heavy buckets of wet mud from the river and carry them to the mosque where it is mixed with straw to form a durable gluey coating. Then boys and men hanging from timber scaffolding slather the entire mosque in a fresh new layer of clay. It turns into a friendly competition between villages to see who can supply, and apply, the most mud.

Our small expedition made up the total handful of travelers in Djenné at the time, so we were prime targets for the hat, blanket, and trinket sellers who plied the marketplace. They walked the streets laden with dozens of conical hats and colorful blankets perched on their heads or draped over their arms as they searched for customers. One such seller spotted us on our first day in Djenné and seemed to find us wherever we were—in the market, in a restaurant, near the mosque, or outside our guesthouse each morning. He didn't speak

English but tried communicating with us in French, German, Arabic, and a few other languages I didn't recognize. One of his blankets was particularly beautiful. Scott and I both liked it, but it was far too large for us to carry in our backpacks, so we shook our heads and said, "No, thank you." But the blanket seller was persistent. We knew enough French to understand that it was a special "wedding" blanket. Such a blanket would be given to a Malian couple at their wedding ceremony.

"Trés chic. Beautiful," I said while insisting that regrettably, we could not carry it. Yet our twosome became a threesome as the blanket seller followed us everywhere we went over the next few days.

On our last morning in Djenné, the blanket seller stood predictably by our guesthouse gate. "No, no, no," we said firmly while showing him how small our backpacks were.

Never underestimate the power of a blanket seller in Djenné. The blanket looked lovely on our bed at home in California and it will always remind me of the mud mosques and markets of Djenné.

I will also always remember Djenné as the place where Mike and the Mechanic came to blows. I never knew exactly what the argument was about, but Mike and Suzanne spent the evening discussing it over beers. When I finally asked Mike about it, all he said was, "You know, the guy is an asshole," he paused. "But I would still have a beer with him."

After Djenné, almost all the positive vibes we had felt while driving through the desert were gone. Tensions were higher than ever. The expedition was starting to resemble a bad marriage, and the Mechanic was getting the silent treatment. No one was ready to utter the D-word, but it was more obvious each day that the relationship just wasn't working out. No one had the energy to mediate any longer, and we hadn't had a group discussion in several days. I again wondered if we would be able to keep it together as a group until we at least reached Ghana.

Meeting Aliens in the Dogon

Failing to find a solution to the dysfunctional dynamic, the trip took on a new vibe after leaving Djenné. Everyone seemed more resigned to live in the moment. There was an acceptance that we were going to take it a day at time and let the chips fall where they may. As nice as that sounds, the "go with the flow" mentality doesn't work particularly well on an expedition that is supposed to reach a predetermined goal. But even Sam had given up the push to stay on schedule to avoid the monsoon. No one talked about it, but maybe we all thought that if we got stuck, or were forced to take a long detour around impassable roads, we could handle it. Or maybe everyone accepted that the trip might end long before we felt the first raindrop. Whatever the reason, we suddenly stopped worrying about our progress.

With the pressure off, we agreed to spend a week trekking up and down a steep escarpment to villages in the Dogon region of Mali. Again, the Mechanic stayed behind with the truck. This time he didn't even use the excuse that the truck needed work. Suzanne also stayed behind because she was worried that she wouldn't be able to handle the heat. Her concern was valid since we were starting our trek at the hottest time of year, and temperatures were routinely over one hundred degrees Fahrenheit.

Built high above many of the villages in the Dogon Valley are the abandoned cliff dwellings of the ancient inhabitants known as "the pygmies of the Dogon." To imagine the compact houses, think Mesa Verde or Chaco cliff dwellings, or picture small adobe buildings built from homemade brick or carved out of solid rock perched impossibly high up on the side of an escarpment. In some places the hundred-mile-long escarpment rises a thousand feet from the valley floor. The scenery alone is enough to entice one to endure the blistering heat, dehydration, and sore feet. But its origins in the region and its people are what make the Dogon especially fascinating. The Dogon people believe that their ancestors are descended from outer space—from somewhere near the star Sirius to be exact. They had oral history about Sirius long before astronomers even knew the star existed. The Dogon people don't look like ET, but they *are* different.

The present-day inhabitants build their dwellings at ground level in close proximity to their fields. Many of their little huts have straw roofs shaped like tall and pointy Merlin the Magician hats. The open-air structure where the elders of the village meet to share news or discuss village matters consists of several elaborately carved posts holding up a flat straw roof. But the posts are so short that it is impossible to stand up in the shelter. "We build a low structure so that everyone must sit down during a meeting. You see, it is impossible to have a physical fight while sitting down," one elder explained.

It was far too hot to sleep inside. Instead, in every village we slept out in the open on the roofs of houses. There was a full moon during our trek, so at night we were able to watch the escarpment slowly appear as it was illuminated in the moon's reflection. Women and children sang and danced in the moonlight and the music drew us into their circle too. Music is such a big part of life in West Africa. Even today if someone says *West Africa* to me, I automatically think *music* or *dance*. It seemed everyone in Mali danced. It didn't matter how hot it was. In one village I watched a small boy pick up a two-string guitar-like instrument at the hottest part of the day and begin strumming. Within a few moments women and children came out of nowhere to dance. We always danced with them for a few minutes, until the searing heat smothered the urge.

For the duration of the trek, we usually walked a few hours in the morning and then took a break in the heat of the day before continuing on to the next village where we would spend the night. The 110-degree heat burrowed into my brain and worked its way through my pores and into my lungs making it hard for me to breathe. I began thinking I should have stayed back at the guesthouse with Suzanne. The six-foot-long Taureg cloth that I had purchased in Timbuktu and small amounts of water were what saved me. Several times a day I soaked the cloth in handfuls of water taken from covered clay pots in each village. Then I wrapped myself in cool damp blue fabric before heading out again into the shimmering Dogon heat. I enjoyed imagining that I looked like a blue ghost floating in the desert.

We were fortunate to arrive at one of the villages on market day. I watched the hustle and bustle of people coming and going, and I laughed at goats as they tried to snag a leaf of spinach or a mouthful of carrots from atop the low homemade tables. Everyone and everything was in motion. Vendors arranged and rearranged their product for best effect, and buyers moved through the crowded stalls inspecting each item carefully before making their purchases. Most of the market-goers were engrossed in laughter punctuated conversation or story-telling. Market day in Africa is just as much about sustaining friendships and trading information as it is about buying and selling goods. I sat on a rock near a group of women who had walked long distances from villages strewn along the valley floor. While they worked on their vegetable displays, they caught up on the latest gossip and laughed and greeted others as they entered the marketplace. One woman had a very profitable day because she had Mike as a customer. He sat on a short stool near her stall and bought cup after cup of her homemade beer. It smelled and tasted horrible.

"Mike, haven't you heard that homemade hooch can cause brain damage?" I asked.

"Yeah, I know," he answered holding his cup up for more. "I should have gone to Thailand where beer is reliable and cheap instead of coming to Africa." He then went on to tell the story of the time a girlfriend stabbed him with a kitchen knife.

"You already told that story," I interrupted.

"No this is a different story," he insisted.

"You were stabbed *twice* by the same woman?"

"No," he answered with exaggerated patience. "I was stabbed by two *different* girlfriends."

I shook my head in bewilderment. "How could one man be stabbed by two different women?"

"Well, if I knew the answer to that I probably wouldn't have been stabbed the second time." Mike answered pragmatically, as if there wasn't anything in particular that inspired women to stab him. "Some people are just born loveable and some are born stabable, I guess," he added, taking another sip of beer. I walked away thinking Mike took the cake as the most complex character on the expedition.

Many of the villages in the Dogon are nestled against the base of the escarpment situated on the valley floor, but one night we slept at a village on top of the escarpment where there wasn't a tree, bush, or blade of grass in sight. The entire stone village was built of—and on—solid rock and was routinely subjected to strong gusts of wind. Villagers had to make their way down the escarpment through a wide gully in order to farm their millet or vegetable patches and farther still to get water. While the view was great, it was not the easiest of villages to live in. The latrine was often just a patch on the rock. There were pigs to take care of clean up. After I saw that, I gave up eating pork for a while and haven't looked at a slice of bacon the same way since.

Timing is everything, especially when you are out in the boondocks in a place you may see only once in your lifetime. We were nearing the end of our trek in a tiny village on the valley floor and hadn't seen a vehicle in a week. Suddenly far across the Dogon desert we saw plumes of sand and dust rising in the air as a convoy of vehicles sped toward us. Soon photographers, reporters, and dignitaries spilled out of Land Rovers and formed a brisk procession into the village. The parade happened to go right past the door of our guesthouse. Scott and I looked at each other and had one of those silent conversations. "Why not?" our eyes said, and we joined the tail end of the procession. When we arrived at the center of the village, we found heavily costumed men on stilts and a group of around thirty dancers sporting elaborate purple masks. They began dancing up a dust storm for the benefit of two nicely dressed women seated in the shade.

We had no idea what was going on, so we watched the dancing and the crowd to glean an explanation for the celebration. Before long we were incorporated into the atmosphere of the festival when the entourage of photographers migrating among the dancers capturing close-ups of the action invited us to do the same.

After taking a few images that were shrouded in a dusty haze, we sat with a group of school children and enjoyed the performance from their vantage point at the feet of the dancers. We received gentle elbows in the ribs as cues on when it was appropriate to clap and when to be silent. I could only guess what story the dancers were telling. I yearned to speak the Dogon language so that I could ask someone to translate the wild spinning, dipping, and ferocity involved in the scenes. It was only later that we learned we had seen the Dance of the Festival of the Harvest (such energetic reaping!) and that the finely dressed women spectators were very special guests. One was the wife of the president of Mali and the other was Princess Mathilde of Belgium. Scott and I slept well that night, happy that serendipity had brought us to such a special event. I suddenly wanted nothing more than to linger in Mali a little longer before continuing the journey to South Africa at a slower Dogon pace.

Architecture, outer-space lore, and unexpected fetes aside, I was most charmed by the elaborate greetings people give one another in the Dogon. Often in America, it's "How's it going?" or the even more abbreviated, "S'up?" and we barely wait for an answer before carrying on down the hallway or street. In the Dogon, the greeting starts while you are still some distance away. It goes like this. Each question receives an answer. "How are you? How did you sleep? Did you eat well? How is your husband? How are the children? How is your mother? How is your father? How are your crops? Where are you going? Where have you been?" Greeters are well past one another as they continue saying hello. I regret not making a recording of the daily greeting of the Dogon people. It is such a delightful sound. It's as if they are singing a duet each morning with every person they meet.

It's Not Hell—It's the Harmattan!

If anyone ever tells me to go to hell, I can tell him I've already been because I've been to Burkina Faso. It's not that the people there are bad or that it has nothing going for it. The people we met were kind-hearted and there were interesting things to do. In fact serendipity struck again. Our arrival in the capital city of Ouagadougou (pronounced *Wa-ga-DO-goo*) coincided with the start of FESPACO, the African film festival, and we managed to talk our way into a screening and party. Not exactly Cannes, but whenever presented unexpectedly with free drinks and a movie I'm usually guaranteed to love a place. Unfortunately weather trumped free beer in Ouagadougou. Burkina Faso is, or was when we were there, entirely made up of scorching hot brown dusty air. I was miserable. I wilted and whimpered. I didn't even feel like trying to crash another party. Again, I relied on my damp blue Tuareg ghost cloth. Maybe as a ghost I could scare the heat away.

"This is hell!" I said as I dragged my withered body across the inferno that was our campsite.

"Actually it's the Harmattan," Scott explained in a matter-of-fact tone. "It's the wind that blows across sub-Saharan Africa."

I hate that tone of his when I am hot and irritable. "Go to Burkina Faso," I said grumpily. But I kid you not: you can't sleep, think, or breathe in the searing brown dusty air that is Burkina Faso in May. I have never been anywhere as hot. The closest I have come to Burkina Faso heat is when I reach into my four-hundred-degree oven on Thanksgiving to extract a steaming turkey. At least after that I get to eat and take a nap, something you simply do not feel like doing during the Harmattan.

The heat was certainly memorable. But what I will remember most about Burkina Faso is that is where the expedition came to an end. Maybe it was the heat that finally did us in, but it was in that campsite in Ouagadougou that the Mechanic and the lab rats decided to part ways once the truck once reached Ghana.

The experiment could have worked. Everyone started the trip with the best intentions. If the Mechanic had finished the truck in his "own bloody time without pressure from some of you bloody blokes!" and if he had been able to sell more seats and start the trip without such considerable financial stress, maybe it would have worked. If everyone on board had pitched in to the satisfaction of the Mechanic (an impossible feat), it may have worked. And those "respectful discussions, like in a family"? Well, it turned out we were pretty dysfunctional as a group. The Mechanic started each group meeting with, "This isn't a bloody holiday! It's an expedition"—only he put the emphasis on the *p* so it came out "ex-*pee*-dition." There was too much discussion and not enough action. The lack of cooperation after the Dogon drove me figuratively nuts. But it almost drove Luis literally nuts.

Luis is a kind soul who felt sorry for the Mechanic. Unfortunately the Mechanic took advantage of his empathy and made Luis feel he could somehow fix the human element of the expedition. Luis always tried to smooth things over and make things right between the group and the Mechanic. He was such a good person, and it was his nature to problem solve whenever possible. I admired his character, but he was no match for the Mechanic. The burden Luis felt he was under to keep the trip together came to a head after we hiked out of the Dogon. While on the hike, others hinted that they were thinking about leaving the trip in Ghana. Scott and I had not told anyone our plans, but it didn't surprise us when others said they were thinking about voting themselves off the island too. We all felt guilty because we all suspected that without every last one of us stay-ing, the trip would have to end. Luis was noticeably upset. He spent more time than any of us in the cab with the Mechanic and was most affected by the Mechanic's angst, bitterness, and disappointment. I know dehydration was a factor in his breakdown, but when we came out of the Dogon and saw the truck, Luis announced he was leav-ing the expedition immediately and began to gather his belongings. No one said a thing. Not even the Mechanic tried to talk him out of it.

"Luis, can we talk outside?" I asked, surprised that no else seemed upset over Luis's sudden departure. I knew that people didn't really care about what happened to the expedition any longer, but to show no concern for a fellow passenger boggled my mind. Didn't anyone give a damn?

"Sure, Trriiis," said Luis, setting his nearly full backpack down on the seat.

We walked a short distance away while Luis tried to articulate his feelings of stress and disappointment that we couldn't be one happy family. "I feel responsible," he said. "I let the Mechanic and everyone else down."

Resisting the urge to suggest that his cornrows were too tight and that he should go back to the Jesus Christ look and all would be right with the world I said, "Luis, you are in no way responsible for people wanting to bail on the trip!" I felt terrible for Luis. He was utterly inconsolable over a failure that wasn't his to own. Luis was a genuinely nice person who cared how others felt. "Maybe the Mechanic led you to believe you are somehow responsible for making him happy or that you could fix the expedition, but this is not your burden." He broke down and sobbed the kind of sob where snot runs down your chin.

While I held him, he said, "I really think I should leave the trip."

"Luis, we are in the middle of a desert! You'll die if you stay here."

Patty walked over and we both shifted into maternal mode, enveloping Luis in a big protective hug. We were shattered to see him suffering so. It took some time, but together we convinced him to get back on the truck. Luis re-hydrated for the rest of the day and told me that night, "Trriiis, you saved my life." Then I sobbed. I was so pissed off at the Mechanic. I thought of him as a bully after that. I couldn't wait to get to Ghana.

The straw that really broke the camels back for me though was when the Mechanic tried to kill Sam in the desert. I hate to admit it, but it all started because I was jonesing for a cookie. Sam had cookies but he wasn't sharing. There were more cookies on the truck, but to get at them would involve making everyone move and trying to lift the heavy plywood floor while the truck was careening at excessive speed through the desert. Impossible.

"Jesus *Christ!*" I said with frustration after I had already politely asked Sam twice to pass me a cookie.

"Yes, Trriiis?"

"Not you Luis. Damn it, Sam, give me a cookie." Sam wasn't worried. Everyone (except the Mechanic) loved Sam, so he knew I couldn't stay mad at him even if he teased me a little. "If you want a cookie you're going to have to come and get it, Trissie," he said laughing. He was enjoying watching me beg. I hadn't had anything sweet in ten days, and I was angry at myself for not remembering about the cookies below the floorboards earlier when I could have gotten to them.

I glared at him with all the seriousness I could muster. "Sam, give me one fucking cookie."

He laughed harder. Though I used it practically non-stop for two weeks after my beloved sister-in-law passed away prematurely, I hardly ever drop the f-bomb. (I'll take this as an opportunity for a public mea culpa to my family, friends, and especially to that poor DMV clerk who I unloaded on the week after my sister-in-law died.)

"Nah, Tris," Sam said with a devilish grin. "I was just about to give you a cookie, but you've been so unladylike, now you can't have one."

This really made me angry. It surprised me how badly I wanted a cookie. I was consumed with cookie lust. I stood up and tried to make my way over to Sam. He was already on the move. The Mechanic was driving way too fast across the open desert and the truck was lurching violently side-to-side so I wasn't making much headway. I irrationally decided that if I moved more quickly I would have better footing, so I took a flying leap at Sam. But Sam was younger and faster, so he easily skirted my grasp. By now everyone was laughing. Except Scott who claims he said something like, "Tris, sit down. Someone is going to get hurt."

I lunged again. To get away from me, Sam jumped up on the bench seat and leaned out the side of the truck. Soon he practically had his entire body outside of the truck and was hanging on to a support bar with only three fingers. His other hand dangled cookies over the open desert far from my reach.

I was just about mid-leap when the Mechanic slammed on the brakes. In his side view mirror, he had evidently noticed Sam laughing uproariously and decided to teach him a lesson once and for all. Everyone flew off their seats and tried to grab on to something, anything, to break their momentum. I went airborne across the inside of the truck and hit the wall of the spare parts locker hard. But poor Sam went flying out the truck and into the desert.

As the truck came to a stop, everyone crowded over to the window to see how many pieces of Sam were left to pick up. After a minute Sam stood up briskly, brushed off the dust, and with an enthusiastic wave and a big grin exclaimed, "I'm all right!"

The Mechanic was unapologetic. "You could have killed him!" said Scott, stating the obvious. "Tris might have been seriously hurt too. Anyone could have been hurt because you slammed on the brakes suddenly like that."

"Well, I feel bad that Tris might have been hurt," he said sheepishly. "But how was I to know she was standing up?"

Sam bounced back on board, still smiling. After we had tidied the inside of the truck and began proceeding through the desert at a much slower pace, Scott repeated, "Sam! He tried to *kill* you."

"Nah. I'm OK. Here Tris, have a cookie," he said laughing.

That's what did it for me. The expedition had already suffered too many delays to avoid the monsoon. We had endured several broken springs, two cracked radiators, one fistfight (Mike vs. Mechanic), and Luis's emotional breakdown, but when the Mechanic tried to kill Sam, well, that was the end of the expedition with the Mechanic for me.

Ironically, before Scott, or I, or anyone else had a chance to tell the Mechanic we were going to leave the truck in Ghana, he presented each person with an "ultimatum letter" that he had prepared while the rest of us were in the Dogon. The letter stated that there would be certain (undisclosed) requirements for continuing the trip beyond Ghana. At the end of the letter he gave everyone twenty-four hours to come and speak with him privately about "his or her decision." We were nonplussed. Sam read his letter and said, "Well, Petra and I definitely want to stay on the truck with the Mechanic to Cape Town."

Sam never got it that the only person the Mechanic *didn't* want on the trip was Sam.

When Scott and I met with the Mechanic the next day to tell him we would not be carrying on past Ghana, he was noticeably disappointed. He appealed to Scott, "I thought you, and Tris, and me could drive across Nigeria, Chad, and Sudan to Ethiopia, and take the truck down to Nairobi together." Next to the Mechanic, Scott and I were the ones with the most overland experience so I suppose he hoped he still had a chance of success with us on board. He tried to negotiate with Bill and Maggie too since they were heavily invested in not only their romance but had contributed time and money in England to help the Mechanic finish the truck.

I was speechless. Scott stared at the Mechanic as one might look at a person who had lost his marbles. "No, Tris and I won't be staying on the truck and here are some of the reasons why. You said you wouldn't allow drugs to be transported across borders, but you did. Sorry we were such hard-asses about that, but the possibility of spending time in an African jail was never our idea of an expedition. Every time you smoked dope with the locals, you made yourself and the expedition vulnerable to theft or police extortion. Second, we know you think things aren't working out for you because you didn't postpone the trip or sell more seats. But you could never put that behind you. You never got over your bitterness with the initial group, and that attitude affected the success of the expedition from the beginning. Third, as far as Tris and I helping you take the truck to Nairobi, don't you know how risky it would be for three people to take this truck across central Africa alone? And, lastly, most importantly, you tried to kill Sam! I'm very sorry you aren't going to reach your goals, but we are no longer the people to help you reach them."

If there was one thing you could say about the Mechanic, it was that he could shift gears on a dime. He barely let Scott's words sink in before saying, "When we reach Ghana I want you two to help me come up with a business plan for the truck." He was obviously already on to the next venture.

Two days later six of us lay in one hammock drinking beer at Big Millie's Place on Krokrobite beach in Ghana and all was forgiven. We reminisced about the trials and tribulations, and we thanked one another for making it a memorable trip.

The Mechanic was unsure what to do next. He asked us what we thought of his "plan." Maybe he would drive the truck to Nairobi alone (nuts), or maybe he would just leave the truck for the time being in Ghana and run West Africa tours from there (really?), or maybe he would sell the truck, start over, and "do it right next time" (uh, what was that about never finishing something you start?).

He asked me what my favorite parts were of West Africa to Ghana. I didn't even have to think about it. "Oh, the camel trek in Morocco was unforgettable! And I loved that week in The Gambia. Oh and trekking from village to village in the Dogon was incredible!" Looking hurt, he said, "Those were the times you were away from the truck." It was a realization that gave me all the confidence I needed for Scott and me to tackle the rest of Africa independently.

Not one person continued on the expedition with the Mechanic. Most flew home. Sam went home to start a new job. Luis went happily back to Spain, presumably to eat more ice cream. Petra and Suzanne, separately, continued to travel in Africa for several months. Mike hightailed it to Thailand.

A few weeks after the expedition ended, Suzanne copied us all on an e-mail she had sent to the Mechanic. In it she read him the riot act about how she didn't appreciate being hit on while the rest of us were away in the Dogon and what a chauvinistic pig he was. Everyone also received e-mail from Mike in Thailand that said, "I forgive you all." I'm still not sure what he was forgiving us for. Had he been upset that we only had one beer kitty? That one remains a mystery. I am happy to say that shortly after Bill and Maggie returned to England, they bought a truck and commenced driving around the world in their very own love shack on wheels. As far as I know, Bill is still married to the women whose name sounds like Tris. And the Mechanic's truck? For all I know, it is still parked at Big Millie's in Ghana.

There were lots of advantages and few regrets about our group overland experience. I doubt we would have gone to Timbuktu without our trusty truck or our hardworking Mechanic. He really was a very fine mechanic, which we noticed because he always seemed to have to fix something on the bloody truck.

Scott and I were excited to continue the journey on our own. We intended to transit the rest of Africa overland as much as possible and on any type of local transport we could find. This turned out to include bush taxis, rickshaws, dugout canoes, and ox carts, to name a few. I couldn't wait.

PART 3
AFRICA ON OUR OWN

EARPLUGS AND FAITH

Ending our journey with the Mechanic in the English-speaking country of Ghana made it easy for us to arrange onward travel. Well, easier than it would have been in French-speaking Mauritania or Burkina Faso. It definitely made exchanging money less stressful. All through French-speaking West Africa, there were always young men at the border crossings ready to sell bundles of currency. They swarmed around us like locusts. The crush of bodies made it hard to concentrate and because we are far from fluent in French, transactions were nerve-wracking. Somehow we always felt like the mark in a three-card monte game. In Ghana we were able to change traveler's checks at established foreign exchange offices with a security guard present. The only bad thing about Ghanaian currency was that the largest note at the time was twenty thousand cedi, but it was only worth about two U.S. dollars. We needed to carry a stack of cedi the size of a brick just to get us through the week. It was an incredible amount of cash to lug around to pay for the odd corncob, bus ride, or bag of water. I remember the day we spent over a million cedi before lunch.

Of the twenty-four African countries I've visited so far, Ghana is by far the loudest. Even the animals are loud. After the expedition ended, Luis, Scott, and I traveled down the coast. After a disheartening visit to a slave fort located in a compound absurdly named The Cape Coast Castle, we spent a night on a wooden platform under a mosquito net in the tropical rainforest surrounding Kakum National Park. Sleep was impossible. In addition to a cacophony of noise coming from every jungle insect you can imagine, we had to endure the round-the-clock shrieking of a rodent-like animal the size of a marmot called a rock hyrax. Its call sounded *exactly* like Meg Ryan when she performed the fake orgasm in the coffee shop scene in the film *When Harry Met Sally*, only much louder.

Outside almost every shop in the bustling capital city of Accra, gigantic speakers blasted the latest pop song "Wakka-wakka-wakka!" which consists solely of the lyrics "Wakka-wakka-wakka!" This was played at full volume. Consequently I think the people of Accra were all a little hard of hearing. They tended to shout when speaking. It's absolutely deafening when everyone starts hollering at once in a crowded *tro-tro*, the bush taxi of Ghana. I'm positive even the most eager of rock hyraxes in heat wouldn't be heard over the din in a tro-tro.

A tro-tro is a usually dilapidated but convenient form of transport that will stop anywhere you want to get on or off. It seems someone is forever shouting to be let in or out of the van. But there are advantages to traveling by tro-tro other than getting from A to B. For one thing, you can do all your shopping while you are stuck in Accra's mind-numbing traffic without leaving the vehicle. Scads of women and children sell bananas, avocados, toilet paper, bread, and oranges from huge bowls balanced on their heads while they weave in and out of the bumper-to-bumper traffic. I also saw people selling the Thigh Master, a light fixture, a ceiling fan, handkerchiefs, maps of Ghana, you name it, as they walked between the vehicles, hawking their wares like vendors to a circus crowd.

If you aren't conveniently located next to a window in a tro-tro— the sweet spot for a wisp of a breeze—and you want to purchase something, you hand the money to the person next to you who hands it to the kid in front who gives it to the vendor and you get the goods passed back in reverse direction. It's like being at a baseball game back home, but with no chance in hell of scoring a malted or a giant pretzel. Ballpark food would have been worth its weight in cedi if it could be had in Ghana, because Ghanaian cuisine is not great. I even went vegetarian for a time because I read somewhere that they eat cat. C-A-T. Kitty cat. Before I went meatless, I would ask the waiters what kind of meat was in the "Spaghetti Bolognese." There was always a long pause before they would answer with an indifferent shrug, "Beef." Fortunately we could often find something called Club Sandwich on the menu that actually resembled a club sandwich you might find in any small town U.S. diner. It contained chicken and pork, though most of the time we ordered it without pork, or lettuce, or tomato. Oh, and hold the mayo—so it was basically a dry chicken sandwich.

Aside from keeping our eyes on the lookout for a vendor selling anything that would provide salty crunch (my kingdom for Doritos), reading the names of businesses in Ghana provided an entertaining diversion while stuck in traffic. Most of them referenced Jesus or God in some way or another. My favorites were, "Clap for Jesus Hairstyling," "See What God Has Done Fashions," and "Blood of Jesus Sheet Metal." The optimistic political slogan at the time was, "So Far, So Good!" It seemed that Ghanaians' reliance on religion is what got them through the day. It's how they filled up their hearts and minds with hope.

Often, people would share their problems with us. Sometimes I asked, "What will you do?" In southern Ghana, which is predominantly Christian, the answer was always, "Jesus will solve my problem." Often it seemed there was nowhere else to turn *but* faith. That may be true in many places in the world these days, but I think it has long been true in Africa that people turn to religion for an answer. Sometimes there aren't too many other options available—certainly nothing tangible. And in Africa, where most things are consumed the day they are acquired, hope and faith have inexplicably long shelf lives.

The joyous moments in West Africa are unforgettable and the heartbreaking ones are impossible to forget. In Accra, a tired and overburdened mother thrust her child into my arms. The child looked healthy, well fed, and cared for, yet the mother wanted me to take her. I don't mean for a few minutes, I mean forever. My jaw dropped as I looked at the woman in dismay. Scott and I had tried everything possible to have children of our own. I consider them a precious gift. Now here was a woman just giving hers away. I looked down at the baby and was devastated to think about what would drive a woman to give her child away to a total stranger. When the mother saw my reaction you would have thought someone threw a bucket of cold water over her. She didn't understand English but she did get the meaning when I said the obvious, "You will miss your baby." She took the child into her arms and cooed reassurances not only to the baby but also to herself. She raised her tired eyes and smiled at me. She gave me a look that said, "Sometimes life is just too hard, you know, sister?" I nodded. I had been in Africa long enough to know. I hugged her then pressed some cedi into her hand knowing it would help make things a little easier for she and her child at least for a little while. I later wondered if I did the right thing. Could I have done more? She seemed so desperate. I knew I could drive myself batty thinking about the butterfly effect and how my choices and actions could affect a life in Africa. It wasn't the first time, or last, that this happened to me in Africa. But I often wonder what became of *that* mother and baby.

Children all over Africa approached me every day chatting away, prancing around my legs, and asking limitless questions. But in West Africa they also did something that might have bothered some. They studied me. And in Ghana, they did more than scrutinize me visually. They performed a tactile examination too. They petted the hair on my arms, they counted my freckles, they combed my hair with their little fingers, and they stared into my eyes from two inches away saying, "You have flowers in your eyes," or "White lady, give me your hair. I like your hair too much." I never minded this attention because if they were studying me, they weren't dodging traffic selling small sachets of water or peanuts. Some of these children had been forced into this life by the realities of poverty. Desperate parents who can't find some better-off relative to take their child sometimes sell them to a middleman who promises "education and opportunity." And this is their "opportunity."

THE ELEPHANTS WILL MAKE
YOU FEEL BETTER

Birthdays still happen even when you are away from home, friends, and family, and Scott has, since the first year I knew him, always strived to make my birthday special. Years ago when we were first running our health clubs, he surprised me at work by whisking me away to Lake Tahoe for my twenty-first birthday. I was thrilled. As we drove on to the highway, I looked down at my work attire, a wraparound skirt, leotards, and tights, and asked, "Shouldn't we stop by the apartment so I can change and pack?" Beaming at me with the pride of one who had planned every detail to perfection he said, "No need. I packed for you!" This worried me. Scott is a brilliant guy. Smart, well read. But he is not a man overly concerned about the details.

Four hours later, we arrived at the hotel and went up to our room. I peered with trepidation into the tiny bag he had packed for me for the weekend. The total contents of the bag were a long black evening gown and a pair of sneakers.

Many years later, on my fortieth birthday, Scott once again planned a surprise trip, this time to Paris. And once again, his plan was to have a packed bag in the trunk, drive to the airport and say, "Surprise! We're going to Paris for your birthday!" Fortunately, forty-eight hours before the flight, his mother convinced him to tell me about the trip. Thanks to her, I had a day to call my girlfriends, buy "Paris clothes," and lose ten pounds. Well at least he gave me enough notice for the first two. Anyway, Scott is really great about making birthdays special, and I love him for it. That he does this in addition to bringing me coffee in bed every morning makes his absent-mindedness just another endearing trait.

There have been times when he is the victim of his own lack of concentration. Once, during a thirteen-hour flight to Auckland, New Zealand, he turned to me and said, "Thanks for setting out all my clothes for the trip."

I looked back at him bewildered. "I didn't put any clothes out for you to pack."

For weeks I had been nagging him to pack for our two-month trip to New Zealand and Australia. Scott thinks it a waste of time to prepare ahead and would rather sit down to a rerun of *Law & Order* while I am upstairs packing my bag for the fourth time. For me it's almost as much fun to prepare for a trip as to go on it. I take pride in packing light and bringing exactly what I think I will need and no more. That takes a lot of planning, packing, and re-packing—an exacting routine Scott says comes from my German side. Scott, who is of Swedish, English, and Eagle Scout descent, is the exact opposite and will pack at the last possible minute and take loads of superfluous things "just in case."

Anyway, there we were at thirty-five thousand feet, and he was thanking me for laying out his clothes for the trip.

I began to chuckle. "Oh, I cannot *wait* to see what you have in your bag." He spent the rest of the flight with a quizzical look on his face periodically staring off into space. I knew he was trying to visualize just what it was that he had packed.

It wasn't until we were in our hotel room in Auckland that the mystery was solved.

"Sheets and towels?" I asked in disbelief as we both stared into his duffle. "How could you pack nothing but sheets and towels?"

I studied his face as he studied our linens. I could tell he was mentally retracing his steps in the moments leading to our departure.

"Well, as you know, I had all these last-minute things to do to prepare the house for our absence, which I worked on up to the time you were in the car waiting to go to the airport. But I hadn't packed yet, so I went upstairs and saw all these clean things neatly folded the way you do, and I thought how nice it was that you put it all out for me to take, and I opened my bag, and swept it inside. That's how," he said as if it made perfect sense.

I suddenly flashed on the days when my morning cup of coffee tasted funny and it made me wonder what he had put in the grinder instead of coffee beans. A jar of granola and another of Cheerios sit next to the jar of coffee beans on our kitchen counter.

"How can you look at something and not see it?" I asked with exasperation.

We went to the Canterbury Store in Auckland and bought a complete set of new clothes for Scott. The only drawback was that Canterbury is a rugby-wear outfitter, so almost everyone we met asked him what time his game was starting. The fact that Scott is built like a rugby player and even broke his nose while playing rugby in college made the whole picture more believable. One of the shirts looked particularly odd on him. "I'm going to give this one away," he said. "It makes me look like Pugsley from *The Addams Family*."

I know my husband may sound like a dolt, but it's just the opposite. He's like one of those geniuses who, let's say (because I still want to have my coffee brought to me in bed, even if it is occasionally ground granola), is easily distracted. He's my very own absentminded professor. When I find a half gallon of ice cream in the oven or one of his to-do lists where the first thing on the list is "Make a list," I smile and know that the next suitcase we unpack will have some surprises in it.

Now another birthday was just around the corner. I was about to turn forty-seven in Ghana, and Scott, wanting it to be special, researched where we could go to see my favorite African animals, elephants. Not an easy task since Ghana and West Africa in general is not where you go for wildlife in Africa. That is where East Africa shines. But Ghana has Mole National Park where there are herds of elephants and troops of baboons, so that's where Scott was determined to take me for my birthday. It would take several days to get there by bus and bush taxi, "but it will be worth it!" Scott said with enthusiasm. I must say I love it that he gets more excited for my birthday than I do. Perhaps that's the reason getting older has never bothered me much. Scott makes sure my birthday is not just a day to mark another year gone; it represents another wonderful adventure together that we can recall over and over in the future.

We took the early bus, anxious to be on our way to the elephants. I felt happy and tingly. I even thought I could feel it in my bones. Soon the tingling spread from my bones to my head and I was suddenly as dizzy as a college freshman after her fourth time at bat during a game of beer baseball. I spent the rest of the day with my eyes shut tight, willing my world to stop spinning. No luck. After a long nauseating day, we got off the bus and checked in to a small inn on the banks of Lake Volta with hundreds of miles still to go between Mole and us. It might as well have been thousands. I didn't see how I could possibly get to the national park feeling as weak and dizzy as I did. I certainly wouldn't be able to endure three more days on crowded bush taxis.

After pouring me into bed, Scott went to the guesthouse owner, Kwame, to ask if there was a clinic nearby. In typical African fashion, instead of merely giving directions, Kwame drove us to the hospital. As we sped away from the guesthouse, his wife thrust bananas at me through the car window saying, "You must eat lots of bananas. They are good for malaria. They will cure you!" She had taken one look at me and concluded I had malaria.

"Malaria? Pfft," was all I had the energy to say.

After the doctor questioned me about which areas in Africa we had visited, he ordered a blood test. The results confirmed the diagnosis of

Kwame's wife. It appeared my first birthday present that year was to be malaria, which I had probably picked up from a mosquito somewhere along the coast.

Scott and I were using a drug called Mefloquine (Larium) to kill any malaria parasites that entered our bloodstream. That's the way malaria medicine works. There is no vaccine or drug yet that will prevent malaria. But there are several medications that can kill the parasite once it has entered the bloodstream. Some malaria drugs are taken daily. Larium is taken once a week on the same day, and it can have some pretty nasty side effects. People who have psychosis of any kind or tend towards depression can't take it because it can induce hallucinations or make people do things they wouldn't normally do. We once traveled with a woman who had nearly all the negative side effects of Larium. She was miserable. She experienced extreme depression and cried almost constantly. She stopped taking it and immediately felt better. "Malaria can't be worse than this," she said. "I'll take my chances." Another man on Larium claimed it was the drug that made him walk out of a third floor window. He lived only because he was also extremely intoxicated at the time.

Fortunately Scott and I had none of the bad side effects but all of the really interesting (dare I say enjoyable?) ones. The oddest one was that after a month I no longer had to shave my legs. The entire time I was on Larium, I never had to shave my legs. My eyebrows no longer needed plucking, and the hair on my head and arms thinned. I started to resemble a hairless cat. My baseline hairiness returned to normal shortly after discontinuing the medicine, but I thought it was a rather convenient side effect to have on a long trip.

We found that Larium made us drowsy, so we began taking it at night. This led to wild dreams. Sometimes we would wake up from a dream and still be dreaming with our eyes open. Okay, yeah, hallucinating. But they were amazing dreams! One night Scott dreamed that he was McLean Stevenson from the *M*A*S*H** television show, only he was a vampire, not an army surgeon. It took Scott twenty minutes to relate the entire dream scene by scene. It was so vivid and detailed it was more like a feature film than a dream. I dreamed that Edward G. Robinson and I were in Europe serving in World War II together. We were due for R & R but only the king of Thailand could authorize our leave. After flying to Thailand and meeting the king, Robinson (even before requesting R & R!) got in his face and said in his classic Little Caesar way, "Mwaaah. What do you think I am, see? Some kind of schmuck? Mwaaah." So much for the R & R. Another night a fellow traveler in the next tent and I had the *exact same dream* involving enormous acid-spitting bugs. For fun, everyone on Larium began taking it on the same night, Wednesday. The next morning at breakfast we would take turns telling our dreams. We always had a later than usual start on Thursdays. We had what we called Delarium Dreams every night, but on the nights we took Larium they were especially good.

It is definitely not for everyone. The side effects can be very serious so, though tempting, I wouldn't take it just for feature film inspiring dreams at night in the tent. Also, as I was finding out in Ghana, it didn't always prevent malaria.

"I will give you some Artesunate to take," the Volta Authority doctor said. "That, on top of the Larium should cure you. Do not stop taking your weekly Larium tablet."

The doctor was surprised when Scott said, "We happen to have some Artesunate with us."

Because we were outside of major cities for long stretches while traveling in Africa, we tried to be prepared for any illness (or at least the ones we could imagine), so in addition to the antibiotics, pain relievers, syringes, and rubber gloves that we had in our medical kit, we had several courses of Artesunate, an inexpensive over-the-counter Chinese herbal drug that the World Health Organization recognizes as an effective malaria treatment. We had bought the Artesunate in

Accra because we had been routinely meeting other Westerners who took Larium but still became sick with malaria.

So there we were in the Volta Authority Hospital, me feeling the lousiest I'd ever felt in my life and Scott worrying that this was to go down in history as my worst birthday ever. After a few hours, the doctor sent me away with explicit instructions on how to take the course of Artesunate, adding that it would be at least a week before I would begin to feel better. Scott, who wasn't willing to let a few malaria parasites get between elephants and me for my birthday, remained focused on getting to Mole. I didn't see how I could tolerate the journey. All I wanted to do was go back to the guesthouse and lie in bed while someone fed me malaria-murdering drugs and bananas until I felt better.

Serendipity struck again. Kwame turned out to be more than a guesthouse owner. He was also an employee of the Lake Volta Ferry. And the Volta Ferry was going in the direction of Mole National Park the next day.

One of the items on Scott's "one thousand places to see before I die" list was the Lake Volta Ferry, and he was becoming increasingly anxious that he would miss his chance. In an effort to get me on board with his plan and the ferry, he urged, "Once you are around elephants you will feel so much better!" True, elephants are my favorite of the African animals. But since I couldn't even open my eyes without going into a nausea-inducing head spin, I doubted very much I would be able to zero in on anything, even something the size of a bread truck.

Nonetheless, when you are determined to travel the way we do, you can't sit around waiting for drugs or bananas to take effect, or you'll miss out on opportunities. If we didn't get on the ferry the following day, then we would have to wait more than a week for the next one. As lousy as I felt, I appreciated that Scott was trying his best to make my birthday special, so I was determined to at least try to meet him halfway. Scott asked Kwame to help us secure passage on the ferry leaving the next day. Kwame not only arranged tickets, he made sure we would be permitted to stay in the only air-conditioned cabin on board, and his wife made sure we had plenty of bananas.

But Kwame was concerned. "Under maritime law, we aren't allowed to transport people we know to be ill. If the crew sees you, they might not let you on board because you look very sick."

Malaria isn't contagious, but the appearance of someone who has the disease is not a pretty sight. In the state I was in, Scott would practically have to carry me on board. I began thinking that a week in bed at the guesthouse while Kwame's wife provided a steady supply of bananas sounded like heaven. "It's too obvious I'm sick," I said. "Anyway, all I want to do is sleep."

Kwame came up with a plan. Just before the ship was to pull away from the dock the next day, I would muster all the strength I had and, with Scott's help, propel myself like a drunken sailor (that part was unavoidable) up the gangway. Kwame assured us that the crew would be too busy at the time to notice. "I am hoping that anyone who happens to see you will think your unsteady walk is due to intoxication, not a mosquito bite."

The following morning I was kept out of sight in Kwame's office until the ship was almost ready to cast off.

When we travel we always bring inflatable globes of the world with us to give away to teachers and students throughout Africa. They were always hugely appreciated, so we gave Kwame one of the globes. It held his fascination for over half an hour. His first comment after Scott inflated it was, "I have always wondered, where is the Bermuda Triangle?" And then he showed us all the places around the world he sailed to while in the merchant navy. When his co-workers entered his office and spotted the globe on his desk, Kwame said protectively, "Only look. Don't touch!"

All over Africa it seemed people young and old had an appreciation for geography and of their place in the world. Many children we gave a globe to could identify not only his or her country but also most of the countries and oceans of the world near and far. Then they would do what every African child does when they get a hold of something round and filled with air. They used it to play soccer or football.

I will be forever grateful to my savior who took me to the hospital, arranged comfortable passage for us, and let me rest in his office. But I remember very little about boarding the Lake Volta ferry or the three days we spent on it. Scott reported that the boat was crammed from stem to stern with humanity. Surrounding the families with their cardboard boxes and sacks stuffed with worldly possessions were enormous wooden pallets overflowing with produce, goods, and cockroaches. Temperatures were well over one hundred degrees. In a malarial haze, I was cocooned in a down sleeping bag in the air-conditioned cabin, drifting in and out of sleep and missed it all. Good thing the Volta Ferry was on Scott's list and not mine.

At the exact point when I felt so sick and weak that I wished I could transport myself back to California, we arrived at the end of the line on the Volta Ferry and had to disembark. We still had a ride on a small leaky boat, and two filled-to-capacity buses to endure before reaching Mole. To this day I honestly don't know how I managed.

After disembarking from the Volta Ferry, we waited an hour before transport arrived to take us to Tamale, the town where we would start our final leg to Mole. The bus that eventually arrived was in worse condition than usual. The seats had at some time all been removed then re-bolted to the floor but not before adding at least three more rows of seats. We literally could barely get into the seats and, once we had shoehorned our bodies into the space allotted, we found it impossible to move even an inch. Plus, whoever re-installed the seats had no eye for symmetry because the seats zigzagged haphazardly down the length of the bus. The passenger who chose a zig seat was squished in so close to the person seated in one that zagged they were practically cheek to cheek. To add insult to injury, we were required to pay the cost of two more seats to have our bags stored on top of the bus for the duration of the journey.

Worse still, there was a crazy woman sitting in the back of the bus who screamed at everyone. Whenever she needed to disembark during the seven-hour bus ride for a pee or to stretch her legs, she would let out an ear-piercing screech and climb on the rest of us to get out. She stepped from shoulder to shoulder, howling as she made her way to the exit at the front of the bus. I suggested that someone in the front seat should trade places with her, but that only led to more shouting. It was the most trying bus journey of the trip so far, made worse by the effects of malaria. I had never felt that bad in my entire life.

When the bus entered the Tamale city limits around five in the afternoon, I looked at Scott and said, "God help me, I need to get off this bus right now." He pulled out the *Lonely Planet* guidebook and found a sufficient hotel just off the street we were traveling down at almost the same time the bus pulled over to let a few women out. Scott checked the map of Tamale in the guidebook to see that the hotel was just a short walk away if we got off the bus right then. We pried ourselves loose from our seats and stood by the road while the women waited for the driver to hand down their satchels, burlap bags, and cardboard boxes from the roof of the bus. When that was done the driver asked us to return to the bus.

"We're getting off here too," said Scott tiredly. But the driver insisted we re-board the bus and continue on to the bus station.

"But we are planning to stay at a hotel very near here. My wife is very sick and needs to rest. Give us our bags so we can go." Again, the driver refused. He returned to the driver's seat and started to drive slowly away from the curb. We got back on board as fast as we could. Scott practically had to lift me up the two steps and carry me to a seat. Ten minutes later we pulled into the frenetic Tamale Bus Station, now too far away to walk to our hotel. I was incensed. I was on the verge of collapse. I was upset that I had let Scott talk me into leaving Kwame's guesthouse where I knew his wife's bananas would have eventually worked their magic if I had only stayed a few days longer. But I was mostly upset at the bus driver for refusing to let us off the bus when we had asked. Now touts and taxi drivers in the bus station swarmed around us to such an extent I couldn't draw a full breath. To top it off, the bus driver refused to get our bags down unless we paid him some more money.

The women who had just left the bus not ten minutes earlier hadn't been required to pay extra to have their bags taken off the roof so I said, "But we already paid for transporting the bags when you put them up there. We aren't going to pay you twice."

"You have to pay. Now we are in the bus station so you must pay."

Thoroughly exasperated, I began to argue with the driver. It was now clear that the reason he hadn't let us off the bus earlier was so he could extort more money from us. Scott began to get angry as well and tried to make a move to get our bags off the roof himself even though the crush of passengers and touts standing next to the bus made it impossible.

Maybe it was the excruciating back pain I was feeling from sitting on the crooked seats for seven hours. Maybe it was the malaria. But I completely lost it and began to cry. I glared up at the driver on the roof and said, "You are a very bad man."

He looked down at me and through tight lips uttered, "Lady, you should be careful. You never know what can fall off a bus roof onto your head and kill you."

"That's it," said Scott as he pushed his way through the crowd to the rear of the bus and clamored up on top of the roof. He forcefully tugged our bags away from the driver and handed them down to a suddenly sympathetic passenger to hold until he could climb back down. Then we realized all at once that almost every eye in the bus station was on us. A taxi driver quickly made his way over to us and said quietly, "Where do you want to go?" We followed him to his taxi and were barely settled in the backseat before he sped away from the ruckus. The driver and I made eye contact in the rearview mirror. He looked truly concerned about me. I was still crying and must have looked pathetically distraught. "He was a very bad man," I repeated again quietly.

At the hotel Scott poured me into the bed and went out to try to find some food. I don't remember eating. I don't remember much from that night except for falling into a deep sleep.

By the time we finally arrived at Mole after dark the next day, I had the strength of an over-cooked noodle. I realized I should never have undertaken such a journey feeling as rotten as I did. Malaria isn't something to be taken lightly. My lesson learned, I collapsed into bed thankful that the journey to Mole was over.

Fortunately being amongst elephants on my birthday *did* make me feel better, and each day we were there I got a little stronger. There was a water hole-viewing platform near our room, so I could watch the elephants as they drank and cooled themselves, and the baboons came to us. Annoying little guys. I thought of my mom and how aggravating we must have been at times when we were kids. When a juvenile baboon jumped up onto our patio wall and stole a loaf of our bread, I looked him in the eye and muttered, "So you think you're funny..."

GIVE ME PEN

After spending an entire month in Ghana, chilling out on her beaches, visiting national parks, and getting elephant therapy for malaria, we had to accept we had put off taking the plunge deeper into Africa long enough. We needed to get moving if we wanted to reach our goal of South Africa by the end of the year. To avoid the west and central African monsoon (the same weather pattern that Sam was rightly so concerned about on the expedition) we thought our best bet would be to travel overland east—from Ghana to Ethiopia—then make our way through East Africa to Cape Town.

Unfortunately several obstacles stood in our way. Togo, the country neighboring Ghana, had just closed her borders and evacuated or expelled all foreigners after an attempted coup following the death of its president and a torching of the German Cultural Center. Angola was experiencing a deadly Marburg virus outbreak, and the Congo—well, call me over-cautious, but a country where you can come face to face with an eight-year-old gun-toting "soldier" high on drugs is a country I would rather avoid. And Sudan was so busy with its own war it was not issuing visas at the time anyway. So through process of elimination we felt we had no choice but to go by air instead of by land to Ethiopia. We were frustrated that we could not arrive there overland, but we were really starting to "get" Africa. People there have a saying, "Africa always wins." Out of necessity we were becoming increasingly more flexible and had come to expect that things weren't going to go according to plan. Besides, Ethiopia and Addis Ababa were on our must-see list in Africa, and we had been looking forward to visiting some of the big game parks in East Africa again.

There was one more thing that was keeping us temporarily bound to Ghana. Scott was having a very hard time shifting gears. It mostly had to do with money—rather, the lack thereof. A flight to East Africa hadn't been part of our budget. Because the expedition ended well before it was supposed to, we all should have received some money back from the Mechanic, but I wasn't going to hold my breath. The Mechanic agreed that we *should* get a share of our investment back, but he claimed there was no more money left to give. As he put it, "I still bloody well intend to take the bloody truck to Nairobi myself, and I need any bit of money that's left to get there!" He humored us by saying he would send everyone a partial refund after he had reached Nairobi and sold the truck and spare parts. He even signed and gave us promissory notes! I knew we would probably never see the money (we haven't) and that we would just have to accept the loss and move on. But Scott was not eager to sink more money into the trip. I reminded him that even before embarking on the expedition we had agreed that even if it got only as far as Ghana, the investment and adventure would be worth it. Still, he was having a very hard time justifying the cost of the flight and felt like we would be paying twice to get to South Africa. Of course, he was right. But the choices were either carry on or go home and leaving Africa was not an option for me. I had already fallen in love with the continent and her people by then and wasn't ready to call it quits. Scott didn't want to leave either. He just wished there was a way to get to East Africa without having to fork over another two thousand dollars for an expensive flight.

Over several days we visited a half dozen travel agents trying to find a reasonable fare and discussed our options in an unattractive (and expensive) hotel room in Accra. Scott buried his head in books as a distraction while I tried to motivate him to take the plunge and agree to book the flight. Finally, though he was quite grumpy about it, we bought the tickets and flew to Addis Ababa. As soon as we arrived he realized it was the right decision.

Addis Ababa. I loved saying Addis Ababa. I liked saying Ouagadougou too, but not many people outside of Burkina Faso have ever heard of it. But anyone who has heard of Bob Marley has heard of Addis Ababa because it is there that he is revered not only as the world's most musical Rastafarian but also as an outspoken supporter of the African unity movement.

Ethiopia was much quieter and gentler than West Africa. Even the way they danced was more laid back. It mostly involved standing in place and pumping the shoulders up and down. (Oddly, it was the *exact* way my brother Sean and I used to dance in our living room under the polka dot ceiling.) For a big African city, Addis Ababa was strangely calm. There was less traffic, less dust, and far fewer scraps of what was left of small blue plastic shopping bags. We had seen those blue bags all over West Africa, torn apart and blown willy-nilly by the wind before inevitably becoming snagged on roadside bushes or fences.

We instantly liked everything about Ethiopia. The air temperature in Addis was cooler and there was far less dusty smog than there was in Ghana. We spent our days walking to museums, restaurants, and twice a day to a café to enjoy a macchiato or cappuccino. We missed our expedition friends, especially Petra, Sam, and Luis, but we loved being on our own. We had the usual challenges that come with traveling independently, such as figuring out how to get from A to B and finding accommodation each night, but we were free of conflict and we had each other for company. If we had an urge to sit and chat with others, we just headed to a café. Café culture thrives in Addis. People sit for hours drinking coffee, reading the newspaper, and participating in the art of conversation. What made Ethiopian cafés different from others around the world is that we were able to watch our cup of coffee being made from start to finish.

Sitting on a short stool near our feet, a woman with flawless skin and perfect posture crushed a small mound of beans by hand. She placed the grounds into a kind of espresso pot that had an elegant spout and a straight handle that stuck out from the side to aid in pouring. After patiently waiting for the grinds to brew to perfection, she poured the dark, steamy liquid into our cups with reverence and a Mona Lisa smile. It's no wonder that the process of brewing coffee in Ethiopia is called a "ceremony." It definitely felt more like a religious rite than a coffee break. Coffee, and the process of brewing it, was invented in Ethiopia and I've never had a tastier cup of coffee anywhere in the world. In the afternoons, we switched from coffee to fresh pureed fruit poured in colorful layers in clear glass mugs. We couldn't guess what the green layer was until the young man making the smoothies asked one day, "Would you like avocado with that?" Our daily Ethiopian smoothie was delicious, healthy, and cheap, at eight cents US for a large mug.

As we walked along the main boulevard from coffee shop to smoothie stand, children ran to us calling out "You!" or "I love you!" followed by a whispered "Give me pen." Several years ago a guidebook or two suggested that instead of handing out candy to children, tourists should give them pens. We heard, "Give me pen!" almost daily.

We were surprised to see scales on almost every street corner. Ethiopians seemed obsessed with weighing themselves. Pedestrians would give a coin to the child tending the scale and then step up to be weighed. This is the country that experienced one of the worst famines in history, so I think they weigh themselves to make sure they are not *losing* weight. Our smoothie wallah told us that in Ethiopia it's a great compliment when someone says to his or her friend, "You are fat!"

"If you ever come to America this kind of compliment will not go over so well," I told him. "If you are going to comment on someone's weight, it's better to say, 'My! You are looking so thin lately!'" He laughed as if I were pulling his leg. It was inconceivable to him that someone would take it as a compliment that he wasn't getting enough to eat. When he saw I was serious he said, "I have heard that in America it is also considered important to have lots and lots of ice. Is that true?"

"Oh, yes! Being thin and having plenty of ice for your Coca-Cola is very important."

Scott gave me a look that said, "Must you?"

"But it's true!" I reminded him.

There is another reason to be concerned about weight in Africa and that is the "skinny disease." It surprised us that HIV-AIDS was openly discussed in Ethiopia. The children proudly pointed out the town's HIV clinic to us and condoms were available from street vendors in most cities.

It was in Ethiopia that we came across people with more disabilities and birth defects than anywhere else we visited in Africa. Sadly many born with deformities had no choice but to turn to begging on the busiest streets in Addis. Their limbs were often twisted in impossible angles. Unable to move without dragging their bodies across the pavement, beggars usually sat upon a bed of long cut grass on the sidewalk and asked, or didn't ask, for money. Most pedestrians bent and gently laid a coin or two down as they passed. They always seemed prepared with their coin, as if it were something they did routinely. Tragically most of the physical maladies we saw seemed like they could have been corrected with surgery at birth. We also saw many people with enormous goiters on their throats. I later learned from a doctor volunteering in Africa that most goiters are caused by an insufficiency of iodine. It blew me away that a simple dose of iodine could change a person's life so dramatically.

The average Ethiopian didn't just treat the needy and disabled with compassion. With a few exceptions they even treated their animals with kindness. Ethiopia got a nine on my donkey scale of African countries. For comparison, Morocco was about a two. They beat their donkeys and overload them to such an extent in Morocco that their legs buckle under the weight. They never make a sound in protest. They are too tired and sad to bray. In Mali (a seven), the donkeys are better treated, especially in the Dogon, but they brayed constantly. It was the saddest sound I've ever heard. We were told there was usually a pack of what our guide called "the beautiful horses" that were away at the time we were in the Dogon and that the donkeys cried because they missed the beautiful horses.

In Ethiopia, donkeys looked healthy and were usually treated very well. The young ones were so fluffy they looked as if they were wearing an alpaca sweater, but one made by a very inexperienced knitter. They hardly ever brayed. It was just a "hee" without the "haw" and only once in a while. A woman bringing goods to market won't overload her donkey. Instead she will carry the extra load on her own back. If the donkey has a foal, it walks alongside its mother. I never saw a woman put anything on the back of a baby donkey. Donkeys in Ethiopia seemed to be treated as an appreciated member of the family rather than like a cart with legs. I figure a country that treats their beasts of burden with compassion is a better country all around.

The cuisine in Ethiopia took some getting used to, but I put it in a category of "fun food" because I got to eat it with my hands. Separate little mounds of vegetables, beans, or potatoes were piled on top of a large flat spongy pancake called *injera*. We tore off a piece of injera, scooped up a little from the mound of spicy food then folded it all into our mouths. It was just before Easter when we were there, so Ethiopians were abstaining from meat. Most of the food bundles atop the injera were cabbage and beans and other highly gas producing vegetarian foods. Only there is a strong taboo against farting in public in Ethiopia. We were lucky my brother Joe wasn't with us because he would surely have made a game of it: "Hey, kid! Pull my finger!" (Which I guess would be one way to keep the ever-present crowds of children at bay.) Despite the bloated feeling we got from the "fasting food" menus, Ethiopian food was very tasty. To satisfy food cravings while on the road we had corn on the cob, which was grilled on charcoal braziers and handed up to us on the long-distance buses. I was hesitant to try it at first because when the boys called out the name of the treat, it sounded like "shit!"

The one thing I bought in Addis was a big red umbrella. Ethiopians protect themselves from the sun under broad colorful umbrellas, and I not only wanted to fit in, I was happy to add to my repertoire of heat deflecting items. Protected by my Tauareg scarf and new red umbrella, the possibility of heatstroke was greatly diminished. The streets of Addis were bustling with pedestrians looking very cool and stylish under their umbrellas.

If Ethiopians aren't carrying an umbrella, they carry a stick. At first I thought the sticks were for herding the many sheep, goats, or donkeys that are ever present. I soon found that they sometimes used sticks on each other; storekeepers took swipes at the boys who lurked by the goods, and teachers raised their sticks in preparation to whack the hands of tardy students. Still, the sticks seemed to be used far more as a deterrent than as a weapon.

I could relate. When I was a child, there was a stick that rested across a windowsill near the washing machine on our back porch and when Mom's threats to move to Timbuktu lost effect, she would sometimes say, "OK. Enough is enough. Get the stick." That really cracked us up because Mom didn't believe in capital punishment. Except in the case of the worms that ate her garden tomatoes. She treated those worms as if they were thieves stealing our last meal, and she would deliver swift justice by picking them off the vine and smashing them with vigor on the cement. Watching those big green worms explode on our driveway is one of the grosser memories from my childhood. Anyway, confident she would never actually use the stick on us, we could usually always get Mom to forgive us by making her laugh. I remember diffusing her frustration on occasion by exclaiming, "The devil made me do it!"

the way Flip Wilson used to, which would always get me off the hook because for some reason Mom thought Wilson's "Geraldine" routine was hilarious. Sometimes I thought Mom said, "Get the stick" just to get us to sharpen our comedic timing. Nonetheless, just seeing the stick there on the shelf each morning as we left for school was enough to keep us in line. I understood the power of the stick.

One sunny morning in Bahir Dar, Scott and I watched local competitors gather for a 10K Race. Several runners prematurely charged off the line a few seconds before the starting gun went off, so a do-over was called, and policemen raised their sticks and beat all the racers back to the starting line. The police were really wailing on them, but not one runner tried to dodge the stick. They merely absorbed the whack and returned to the starting line. I decided to try out the power of the stick on a few of the boys who gathered persistently around us each day. All I had to do was shift the position of my collapsed umbrella (stick to them) and they took off running. But like mother like daughter—they somehow knew I would never use the stick on them because they always ran back laughing. For a few minutes they would keep an umbrella-swing distance between us before once again becoming glued to our sides. With all those boys attached to us, we looked like a pulsating seven-celled organism with fourteen legs moving down the street.

The Ethiopian umbrella is not only a good tool for keeping cheeky boys in line, one day it saved us from being robbed. While walking on the main boulevard near Mescal Square in Addis Ababa, three young men surrounded Scott and tried to pick his pockets and steal his daypack. But we were ready for them. Scott grabbed an arm of one of the thugs while I raised my umbrella and came at them like Mom coming at a tomato worm. As soon as they saw the umbrella they took off running.

Unfortunately the umbrella didn't work in all instances. We were trying to eat breakfast one morning on a guesthouse terrace, but mostly we were chasing annoyingly persistent monkeys away with my umbrella. Suddenly a robust monkey leapt on to our table and startled Scott to such an extent that he bit down too hard on his fork and chipped his front tooth. The monkey refused to budge even though Scott continually swiped at him with the umbrella while shouting "Ya! Ya!" just like John Wayne did when urging his horse to go faster in *True Grit*. The monkey ignored us until he had finished our breakfast. Then he retreated to a tree over the terrace with a disdainful look over his shoulder that seemed to say, "You call that a stick?"

Despite the occasional need to use our umbrella on people or animals, we found Ethiopia to be a country full of charm. Toilet paper was simply referred to as "soft." It always made me smile to enter a shop and say, "I would like to buy some soft, please. Yes, I would like one packet of soft."

In Lalibela, we were in an underground church where twenty or so monks leaned on sticks while they chanted prayers from an eight-hundred-year-old holy book. As we listened, several young boys training for priesthood swayed rhythmically and periodically glanced our way. We were moved by their devotion. On each sway one young priest leaned closer and closer to my ear until finally he was so close I could feel his breath.

"Give me pen," he whispered.

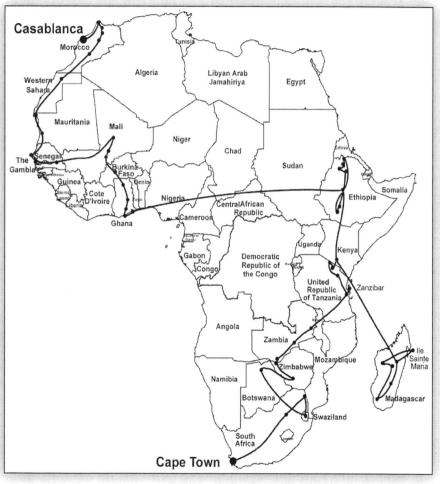

Casablanca

Morocco

Tunisia

Algeria

Libyan Arab
Jamahiriya

Egypt

Western
Sahara

Mauritania

Mali

Niger

Chad

Sudan

Eritrea

Senegal

The
Gambia

Burkina
Faso

Benin

Guinea

Cote
D'Ivoire

Nigeria

Central African
Republic

Somalia

Ethiopia

Sierra
Leone

Liberia

Togo

Cameroon

Ghana

Uganda

Kenya

Gabon

Congo

Democratic
Republic of
the Congo

United
Republic
of Tanzania

Zanzibar

Angola

Zambia

Zimbabwe

Mozambique

Ile
Sainte
Maria

Namibia

Botswana

Madagascar

Swaziland

South
Africa

Cape Town

MAP BY JO FILARCA

CONTENT WITH LIONS, ZIMBABWE

GO EBAY!, SOUTH AFRICA

ARRIVAL IN CAPE TOWN AFTER TEN MONTHS TRANSITING AFRICA.

THE POTATO TRUCK, GAMBIA

THE MUD MOSQUE AT D'JENNE, MALI

MOTHER AND BABY IN THE DOGON, MALI

MALI CHILDREN LOVE TO DANCE

Ethiopian Hat Seller

CAMPING ALONG THE SHORE OF LAKE LANGANO, ETHIOPIA

ORPHAN ELEPHANT SUCKLES THE HAND OF THE
AUTHOR AT THE SHELDRICK WILDLIFE TRUST

KAREN BLIXEN HOUSE

CLASSROOM IN THE SAND, MADAGASCAR

AVENUE OF THE BAOBABS, MADAGASCAR

An Obelisk and an Antonov

Ethiopia has an uncommon distinction. It is the only African country never colonized by another nation. The Italians occupied it briefly during World War II but never officially claimed it as a colony. The extent of Italian influence in Ethiopia was, as far as I could tell, espresso and pasta. (If cappuccino and carbonara are all the Italians ever leave behind, they are welcome to invade my home anytime!) Because it wasn't under foreign rule for long, there is a vibe in Ethiopia that is not found in most other African countries. Most everywhere else in Africa we were paid deference just because we were foreigners or because we are white. In Ethiopia we were treated no differently than anyone else. We were treated less like a teacher and more like a student, and that made us instantly more comfortable. We could immerse ourselves in a culture that was, for the most part, untarnished by colonial influences and without the guilt that plagues some Europeans when they visit a former colony. Suzanne was Portuguese-Australian and in the first days of the expedition she told me she was dreading going to Angola, "...because what the Portuguese did there was horrific," she said. She felt so much guilt about Portuguese colonization that she vowed she would not speak Portuguese while we were in Angola, even though she was fluent. I think part of the reason that she, above all others, was not too upset that the expedition ended in Ghana was that she would be able to skip Angola entirely.

We found present-day Ethiopia and her people thoroughly fascinating. There was a genuine openness among her people and it was the one African country where I felt a cohesive sense of national pride emanating from the people in every city we visited. But when we tried to delve into Ethiopia's ancient past, we found it complex and befuddling. Scott is an avid reader of world history but he'd never even heard of the Axumite civilization before we were in Ethiopia. The Axumite kingdom had its own language and alphabet. Its diverse population included Christians, Jews, and Buddhists, and it had been a major trading hub between North and East Africa. It really bothered Scott that the story of the Axumites had not been told, at least not in the California education system.

We had read about the town of Lalibela (probably in a *National Geographic* magazine in our dentist's office), so at least we knew about her underground churches. The most striking from above is the cross-shaped St. George's church, considered by some to be the Eighth Wonder of the World. The incredibly engineered solid granite churches make up yet another World Heritage Site and are bringing more tourists than ever to Lalibela. The downside of this increase in tourism is truancy. The children of Lalibela view any visitor to their town as a welcome diversion and would rather latch on to a tourist than attend school.

Children are hard to resist anywhere in the world and, for me, children are the very best part of Africa. We loved learning about their world through their unjaded eyes and unguarded comments. They never ceased to enchant us with their endless questions, joyous laughter, and hopes for the future. Invariably they would say, "I want to be a doctor when I grow up!" It didn't matter whether they lived in a tiny village or in a large city. They dreamed of being the person who could treat the sick with the right care and the best medicine. Those children fortunate enough to go to school considered it a treasured privilege. Africa doesn't export much, but if they could somehow export appreciation for education, they would fill a need in most of the schools in the developed world.

Unfortunately in Lalibela where tourism is really taking off, the lure of a foreigner is stronger than the desire to attend school. We usually had a posse of kids trailing after us wherever we went in Africa, but I wasn't prepared for the onslaught of truant children we encountered in Lalibela. The boys were especially persistent. They never left us alone and *never* stopped talking. We were in Ethiopia during low season, so we were only two of a handful of travelers. Each morning children swarmed around us as we left our guesthouse. One boy handed us a neatly handwritten letter stating that his football club was in need of donations for a new soccer ball. Others showed us letters from their overseas "sponsors." Mostly they were just interested in talking with us and practicing their English. But their elders became understandably upset that the children preferred talking with a foreigner than attending school.

One afternoon a little boy walked along with us chatting away brightly as we made our way between the churches in Lalibela. A male relative called him over and twisted his ears while commanding, "How many times have I told you! Leave the tourists alone!" I felt awful for the boy and somewhat guilty that he was being punished. It was the law of unintended consequences. All I wanted to do was learn about Lalibela and see her churches but simply *because* we were in Lalibela, school attendance and this boy's education were altered.

A few minutes later the boy reappeared by my side with a tear-stained face and ears the color of a bright red candy apple. I stopped short. "You must not walk with us! You will be scolded and have your ears twisted again." He looked up with a smile and asked, "What is it like in America or England? I want to go there. Then I will become a doctor."

I sighed. The right thing to do would be to chase him away. I briefly considered using my umbrella but decided to try reasoning with him instead. "If you want to be a doctor, you must stay in school."

"Yes," he agreed pragmatically. "But, what is it like in America?"

"In America, children have to go to school. If they don't, they won't have a chance of becoming a doctor or teacher. They can only get a job..." I paused. I almost said, "flipping burgers," but I knew I had to make it a more relevant outcome of skipping school. "...Tending goats," I finished.

"Oh," he said solemnly. At the next corner he peeled off, probably to search for another tourist, one who wouldn't be such a killjoy.

In the city of Gondar fewer children followed us around the historic sites. Then again, the supply of tourists in Gondar was so low that the boys probably thought it wasn't worth the trouble or scolding to cut class. We walked unescorted to a vast castle built by Emperor Fasilidas and farther on we studied the ceiling of the Debre Berhan Selassie church, which is covered with the worried faces of hundreds of angels. They look like children on the lookout for ear-twisting relatives.

For two weeks we traveled by plane or bus to cities on the "historic circuit" which rims the northern part of the country. Flying to the historic areas within Ethiopia was not expensive, but because the route was purported to be very scenic, we decided to travel to Bahir Dar overland. It was an extremely hot day, and we were the last two to board the stifling bus. None of the windows were open; it was as if we had walked into a hothouse. As soon as we found our seats, we opened the window next to us for a breath of air. An Ethiopian gentleman across the aisle stood up and, waggling his finger and shaking his head at us, closed it. Thinking it must be for a good reason that he didn't want the window open while it was at the station, we waited until the bus departed to open it again. When we did, there were gasps of displeasure and the window was slammed shut. We began to strip down. We removed all the clothing we could decently get away with. Soon we were dressed like a couple of Ed Nortons on a hot and humid New York summer day.

We waited until the bus was far out in the countryside before opening the window a crack so we could breathe. Slam! Everyone on the bus acted as if fresh air was a monster to be kept at bay. By now the sweat was dripping from our bodies, and we had begun to sprout. Finally a man explained, "Please. Do not open the window. We do not want to catch cold."

Bahir Dar is at the source of the headwaters of the Blue Nile, which sounded like a good place to dive in and get refreshed after our steam room bus ride, so we pedaled there on rented bicycles as soon as we arrived. Fortunately the bike ride alone revived us sufficiently because once we saw all the crocodiles resting on the bank amongst the papyrus reeds we didn't feel the need for a swim. Instead we rode back to our guesthouse situated on Lake Tana.

The guesthouse was full when we checked in, but they allowed us to pitch our tent on the bank of the lake near an enclosed gazebo. After we set up our tent, a member of the hotel staff brought us two beers and handed us a key. He told us that whenever we were away from our tent we should put our backpacks inside the gazebo. The next morning he asked that we move our entire tent into the gazebo so that we would be more secure at night. "Bad men walk along the bank at night," he said. I noticed that he looked as if he had gotten very little sleep, and I worried that he had sat up all night watching over us. The gazebo, situated in a flower garden in full bloom, had an even better view of the lake, so we readily accepted his offer. We re-pitched our freestanding tent inside the gazebo and had the best room in the house. Each morning we woke to bird song in the garden and each evening we had sundowners at the lake's edge and watched men in kayak-sized papyrus boats catch fish with a string and a hook.

Lake Tana is famous for the island monasteries which dot the lake, so we took a boat ride out to a different island each day. At each monastery monks showed us eight-hundred-year-old holy books held open in their arms as they stood under colorful umbrellas while leaning on ornate sticks. "Doubly armed," I remarked to Scott.

One of the main cities on the historic circuit of Ethiopia is Axum, home of the world's earliest Christian kingdom. But that's not what it is known for. Axum is renowned for its stelae field populated with enormous obelisks. One obelisk is the tallest in the world. "Why haven't I ever heard of this?" Scott mumbled, as he often did while we explored Ethiopia.

When the Italians left Ethiopia in 1941, they took with them a souvenir in the form of a 1,700-year-old obelisk. The obelisk resided for 68 years near the Circus Maximus in Rome before the Ethiopian government convinced the Italians that pasta for an obelisk was not a fair trade. In 2005 the obelisk was finally being returned to its rightful home in Axum. Interesting things happen when a fifty-eight-ton solid piece of granite (only one-third of the entire obelisk) is flown from Italy to Ethiopia. The only plane big enough to carry the obelisk was one of the largest planes in the world, the Antonov, a Russian cargo plane.

As the Antonov was preparing to fly the obelisk to Axum, we were at the Gondar Airport waiting for a flight to Axum along with five other tourists. Just as we were about to board, a representative from Ethiopian Airlines approached the group. He drew a deep breath before saying, "Due to insufficient fuel, *you* can go to Axum, but your bags will have to follow on a flight leaving tomorrow."

The other travelers became very upset and expressed them-selves in a Western civilization manner by shouting at the airline employee.

He explained, "The obelisk that the Italians stole from us dur-ing their occupation in World War II is being returned today, and the plane carrying it requires all available aviation fuel. So there is only enough fuel on this flight for you, but not your luggage."

This didn't sit well with the others who again began shouting, "I've got to catch a flight back to Europe tomorrow" and, "This is unacceptable! I demand to speak with your supervisor."

I looked at Scott and motioned that we should distance ourselves from the whine fest. "Why don't we stay here another night?" I suggested. Scott interrupted the vocal melee and offered to the airline rep, "If my wife and I stay behind with our bags, will you be able to take the rest of the passengers and their luggage on this flight?"

The other passengers waited anxiously for his answer. "Yes, that is possible," the employee said.

We received grunts of thanks from the other passengers who obviously hadn't been traveling long enough in Africa for their type A personalities to melt into type Bs. But we had been in Africa for more than five months by then, and if we hadn't learned patience, we hadn't learned anything. Besides, we didn't really mind spending another night in Gondar.

We watched the plane take off (barely) without us, and a half hour later the airport was shut down, the doors were locked and we, along with the entire airport staff, climbed into one Toyota Land Cruiser and drove to the Ethiopian Airways office in town. I sat in the front seat next to the driver as he navigated a route congested with pedestrians and vehicles. Then something occurred that sort of epitomizes Africa for me: how Africans can say so much in just a few words. Up ahead I noticed something lying in the middle of the road. As we got closer I could see it was a woman. A car hadn't hit her and she wasn't dead or dying. Our driver, who seemed to want to ignore her presence, swerved just enough to avoid hitting her. He came so close to her that I was sure she could smell the rubber from the tires. No one in the vehicle said anything. Finally, eyes wide, I looked at the driver and said, "Why is that woman lying in the road?"

He cocked his head and thought a while before answering, "I think she is tired."

Tired? Tired of what? Tired of struggling to survive? Tired of watching her children die of disease? Tired of being tired? I had not yet encountered a woman in Africa who was ready to give up so completely. The way the driver endeavored to make her invisible was a method of coping I saw all over Africa, especially in the cities. The men in the vehicle noticed the woman's suffering without reacting to it. If they did, they would have to admit actually seeing it. If they see it they might have to do something about it. And what good does that do anyone? Taking care of one's family followed by self-reliance is how people survive.

"Don't worry. She will get up after a time," he said with conviction.

We never asked about accommodation for the night. We assumed we would stay at the same modest lodging we had the night before. Instead, we were driven up into the hills to a snazzy government hotel. We checked in and had sundowners on a terrace overlooking Gondar's castles. A complimentary three-course dinner and a soft bed followed. Not that I slept that well. I kept thinking about the woman in the road.

The next day we were driven back to the airport for our flight to Axum. We arrived in central Axum just as the locals were beginning to celebrate the return of the obelisk. If we had taken the flight the day before, we might have missed our chance to see the celebration. Serendipity was alive and well. Once again, we were in the right place at the right time.

In addition to celebrating in the street with, well, everyone, we managed to see some of the tourist sites in Axum including the building that is reputed to hold *the* Ark of the Covenant. "Don't you think this would be considered a pretty important piece of historic or at least religious trivia?" asked Scott.

"Never heard of it," I answered.

"Not even in any one of the religion classes you had every day for eight years in Catholic grammar school?"

"Nope. Actually it never even occurred to me to ask. I was too busy putting white polish on my saddle shoes to worry about the location of the Ark of the Covenant. Once a month, the monsignor, a retired Marine, would inspect all of our shoes in a playground line-up. The girl with the whitest shoes was rewarded with one of those candy-coated almonds that brides used to hand out at weddings. Try as I might, my shoes were never almond worthy. I even complained to my mom that she wasn't buying the right polish, but I never once earned a candy."

Scott gave me a look that said he was glad he was a Frisbiterian.

Ethiopian Christians believe that they acquired the ark during the reign of Solomon. As the story goes, during a visit to Jerusalem, King Solomon's son Menelik stole the ark and brought it back to Ethiopia where his mother was queen. King Solomon and the Queen of Sheba had an on-again, off-again relationship (on enough to produce Menelik) so it's as plausible a story as any when it comes to the Ark of the Covenant. In any event, the belief that the Ark of the Covenant resides in Axum is at the core of Ethiopian Christianity. Devotees line the short wall surrounding the structure that houses the ark. Within the structure is a solitary monk who guards the ark for and with his entire life. I stood at the wall looking down on the repository and I had to admit that a chill or two ran up my spine. But it was mostly due to the palpable faith emanating from the women nearby who bowed their heads in homage, unwavering in their belief that the One True Ark was inside.

It is said that more than 90 percent of Axum is still to be excavated, so there are sure to be many more mysteries to discover and treasures to be found. Yet as of 2005, even with all the rich history and fascinating religious sites, each city we visited, was unspoiled by tourism (truancy factor in Lalibela aside). In all of Ethiopia during our month there, we encountered only a handful of Western tourists. When a friend of mine later said she was thinking about going to Ethiopia I said, "Go! But take an umbrella, an open mind, and an appetite for fresh fruit smoothies, Italian pasta, and delicious coffee. And remember how Karl Malden didn't go anywhere without his American Express card? When you go to Ethiopia, it wouldn't hurt to take along a little Beano. Don't leave home without it."

By the Way, Would You Like
to Come to My Wedding?

On our way back to Addis, we stayed one night in the town of Arba Minch, which sits atop a rift valley escarpment. After a picnic lunch high up on a ridge overlooking two of the rift valley lakes, we walked back to town to book seats on a bus leaving for Addis the following day at 6:00 a.m. Just as we were trying to decide how early we would have to get up the next morning in order to secure seats at the front of the bus, a young man approached us. He said he lived nearby and that for a fee he would board the bus at 5:00 a.m. and save two seats for us. This sounded like a good idea since the bus station was nowhere near our guesthouse, and it would save us having to get up at 4:00 a.m. We stressed to him that we would like to have two seats up front, near the driver, so we could see out the window and hopefully get some air. We paid him and hoped for the best.

Back at our guesthouse, mosquitoes pestered us all night long while rain pelted down unabated. After very little sleep, we rose at 5:00 a.m. and made our way to the bus station thinking if the young man came through for us we would at least have good seats to Addis and we might be able to nap on the way. And he did come through. He did exactly as we asked, securing two seats right behind the driver. Only the seats were next to the enormous engine located in the aisle between the driver and our seats. Every other seat on the bus was taken, so there was no choice but to take the seats the young man had reserved for us.

By 8:00 a.m. the engine had heated the space around us to such an extent that we were practically down to our underwear. As usual, no one would open a window. It made me long for the Mechanic's drafty overland truck.

Six hours into the journey, the bus blew two tires at once. Dripping with sweat, we looked at each other then asked the driver to get our backpacks off the roof. "We're leaving," we announced. He and the other passengers tried to talk us out of it, saying it was unsafe. Two boys even offered to go with us to provide protection. We assured everyone we would be careful and after looking at a map, we saw that the bus had broken down near a lake. We decided to camp at the lake for a night before continuing on to Addis the next day. We waved goodbye to the heatstroke-inducing environment of the bus along with the concerned passengers and started off down the three-kilometer sand road that led to Lake Lagano.

Almost immediately we were joined by a group of small boys who insisted that the lake was too far away to walk to. They repeated that at five-minute intervals as they followed us the whole way to the lake. We did animal impressions for one another as we walked, the boys laughing hysterically at my hippo impersonation.

Once we got to the lake, the boys left us with happy waves and a final zebra bark. We saw that there was a hotel on a small hill, but it was very run-down and it appeared to be deserted so we pitched our tent on some grass under an acacia tree near the lake. We went for a walk, a swim, and had a simple picnic dinner. We always had emergency provisions in our pack such as crackers and biscuits. And gin.

We were content with our solitude on Lake Lagano, but we began to feel we might have abandoned the bus in haste. We would probably have to wait several hours (or days) on the road before securing a ride to Addis. The buses, few and far between, would undoubtedly be full and would probably not stop for us. Serendipity would have to be on our side once again.

The next morning our young escorts from the day before joined us for the walk back out to the main road. Only this time they had a donkey cart with them and insisted on giving us a ride. The only problem was that they repeatedly used a switch on the donkey to get it to run. They were really messing up my donkey index for Ethiopia. "No!" I pleaded, taking the reins and coaxing the small donkey with clicks of my tongue while lecturing the boys that beating an animal is cruel and will shorten its useful life. "Every living thing performs better without a beating." They rolled their eyes at me and laughed uproariously.

Back on the main road a replacement bevy of children surrounded us. Immediately a four-door sedan screeched to a stop. A well dressed man got out, opened his trunk, threw our backpacks inside and said, "Get in! Get in! It is not safe for you to be alone out here!" I looked around us. We certainly weren't alone. The kids were still there, smiling, laughing, and bellowing like hippos.

His name was Delasi, and he was dumbstruck that we had asked our bus driver to leave us "out in the country where bad things can happen." He made us promise never to do that again in Ethiopia.

During the three-hour ride to Addis, we talked about many things, but mostly about Ethiopian politics and the upcoming elections. "Ethiopia has never had a peaceful election. That is why it is not safe at all for you to be traveling around on your own. Perhaps this election will be different," Delasi said wistfully. "Promise me you will be careful."

I could tell that Delasi enjoyed having company on the drive to Addis and that he was glad he had rescued us. As he pulled up to our guesthouse, he invited us to dinner that night and added, "Oh, by the way, would you like to attend my wedding in two days?" My jaw dropped. A woman would have told us within five minutes that she was getting married in two days and about all the last-minute details she had to attend to. We had been with Delasi three hours, and he had only mentioned it as an afterthought. We told him we were honored, but shouldn't he ask his bride-to-be first? From past experience we knew that as the only foreigners in attendance, we would probably become the center of attention and that many of the other guests would be curious about what two blond-haired Americans were doing at Delasi's wedding. Any woman knows that to take even a little of the spotlight off the bride on her wedding day is not appreciated, so we told Delasi that while we were greatly honored, we would be unable to attend. When we met his fiancée at dinner that evening, I could tell she was relieved that we declined the invitation. She went on to tell us about all the last-minute details she had to complete before the wedding.

A few nights later we went to a bar, The Milk House, frequented by expats working in and around Addis. We sat with two physicians from the United States who were enjoying their last night in Ethiopia. They had finished their residencies in the States a few months earlier and were headed to South Africa for a little R & R before beginning their practices in New York. One had just spent a month working with a New Zealand couple that ran a clinic in a pygmy village in Uganda. When I asked him what it was like he said, "It was depressing because a lot of them are dying. And, well," he said with disappointment. "The pygmies...they just aren't that short."

The doctor reminded me a lot of Ingrid, a woman we had met on a previous trip to Africa in 1995 when we were lucky to have an opportunity to see gorillas in the Virunga Mountains in Zaire, now the Democratic Republic of the Congo. We were traveling with a group of seven Europeans, two Kiwis, several Australians, and one Canadian, some of whom had come all the way to Africa for only one reason: to see gorillas.

We parked our truck in Uganda, paid men to guard it while we were gone, and walked across the Zaire border and into the mountains. A long line of porters carried our tents, sleeping bags, clothing, and three days' worth of food up a narrow footpath that led into the misty hills. Zaire was in a state of unrest at the time, so it was to be a quick in-and-out trip. Unbeknownst to us, refugees from the Hutu and Tutsi massacre in neighboring Rwanda were spilling over into Zaire.

To make matters worse, there was a recent deadly Ebola outbreak in a nearby village. Our guide had been on the verge of canceling the gorilla segment altogether. But one woman in particular, the Canadian, was very keen on seeing the gorillas, and she convinced the rest of us that we had come too far to miss seeing the gorillas in their natural habitat.

After several hours of hiking, we arrived at a place to camp. As we prepared dinner over a wood fire, a ranger came out of nowhere to talk to us and arrange our trek to see the gorillas. Africans do that. They just appear out of nowhere. I was once in a wide-open plain in Tanzania desperately seeking a tree or bush to pee behind. The landscape was devoid of vegetation. Finally I couldn't wait any longer. After determining that I was far enough away from the truck that one would need binoculars to see me, I quickly scanned the horizon and did my business. As I stood up and zipped my jeans, a Masai warrior appeared, *out of the blue*, not six feet from me. He stood balanced on one leg while leaning on his stick studying me. I looked around to see what blade of grass he had been hiding behind. Eventually he slowly put an invisible cigarette to his lips and inhaled a breath of imaginary tobacco.

"Sorry, I don't smoke," I said shaking my head.

When I arrived back at the truck, I scanned the horizon to see where he had gone. Even with binoculars I couldn't spot him anywhere. It was as if he had evaporated.

It was the same with the ranger in Zaire. He just suddenly appeared. After he said all he needed to, he vanished. Sometimes it seems as if Africans can be in two places at once. They are there, we just can't see them coming and going.

The next morning we separated into two groups. The rangers endeavor to keep the groups small so that gorilla-to-human interaction is minimal. Our group included the Canadian woman who was most excited about seeing the gorillas. It was the main reason she had come to Africa. Our group also included Ingrid from Norway. Ingrid was very pragmatic for a Scandinavian (excuse the oxymoron). Around a campfire one night, Ingrid taught us the appropriate way to club a baby seal to death —a technique she had learned as a child in Norway. A log served as stand-in for a pup seal. Ingrid was in Africa recovering from a recent disappointment. She had spent four years in school preparing herself for a job in the new European Union, but just as she graduated, Norway voted not to enter the E.U. To say Ingrid was bitter is an understatement.

We followed the guide single file through the thick vegetation. A tracker was at the front clearing a path in the forest with a *panga* (machete). After only forty minutes, the tracker pointed to a large nest made of leaves high up in a tree. "They slept here last night," the guide said softly. We walked another ten minutes before coming upon a family of gorillas sitting quietly together in tall grass. The guide motioned that we should kneel down, be silent, and keep our distance. Immediately a baby gorilla toddled over with its arms outstretched the way a young child does when it wants to be picked up. So moved was she at seeing the baby gorilla, the Canadian woman burst into tears. We sat transfixed as the family interacted with one another. The guide motioned for us to back up and give the baby gorilla space while a great silverback, twice as large as the adult females kept a watchful eye over the scene. The Canadian woman continued to weep as she snapped photo after photo. Soon most of the rest of us were sniffling. Except for Ingrid. She barely looked at the gorillas. Instead she sat on her haunches with her head in her hands watching us. After several minutes she broke our reverie and said with a disdainful snort, "Pfft. What's the big deal? They're just monkeys, only bigger."

We all stared at Ingrid as if she had just said, "Mothers. They're OK I guess but we could live without them." The Canadian woman took it personally. She gave Ingrid a look of supreme pity and was cool toward her for the rest of the trip.

Ingrid never lived her big monkey comment down. A New Zealander had the best, though most biting, comeback when he said over dinner one night, "What's the big deal about Norwegians? They're just Swedes, only dumber." Even Ingrid, to her credit, managed a chuckle.

As I sat in the Milk House listening to the doctor complain about the size of the pygmies, I wondered if Ingrid was still single. Here was a man she could relate to!

"What do you think about gorillas?" I asked him.

He shrugged, "Dunno. They're all right, I guess." Changing the subject he asked, "How much longer are you two going to stay in Ethiopia? Things are really heating up here."

The heat he was referring to was the vibe on the street. It was our last night in Ethiopia as well. If it isn't coups, closed borders, riots, the Marburg virus, or the coming monsoon, there is another good reason to leave an African country: impending elections. Ethiopia's Prime Minister Zenawi had been in power for fourteen years, and elections for a new leader were imminent. Ethiopia had never experienced a peaceful transition of power, and the opposition parties were numerous and cranky.

As the day for elections approached, Addis became not so gentle and charming. It was subtle at first. There were huge but peaceful political rallies almost daily. Every bus we rode on was stopped while police searched all the male passengers inside. At the entrance of every hotel or restaurant we, along with all the Ethiopians, were patted down for weapons. It happened everywhere, and we became used to it. The one place I began to avoid because of the pat down was the post office. The lady guard there came at my breasts as if she was turning on bathtub faucets full blast.

There was so much extra security that I began to wonder if we had missed some news about recent violence. I asked a guard at a café as he ran his security wand over me, "Has something happened?"

"Yes," he answered.

"What? When?" I asked.

"Seven years ago there was a bomb in a hotel."

As the days went by, there was a change in the atmosphere on the street, and we were not as comfortable walking around at night. It felt as if something dramatic could happen any minute—that an innocuous car backfire or popped balloon could start a riot.

There is a Gabra word *rubvunzavaeni* that translates as, "the time of day when visitors ask for lodging." Focus on quickly finding shelter was something we saw nightly whenever we were in Nairobi, and it was beginning to happen now too in Addis. Just before dusk, Ethiopian workers stepped double time to clear the streets and get home before dark. Soon front-page news articles warned all foreigners to stay off the streets during political rallies, of which there were many. Hundreds of thousands of Ethiopians attended these rallies. And they were always peaceful. Yet, there was that feeling in the air that told us it was time to get out of Dodge. Madagascar was calling. And we too would be practicing rubvunzavaeni because we would have to travel to Nairobi first. Kenya was the only African country at the time to offer direct flights to Madagascar.

Sadly, while there was so much hope in the newspapers for a peaceful election, this seems to be a very difficult thing to achieve in Ethiopia. I thought about Delasi and how disappointed he would be. Shortly after the election, people began protesting the results. Sixty thousand were arrested. Hundreds were killed and injured or disappeared in the months following the election. Zenawi remained in power.

ELEPHANT TRUST

We spent two days in Nairobi, Kenya, before flying to Madagascar—just enough time to buy round-trip plane tickets, see *Out of Africa* author Karen Blixen's estate, and visit one of my favorite places on earth, the elephant orphanage at the Sheldrick Wildlife Trust. The Trust is not only an orphanage for rhinos and elephants, it is also a leader in conservation in Kenya. Run by Daphne Sheldrick since 1977, the trust rescues and rehabilitates elephants that have been orphaned, usually due to poaching.

The ivory trade is what drives poaching. Daphne Sheldrick believes that the only way to stop poaching is to burn all the stock of ivory that has been taken from elephants. I agree with her. If I ever have the occasion to meet you, please don't wear ivory. I would hate for you to see your favorite piece of jewelry go up in smoke. (I'd also hate it when you pressed charges.) But I'm sure if you knew that an elephant had to die for your ornamentation, you would never have bought it in the first place. Believe me, you only have to see these orphans once to give up wearing ivory or make the switch to imitation.

As I watched the elephants wallowing in a mud bath at the orphanage, one baby no bigger than a large dog ran over, sniffed my toes, wrapped his little trunk firmly around my arm, stuck my hand in his mouth and suckled. It was heart wrenching. Another resident was an eight-month-old elephant recovering from a gunshot wound to the head. Poachers shot his mother for her ivory, then shot the baby because baby elephants go berserk when they see their mothers die. Fortunately the little guy managed to run off and was later rescued and brought to the orphanage. He stood apart from the others a very sad and traumatized elephant. He brushed the ground rhythmically with his trunk while his caregiver stood by and tried to soothe him with a bottle of milk and a warm blanket. Periodically the other young elephants came to him and touched his wound with their trunks, which seemed to comfort him a little.

Each elephant at the orphanage has a group of caregivers who spend 100 percent of their time with the orphans, even sleeping with them at night. The Sheldrick Trust gets most if not all of their funding through donations or sponsorship from the public, and their goal is to return all rescued elephants to the wild. After rehabilitation each elephant gets to decide when he's ready to join another herd and just be an elephant again. In the past they could simply walk away into the adjoining national park. We were told that some female elephants that had been rescued by the trust have brought their offspring back to the orphanage years later to show them off to their former caregivers.

Before we left Nairobi the next day, we adopted an African. Her trunk is gorgeous, and she has the sweetest little trumpet.

BEAUCOUP OEUFS

Madagascar. Where lemurs scream like banshees and look like children dressed in koala bear suits, where bizarre and beautiful sea life abounds, where there are plants and trees that grow nowhere else on earth, where the word for bad is "ratsy," and the top female vocalist is Poopy. That's her name, not a critique of her talent.

Winter had just arrived in the capital city of Antananarivo (even the locals find it a mouthful and refer to it simply as Tana), and the first thing I noticed about this island nation was that Malagasies look Indonesian. We learned that Madagascar was settled from Indonesia and that many Malagasies don't consider themselves part of Africa. The second thing I noticed was that almost everyone was barefoot. Wearing winter coats, but barefoot. Even the *pousse-pousse* (rickshaw) pullers were barefoot.

Our first stop in Tana was the Shoprite Supermarket. After seven months of grilled corncobs, vegetables, potatoes, and rice, I was on the hunt for some seriously high fat content food, specifically Doritos. I'd had a brief sighting of Doritos a few months earlier in Ghana when some embassy workers on holiday opened a bag by the swimming pool at the Mole Park Hotel. "Excuse me, where did you get those?" I asked while trying not to drool. They looked at one another sheepishly before answering, "We have Doritos sent to us occasionally by diplomatic pouch." I wasn't offered a single triangle, even when I played my recovering-from-malaria card. So by the time we arrived in Tana, which had Western-style supermarkets, I had a serious craving for some savory crunch.

At the supermarket, Scott and I split up to search the store for the crisps aisle. Scott located it first. I found him standing in front of bags and bags of salty, crunchy goodness, speaking to three young Peace Corps women who were also there to satisfy their desire for something fattening and spicy.

We had arrived in Madagascar without a guidebook, so after I gathered up five small bags of Nacho Doritos we asked, "What should we not miss seeing in Madagascar?" A woman who couldn't wait and was already consuming her first bag of Doritos said, "I'm finishing my Peace Corps obligation in a week, so you can have my guidebook. It's old, but it should help you in getting around." Then Scott asked where their favorite bar in town was located and asked if we could meet them there at 7:00 p.m. If they supplied information about Madagascar and the guidebook, we'd supply the drinks.

At seven we walked into a pub to find not only the three Peace Corps girls, but also six more Peace Corps workers who were in Tana for R & R. They all had lots of good tips, so it was an expensive night for us. We didn't mind. We make it a policy to buy a beer for any Peace Corps volunteers we encounter on our travels. They get paid very little, and they do have the best insider tips. Now armed with a guidebook, we made a plan to see as much of the country as we could in the time allowed and we began to explore Tana.

We found Malagasies to be incredibly polite. I never heard a single person raise their voice or act without courteous intention. Transactions were done orderly and with patience. There were never any lines! One day at a bank we finally realized why no one ever lined up. There was only one customer at the counter but about twelve people sat quietly in straight-backed chairs against the walls. Puzzled at what everyone else was waiting for in the bank lobby, but happy that there was only one person at the counter, we walked over and stood behind her and waited our turn. After cashing our check with the necessary *bonjours, s'il vous plaits,* and *mercis,* we started out the exit until I stopped Scott with my hand on his arm. "Look," I whispered. We watched a woman rise from her seat and approach the counter. While she conducted her business, a man entered the bank and took a seat along the wall. After the woman at the counter left, the next "in line" rose from her chair and went to the counter. Malagasies are so courteous they don't even make one another stand in line! Everyone somehow knows who is next and waits patiently for their turn from the comfort of their seat. We realized then that we had inadvertently jumped the queue when we stood behind the woman being helped at the counter. Everyone was too polite to say anything. Before we left we pantomimed to the others waiting, "We apologize! We are stupid foreigners, but we get it now!" and everyone smiled and nodded.

"Are they agreeing that we are stupid foreigners or that we get it?" I asked Scott.

"Yes."

I read in the guidebook given me by the Peace Corps volunteer that in Madagascar you travel your palate. I had to agree. After my craving for Doritos was sated, I dove into the local cuisine with gusto.

Madagascar is a former French colony, so an entree is often *en sauce*, and because it is an island nation, the seafood is always plentiful, fresh, and delicious. However transporting all that fish around meant that our backpacks were often on or under enormous wicker baskets of fish piled high on top of the bush taxi. Our packs soon began to take on the aroma of a seafood platter. But the food is really good and most of it is served with rice, which I love. Rice is such a part of daily life that Malagasies refer to the growing cycle of rice in the same terms as gestation of a baby.

Speaking of babies, while lying in bed one morning in Antananarivo trying to pronounce Antananarivo and scratching my various mosquito bites, I discovered a small hard lump on the bottom of my foot. Very small, but as we had learned after seven months in Africa, little things could turn into something big, so off we went to the clinic, which turned out to be a maternity hospital. Since our French is minimal, we had to communicate with gestures and pantomime. I bared my sole to the doctor and *tout suite* she had me up on the gurney in her office/operating room. An attending nurse smeared my foot with Betadine, and the doctor began to cut. I pantomimed, "Ow! This will hurt! No anesthesia first? Numb the foot, *s'il vous plait!* Me no likey pain." The doctor pantomimed back, "We don't normally do that here; I'll cut slowly, and we'll see how much it hurts. It's just a sharp knife, you big sissy!"

While charades were being played between the hospital staff and me, Scott was flitting around the doctor and my foot, trying to be helpful while cheerfully proclaiming, "Maybe it's a maggot!" He said this, believe it or not, as an educated guess since I actually *had* a maggot in one of my toes while in Zanzibar a few years back. "A *maggot!*" said Scott repeating his diagnosis with enthusiasm. He said this in English though, so they ignored him, until he brought out the camera. Then they were all smiles, pantomiming that copies be sent and becoming very cheerful. So everyone was cheerful but me. The doctor began to cut, and all I could think about was the scene from *Gone With the Wind* when the Confederate soldier on the table about to have a leg amputated yells, "Don't cut! Don't cut!" while Scarlet looks on in horror. I think I even whispered, "Don't cut!" but I said this in English and my face was buried in the gurney pillow so everyone ignored me.

Camera clicking away, doctor cutting away, me looking away, when suddenly the doctor shouted, "*Voila!*"

Scott zoomed the camera lens and said with anticipation, "Is it a maggot?"

The doctor, smiling for her close up exclaimed, "*Non! Beaucoups oeufs!,*" which, I learned when she showed me *about a hundred of them* on the scalpel, means, "lots of eggs."

My mom always said what a good host I was, but this was ridiculous.

"Eggs? In my *foot?*" I asked with horror.

The doctor and nurse pantomimed a little insect drilling a hole in my foot and laying her eggs. They also conveyed to us that it was their most interesting delivery of the day.

I most likely acquired the stowaways in the garden of Karen Blixen's home outside Nairobi in Kenya where I guess pregnant insects like to live. The bug must have tested my soft Western sole and shouted, "Eureka!" before depositing her eggs. Anyway, Karen Blixen's garden is a lovely place and if I were a creepy bug I'd live there too.

This wasn't our first encounter with egg infestation. We had already experienced the Zanzibar maggot Scott referred to during my foot surgery in the maternity ward. Back then I didn't remotely imagine the little bump on my toe could be something disgusting or *alive* so, thinking it was some kind of weird toe zit, I had taken a needle to it. When a little worm head presented itself after a single pinprick, Scott went berserk, grabbed his head, and shouted, "Get it out! Get it out! That is the most disgusting thing I've ever seen on you!" I reacted by jabbing away at the maggot like Glenn Close in *Fatal Attraction*, or Anthony Perkins in the shower scene in *Psycho*. After making a fairly deep gouge in my toe, I went to the reception desk where we were staying and showed the clerk. I asked, "What the heck was that?" I wanted to make sure I didn't need to start taking antibiotics or something.

"Oh you shouldn't have done that," he said. "You must remove the worm whole. Next time, just ask a local to tease it out for you." He added, "You should probably have a doctor look at it to make sure you got it all out."

As luck would have it, on that particular trip we were traveling with a doctor. Well, a vet from New Zealand. Anyway, he was able to get the rest of the maggot out of my paw mostly by gouging it more deeply and more professionally than I did. From that experience we learned that "peculiar" could mean anything from infected mosquito bite to full-blown alien infestation, so whenever either of us said, "Hey, does that look a little peculiar to you?" we hightailed it to the nearest clinic.

Therefore when Scott had a peculiar bump on his pinkie toe in Zimbabwe later during that same trip, we headed to a clinic for a look-see. (By then the vet had returned home to New Zealand.) We arrived just as the young doctor, dressed in shorts and sandals, parked his car in dusty gravel in front of the clinic. Third in line, we didn't have to wait long before we were seated in the doctor's office. The doctor looked at Scott's toe, guessed it was a thorn, and said it had to come out. He asked Scott to get up on the operating table and began to prepare his instruments while the three of us chatted about this and that. Before he injected anesthetic into Scott's toe he said, "You will feel a slight jab." Scott's reaction to the jab makes me glad that in Antananarivo they don't do sissy things like numb nerves before cutting. As the needle entered his toe, Scott's entire body contorted in a way I would never have guessed possible. If a scout for the Chinese Acrobats had been on hand he would have signed up Scott immediately. His "YEEEEOOOOWW!" cleared the waiting room.

"Gee whiz, Scott. He hasn't even begun to cut yet," I said supportively.

After the toe became numb, the doctor began to operate.

Then he said something you never want to hear a physician say. "Hmmm. I've never seen anything like this before."

"Don't tell me it's a maggot!" I said thinking we definitely needed to switch to a no flip-flop policy before one of us blossomed into The Fly.

Looking over at me he said, "No, not a maggot. Come take a look. It's lots of eggs."

I walked with trepidation over to the doctor and peered into Scott's toe. "Bluck!" I said, using my word for barf plus yuck. "That's disgusting!" Scott had to soak his foot several times a day and take a heavy-duty antibiotic. Yet we somehow managed to block out that experience because it didn't occur to us that the little bump on my foot in Tana could be eggs too.

We have been very unlucky when it comes to foot infestation on our travels. Every time we leave town, our doctor automatically issues us a course of antibiotics specific to foot infections. He started doing this after the time a bot fly larva took up residence in the top of Scott's foot along the Amazon in Brazil. The swelling was the scariest part—his foot ballooned to twice its normal size. Luckily we were flying home the next day, so Scott dosed himself up with antibiotics we had on hand (not the right kind—I think they were supposed to be for a bladder infection) and made an appointment with the tropical disease specialist at home in California.

A team of doctors in our hometown who specialize in equatorial diseases became practically giddy when they saw Scott's foot. "It's not every day we get to see a bot fly!" one said with excitement. They discussed several options for getting rid of the critter. One favorite was to place a piece of raw bacon or meat over the hole. The theory was that the bot fly would hungrily transfer to the fresh meat. Another doctor heard about the case, phoned, and asked if we would come back after lunch since he was unavoidably detained and didn't want to miss his chance to be in on a real live tropical creepy-crawly case. We complied and upon seeing Scott's foot after lunch, the doctor last to join the bot fly team lobbied for and won the surgery option. Let's just say, I was there, and it was gross. A big fat blob of bot fly is way more nauseating than hundreds of eggs. Bluck.

I think we have this problem with alien implantation because our feet are so soft compared to an average African or Amazonian foot. Also, in my case, my feet are a rather large target.

Anyway, making the most of *my* oeuf extraction, I thought it would be best to recover on a tropical isle, so we flew to Ile Sainte Marie, twenty-five miles off the northeast coast of the Madagascar mainland. We transferred by dugout canoe to an even smaller outer island, Ile aux Nattes, which has a small troop of ruffed lemurs that are black and white with very long black bushy tails and white beards ala Uncle Remus. They leapt from tree to tree looking like teddy bears strung out on Red Bull. It was mating season and of the six lemurs on the small island there was only one female, so there was a lot of yelling, and screaming, and crying going on when a suitor was rejected. The female was very particular, and when her current mate fought off another amorous male vying for her attention, a big verbal fight ensued and the rejected lemur, I swear, cried while the winner gleefully groomed the gloriously extravagant tail of the female. We could hear them all the time, and see them most of the time, from the balcony of our simple ten-dollar-per-night bungalow on stilts perched over the Indian Ocean. We stayed longer than planned, but we were enticed by the turquoise blue sea, the blindingly white sand, and the love struck lemurs. Okay, the real reason we stayed was because it took several evenings to adequately sample all twenty of proprietor Pierre's homemade flavored rums. Punch Coco was the hands-down favorite.

My foot was good as new after a week (sadly, still size nine), so we left our tropical paradise and made our way back to the mainland, then inland via bush taxi to visit some of Madagascar's seventeen national parks and canoe down a river. We wanted to take the train, but we got to our destinations mostly by bush taxi because some ratsy rebels had blown up railroad bridges over much of the country in 2000.

CANOEING THE TSIRIBIHINA RIVER—A
LITTLE FOR SWEET DREAMS

We hadn't had our fill of Malagasy wildlife, and a three-day float down the Tsiribihina (pronounced *sir-a-BEE- -na*) River in a dugout canoe seemed like a good way to enjoy more flora and fauna at a slow paddle pace. Our guesthouse would have made all the arrangements for us, but we decided to organize the trip ourselves. We took a bush taxi to a town located on the river in order to sort out the details.

Our trip was booked even before we arrived. A young man on the bush taxi introduced himself and told us that he ran "very excellent!" boat trips. From then on he wouldn't let us out of his sight. He led us to a hotel in Mirandravazo and arranged a meeting with two men who would ultimately be our guide and oarsmen/cook. The guide, John, spoke very little English and the cook, Katu, spoke none, except for the word "crocodile," which he said with tiresome regularity, especially when he was tipsy.

The next morning while John bought provisions, Katu took us to the mayor's office and then to the police station to sign some "necessary paperwork," none of which we could read, but which we were given a copy of and told not to lose. Then we walked to the river where John was in the process of loading the dugout canoe. Suddenly a procession of elegantly dressed young women holding large golden urns on their heads paraded across the square. We couldn't get anyone to explain who the women were or what, if anything, was in the urns. The best we could make out was that it was something that sounded like *the petticoat festival.*

Scott had explained to John the night before that we would pay for the three-day canoe trip only after Scott had inspected the boat for leaks (a frequent problem) and the supplies were loaded. When we saw the boat the next day, it looked "riverworthy" and the supplies were on board. I sat in the canoe under my big red umbrella, my back resting against a cardboard box filled with food and water, while Scott paid John what we owed him. Immediately a crowd of men gathered around John and began demanding a cut of the action. All seemed to think they had something to do with getting us to go on the trip. There was a attitude of, "You have something and you must share it!" John agreeably doled out some money to a few men and gave Katu his share. Then Katu had to leave to buy rice for his wife and children. We waited another forty-five minutes for Katu to return before we finally cast off.

The river was wide, but there was a very strong current pushing us down the river. Katu didn't have to paddle much at all. Instead, he used the paddle as a rudder to steer the canoe close to the bank. That was where the current was strongest and the scenery most interesting. Along the way naked children ran to the edge of the river to stare at us shyly from behind tall reeds. We waved at them, but they were obviously not used to seeing many foreigners because they appeared wary of us and only a few waved back.

As we floated down the river, John educated us on the local customs. We were told how to behave as we passed by certain villages. In one village it was taboo to point, so if we saw a chameleon or a lemur we had to indicate with our elbow. In another village it was taboo to wear anything red, but only on that particular day of the week. I kept my red umbrella collapsed and out of sight that day just in case. Periodically I noticed that Katu dropped crumbs of food in the canoe behind his seat. The superstitions and rituals along the river were so numerous I interpreted this as some kind of offering to ensure our safe journey.

About an hour before sunset, John found a sandy spot on the bank to camp for the night. When I helped unpack the canoe I found out why Katu had been dropping morsels of food in the canoe. Behind his seat sat a live chicken that was to be our meal the next evening.

While John and Katu cooked zebu steak with garlic and ginger sauce for dinner (unbelievably delicious), we pitched our tent and prepared sundowners of rum and coke. John and Katu would only take a little. "Only a little!" John said when we offered some to him and Katu. "A little for the sunset," John said. Then, "A little for the river." Then, "A little for the food." They held out their cups out each time for a refill while Katu ran around laughing and yelling "Crocodile!"

After dinner we carried the empty bottle to the canoe, bid goodnight to the chicken, and retired to our tent. As we settled into our sleeping bags, I called out, "Good night. Sweet dreams," and I heard John mumble, "A little for sweet dreams."

Dawn the next morning was a silent event. John and Katu were still asleep when Scott and I walked a short distance and sat down on the sand to watch the sun rise over the river. There was not a sound that morning! Was every creature still asleep? Nothing stirred in the thick reeds behind us on the high bank, not a bug nor a fly. There was no bird song. Nothing affirmed its presence or territory with flight or sound. Even the river seemed to sneak by as if it did not want to get caught in the act. It seemed everything around us, except the quietly rising sun, was frozen in time. I have never experienced such profound silence and stillness.

Later, after packing the canoe, I made an offering to that night's dinner, and we continued our float down the river. The feeling I had during the morning's silent sunrise stayed with me. The day wasn't marked in hours but in how much farther away I felt from my life back home. Each bend in the river took me to a place I was afraid I wouldn't be able to find again. A place of such stillness exists, I imagined, only in the mind of a person who had mastered the art of meditation. I had tried meditation a few times in the past and decided it just wasn't for me. I am too eager to be distracted by sights or sounds around me, mostly because I actually enjoy what and who is around me in my everyday life back home. But there on the Tsiribihina River, I could see how groovy and healing meditation could be. I felt positively drugged. And it wasn't something we ate because while Scott admitted he was super relaxed, he didn't feel the trippy calm that I did.

The next morning, after another silent sunrise, we sat in the sand drinking our coffee, glad that we had decided to come to Madagascar. Out of nowhere three children appeared seventy-five feet down the beach. They sat in the sand watching us as we sat watching them. Every few minutes they moved closer until they were not ten feet from us. I got up and took them some bread. Then we drew pictures of things familiar to each of us in the sand; I taught them and they taught me.

I often created a classroom in the sand or dirt while waiting for a bus or bush taxi in Africa. Twigs in hand, the children usually drew a boat, a bird, a hut, or house. Then I would add something to their drawing. If they drew a bird I would add a tree branch under its feet. If they drew a boat I would add some waves. Then the children would add a trunk to the limb or sails to the boat and so on. Pretty soon, along the side of the road we had a whole storyboard, like the Bayeux Tapestry, about birds and boats and huts. As much as I enjoyed riding in a bush taxi, I was always disappointed when it arrived and took me away from such creative children. Then I remembered I could pretty much count on being able to start a new story in the next village. All I needed was a twig.

The day our canoe trip ended someone turned the sound back on and there was no going back. Fortunately the increasing volumes of noise radiating out from the Tsiribihina came on slowly, like a dimmer switch making light glow with more intensity the more you turn it on. The farther we got from the river the louder our world became.

First a zebu cart rumbled into sight to take us to a nearby town where we could wait for a bush taxi to take us to our next destination. The cart driver loudly urged the lumbering zebu to keep moving. The cart creaked, and groaned, and rattled as the road became more deeply rutted. At the village, the obligatory posse of happy squealing children gathered around us to draw in the dirt and wait with us until the bush taxi arrived. Sounds grew in volume until they were once again at normal Madagascar levels (which are still *much* quieter than the usual noise level of Ghana).

Since that trip down the Tsiribihina, whenever I get the mood to meditate, or even if someone just mentions the word, I remember the quiet of the Tsiribihina River—especially the stillness of that special morning when the world stood still—and I am there.

THE WA-BENZI TRIBE

We went reluctantly back to Kenya after a month and a half in Madagascar. We missed her as soon as we left. How can you not love a country whose people are so polite, rivers are so quiet, and one of her lemurs is named "Indri," which translates, "Hey! Look up here!"

The backpacker hostel we like to stay at in Nairobi (appropriately named Backpackers) was overbooked, so the first night we had to sleep in our tent in the backyard. A very good sleep. Quite comfy. As anyone who travels with me knows, I sleep well anywhere. My secret? I always use eye patches and earplugs—and a Tusker beer or two before retiring doesn't hurt either.

On the second night at the Backpackers, the manager moved us to his annex building down the street. We had a one-bedroom apartment with kitchen overlooking a beautiful pool and garden. It was a far cry from sleeping in our tent and sharing a bathroom with twenty people. Did we get the upgrade because he was impressed that a couple of Americans would attempt transiting Africa from top to bottom? Was it because we were a little older than the average backpacker? Who knew age and reckless abandon had their advantages?

"Staying here is nice, but it is going to make us soft," I said to my husband as he returned from his second dip in the pool that day.

The next morning we took a bus to Tanzania. Well, it wasn't exactly a bus. After the bush taxis in Madagascar, I had begun to enjoy the comfort and added safety of getting around Africa in private vehicles. So we joined the Wa-Benzi Tribe. "Wa" as in "Tribe of" and "Benzi" as in "Mercedes." Scott was surprised at my change of heart because since leaving the Mechanic's truck my mantra had been: "We *must* travel the way the Africans travel! We must get from A to B through Africa by bush taxi to really experience the *true* Africa and meet *real* Africans. No matter if it takes the vehicle three hours to fill up before leaving and that some kind of livestock is often on board or that someone is always being sick out the window (hopefully out the window) at least once! We have perfected the Bush Taxi Squish and met so many nice people!"

I don't know what it was that finally pushed me to join the Wa-Benzi. It might have been the ultimate over-squish of the small truck in Madagascar where we encountered not only the obligatory live chicken but a tire on my feet, an old lady and three others who had nowhere to sit but on the tire, a cute kid with the most amazing double snail trail running from his nose (left nostril occasionally managing an impressive bubble), and a nut-less bolt sticking in my back for six hours. Or maybe it was that man who fell off the back of the bush taxi unnoticed. But when we had a chance to take a Mercedes with driver for an eleven-hour journey in Madagascar at only ten times the cost of a bush taxi, I jumped at it.

I used to scoff at drivers who made us this offer. "We want to *hire* the car not buy it!" And, "I'd rather ride with the *real* Africans, thank you!" But before long I became a shameless member of Wa-Benzi Tribe whenever the opportunities arose. Which is why we took a First World, book in advance, only one butt per seat, twelve-passenger shuttle bus from Nairobi to Tanzania.

Tanzania. Where the wild things are and the bathrooms are called "choo." Every time I saw one I turned to my husband and said, "Ah! Choo!"

Our drop-off point in Tanzania was a five-star hotel parking lot in Arusha, so we didn't even get to experience the usual bedlam we had become accustomed to when arriving by bush taxi. The welcoming committee when one arrives by bush taxi consists of a mad rush of touts, pousse-pousse drivers, and safari operators, all desperate for business who run along the bus or bush taxi as it enters the transit lot. When they spot two *muzungu* (white foreigner) faces, they force open the window and stick their heads into the vehicle while shouting, "Safari? Taxi? Hotel? I have the best! Remember me! Ramón!" They always have made-up Western names like Ramón or Philippe. Then when the bus stops, they try to grab our bags off the roof. We kind of missed the crush of bodies, noise, and five-second sales pitches.

We left the luxury of the Impala Shuttle and the five-star hotel parking lot, and checked in to the much less luxurious but sufficient Flamingo Hotel in the Muslim Quarter of Arusha.

The call to prayer in Arusha is something not to miss. Why? Because it's *impossible* to miss. The little Flamingo is surrounded on three sides by mosques, so we got to enjoy the call to prayer five times a day. It was so loud it was as if the muezzin was *right next to us* shouting sweet nothings in our ears. Only it's not sweet. Some Muslim sects have a belief that the call to prayer should not sound pretty. The Flamingo seemed to be the hub for this sect, and they are doing a great job of sounding very loud but not very pretty. On the other hand, ten years ago in the desert in Palmyra, Syria, we were awakened at dawn by a call to prayer so beautiful and so lyrical it made me weep. The muezzin sang with so much emotion it almost sounded more like a love song than a reminder to join him in prayer.

Arusha is a good place to take a break from travel. At the same time, it's also a good place to plan onward travel. It has Internet cafés, coffee shops, a small outdoor venue for concerts, and plays, and more than three hundred safari operators vying for your business. I think all three hundred (not counting the dozens of batik and banana leaf art sellers who trailed along behind us) had approached us by the second day.

The main reason there are so many Western-style cafés in town is because Arusha is populated with lots of expat types who are working either in the prolific NGO (non-governmental organization) arena or who are trying cases or doing internships at the United Nations War Crimes Tribunal for Rwanda that has been located in Arusha since 1996. I have never seen so many expensive four-wheel-drive vehicles in one place at one time. Why someone needs a 4X4 Land Rover to drive around Arusha, to and from the courthouse, I'll never know.

While we were enjoying drinking cappuccinos and chatting with safari and batik sellers, we decided it would be horrifyingly informative to attend one of the war crimes trials as observers, which is allowed as long as you turn over your passport and camera to the man with the AK-47 at the door. Then another man with an AK-47 leads you upstairs where you collect earphones so you can hear the translation of the proceedings from French into English. Then you take a seat behind soundproof (bulletproof?) glass to watch the trial.

There were three judges, a prosecutor, a defense attorney (he was British, with a little white *Rumpole of the Bailey* wig and everything), two court reporters, three translators, camera operators, lots of interns, note takers, and the clerk who says, "All rise" when the judges entered or left the courtroom. The witness, behind a curtain and seen only by the court, was addressed under an assumed name. This was because the Tutsis and Hutus were still killing each other and people were afraid to testify.

The testimony we heard was from a man who lost almost his entire family to machete blows during an orgy of murder. The crazed killers then went to the hospital and hacked to death all the patients. But as the testimony went on, we learned that he did his share of killing, too, turning his machete on his own neighbor.

Today there are still refuges over the border in the Congo, and the Tutsi government in Rwanda says it wants to wipe out the Hutu forces there. The bloody competition for resources and power goes on.

We happened to have this day in court on July Fourth. After hearing brutal testimony all day, we longed for something to distract us from thinking about it all night. All afternoon I had been on the lookout for other Americans to say, "Happy Independence Day!" to. After one case of mistaken identity (gee, you'd think the Brits would be over it by now), we finally found John from Virginia back at the Flamingo, and we managed to enjoy a barbeque after all. We had it African-style, though, with a chapatti instead of a bun and goat instead of beef. But with a few beers and a lucky find at the Indian market down the street of not one but *two* packets of stale Reese's Peanut Butter Cups, it was a pretty good night and, after the courtroom events of the day, a reminder of how fortunate we are. It also reminded me that we had a bloody and brutal fight in our own Civil War. For different reasons but atrocious nonetheless.

KARATE!

The safari touts eventually wore us down. After a few relentless days of hounding, we joined forces with a young couple from Argentina and arranged a three-day safari in a Land Rover to Lake Manyara and Ngorongoro Crater.

One has to see Ngorongoro Crater to believe it. It is the world's largest collapsed volcano with a caldera of more than one hundred square miles. It is a wide-open plain filled with twenty thousand to thirty thousand animals. Sightings of lion, cheetah, elephant, hippo, warthog, wildebeest, hyena, jackal, and leopard are almost a guarantee. We even saw a leopard with a full tummy draped in a tree in the classic pose.

It was in the Ngorongoro that we saw our first kill ever. From the Land Rover we watched a cheetah stalk, chase, and kill an impala. At home when watching Animal Planet, I never cheer for the cheetah. But being there, seeing the real deal, and watching her patiently stalk her prey for twenty minutes, I found myself saying, "Go-go-GO!" when she sprang after the impala and chased it around and around the plain before catching and quickly killing it by clamping her jaws over the impala's windpipe.

The only people allowed grazing rights inside Ngorongoro are the Masai, so there are plenty of warriors to see in the area too. The primary occupation of the Masai is tending cattle and acquiring more cattle. Cattle are wealth to the Masai. Masai boys spend their youth watching over their cows as they graze the lands surrounding the village. When the boys reach the age of fifteen, they go through a ceremony that makes them men. They are circumcised. Wouldn't that be the most excruciating thing a boy of fifteen could endure? But a Masai boy must not show he is feeling any pain. He must not cry or make a sound during the procedure, which "takes around ninety seconds" we were told. We asked our guide if anesthesia is administered. "No," he said. "But the boy is allowed to bring his own knife."

Masai girls also undergo circumcision when they are twelve or thirteen, soon after they have their first period. This double whammy removes all doubt from a young girl's mind that life is, or ever will be, fair.

"Isn't female circumcision illegal in Tanzania?" I asked.

"Yes. But Masai men can have many wives, and it is very difficult to control all of them. Therefore the practice continues because the women are easier to control after they have been circumcised. Also a girl will have a very hard time being accepted in society or finding a husband if she has not been circumcised," he answered.

"Oh," I said, trying my best to be culturally sensitive and still speak though my body language, especially my crossed legs, expressed how I really felt. I wasn't only empathizing with the physical pain of the young boys and girls. Did I dare get into a whole "controlling your womenfolk by circumcision" debate when I knew that it's the women who are the ones performing circumcision on the young girls as part of their social identity and culture? Instead I asked, "Do they get to bring their own knife?" He said he didn't think so.

On the last day of the mini-safari, we decided against returning to Arusha with the Argentineans and asked our guide to leave us at a campground on the rim of the crater so we could spend one more day on our own in Ngorongoro. He was concerned about leaving us because it meant we would have to take a public bus back to Arusha the next day. (We never could get Africans to understand that we actually enjoyed riding on public transport.) But our guide had a more legitimate worry that we couldn't argue with. We were sure to encounter some aggressive elephants on the road while walking the half-mile to the bus stop. He asked the campground *askari* (guard) to ensure we would have a ride to the bus stop at the police compound the next morning where we could wait for the bus without risk of being trampled by *tembo* (Swahili for elephant).

That night we enjoyed a quintessential African sunset (orange and quick) before eating a picnic dinner and retiring early. During the night, Scott had to use the toilet. As he walked through the campground, I heard an askari approach him and say repeatedly what both Scott, and I from the tent, understood to be *"Jambo,"* which means hello. I heard Scott cheerfully respond, "Jambo! Jambo!" It wasn't until Scott was on his way back from the toilet and his eyes were adjusted to the dark that he realized the guard had been saying, "Tembo! Tembo!"—for now he could make out a big bull elephant standing not far from our tent.

Scott slowed his pace, keeping his eyes on the looming hulk of unpredictability. He made it to the tent without inspiring the elephant to move. Unzipping the tent as quietly as he could, he exhaled and said, "I hope you don't have to use the toilet tonight because there's a big elephant out there. I think he may be asleep right now, but I would *not* go out there if I were you." Instantly I had an urge to use the toilet. For the rest of the night I kept my ears on alert for tembo and my bladder on hold.

At the crack of dawn the next morning, with only my head poking out of the tent door, I took a good look around for tembo before running to the loo.

As promised, the askari procured a driver to give us a lift to the bus stop at the police station compound. When we arrived at the compound, another askari took over guard duties, making sure we wouldn't be eaten by anything bigger than a mosquito. While we waited for the bus, a group of boys came out of the compound to catch the bus as well. It wasn't a school day, so I asked the boys where they were going. "To karate," I was sure I heard them say. "Ah, karate!" I said while performing a very nice, I thought, karate chop with a "Hi-YA!" thrown in for good measure. It might have had something to do with the sleep-deprived state caused by the previous night's tembo alert but I carried on talking, kicking, and chopping even though the boys didn't seem nearly as enthusiastic about karate as I was. "A very good discipline!" I said. I encouraged them further by doing a few high kicks with even more enthusiastic "Hi-YAs!" Watching me very carefully and with some hesitation, the boys performed a few chops and kicks. But they weren't very good. "I guess they are new to the practice and just haven't got the hang of it yet," I whispered to Scott. But I still gave the boys one more supportive chop-chop!

The bus arrived, and I was immediately re-sold on the whole "ride with the real Africans" concept. Because the bus was full of not just real Africans but real Masai Warriors! Fantastic- looking men with flowing red blankets, red dye in their hair, great hanging ears with big holes the size of silver dollars cut out of their stretched-from-birth lobes, and a spear or stick—the only thing a Masai carries—on their shoulders. Nine small boys (going to Karate class too?) sat across the backseat of the bus, and in short order a Masai standing in the aisle made them evacuate their seats with just a glance and a shift of his spear. One warrior slowly but deliberately sat on a boy who didn't get the message. He eventually appeared sometime later from under the Masai's hip. And the women! Gorgeous! Very dignified with shaved heads, long jingling earrings, hats perched with ease on top of their polished heads, and bright beautiful cloth wrapped around their lean bodies.

I studied the Masai to see what they would do to occupy them-selves during the ride. The warriors seemed to be trying out warrior jokes on each other in their tribal language. One would tell a story, and then they would laugh and laugh. Then another seemed to start a new joke. I also noticed their scent. The traditional diet of the Masai consists of a mixture of blood and milk from their cows, so they some-times take on the aroma of a very rare steak or carpaccio.

The Masai also stared at us and I heard them say, *"muzungu,"* which is the Swahili tag for a white foreigner. It's a good thing the Masai word for foreigner didn't stick because when the Masai first saw the white man wearing trousers, they christened him *iloridaa enjakat* which means, "Those who confine their farts."

An hour into the bus ride, I turned to Scott and remarked, "These boys sure have to go a long way for a karate lesson!" A half hour later, we pulled into a town and the boys who I had practiced karate with at the police station all said *"Kwaheri!"* (Goodbye) with sympathetic smiles and pretty weak karate chops, and got off the bus. It was then that I noticed the sign at the station: "Welcome to the city of Karatu."

It wasn't the first of what we have come to call my "Karatu moments." During a trip to Rome, we rented a flat in Trastevere for a week. We were following directions from the flat owner (...take the train to the tram...), and we were up to the tram part with our stop fast approaching. I thought it would be wise to ask a local if the next stop was indeed the one we were looking for.

"Bello?" I said smiling at an attractive young man standing in the aisle. He smiled down at me and drew closer. When he noticed Scott standing behind me, his expression became quizzical. The tram was about to stop and I was getting anxious so I repeated with even more urgency, "Bello! Bello!" while pointing at his chest then out the window, which in my mind was a completely clear pantomime of, "Tell me if this is the Bello stop, will ya!" I said it a little louder and a little slower each time for beeettter commmmpreheeeensionnnn. With sudden recognition and a big smile the young man said, "Belli! It is nice of you point at me while saying, 'Bello! Bello! Handsome! Handsome!' But the stop you want is Belli. Beeeeelllllliiiii."

A week later we were in Berlin at the same time as the Dalai Lama. There was a poster about a Free Tibet rally happening that afternoon and I wanted to go, but I needed someone to tell me how to get there. I walked briskly over to two Tibetan men at a tram stop and said,

"Dalai Lama! Free Tibet! Today?" while raising my shoulders and extending my hands in what I thought was an appropriate "where?" shrug. They just stood and stared at me. "Free Tibet!" I repeated more loudly, surprised that they didn't seem to know anything about it. The "Tibetans" and I suddenly realized at the same moment that I was an idiot because they were not Tibetans. They were Chinese and not at all amused about me asking them to free Tibet. After a few awkward moments I exclaimed, "Good luck in the Olympics!" and retreated to the safety of one of the many Starbucks located in Berlin.

Back in Karatu, Scott watched the boys exit the bus, then looked over at me. "Karate, eh? Do you have to talk to absolutely *everyone* we encounter?"

Quickly recovering my dignity I said, "Yes! Isn't that the spice of life?"

Coach Kilimanjaro: A Fairy-Tale Hospital Stay

After our bus ride with the Masai and the karate kids, something happened that taught me that the real Africa is nothing like the *Out of Africa* version. You know, like the one where Robert Redford washes Meryl Streep's hair while completely unaware that there are tembos and mosquitoes lying in wait just beyond the acacia tree.

We arrived back in Arusha feeling incredibly weak and dizzy. I didn't want to believe I could be unlucky enough to get malaria twice. We walked to a clinic down the street and asked for a blood test. Testing for malaria is practically a drive-through operation in East Africa. A prick of the finger, a smear of the slide, and twenty minutes later you have the results and are sent home with a box of parasite murdering pills to take over the course of three days. However it turned out we were not only positive for malaria, but we had picked up a particularly drug-resistant strain from mosquitoes in either Madagascar or Tanzania.

Two weeks went by. We had exhausted all the usual malarial remedies in Arusha to no avail. Thinking that we might be better off being treated in a city where there were tourists in greater numbers we decided to try our luck with the curative skills of doctors in Moshi. Moshi is a village near the base of Mount Kilimanjaro bustling with trekkers preparing to climb the mountain. We planned to climb her too, as soon as we felt better. Climbing Kilimanjaro was one of the reasons we decided to go to Africa. Since it was a destination actually on our loose itinerary, we felt an obligation to summit her peak or at least try. Knowing that visualization sometimes works as a motivator, we took a room facing Kilimanjaro so she could encourage us while we lay in our bed trying to get well.

Feeling sluggish and discouraged, I stared at the mountain from under a heavy pile of blankets. I began to see Kilimanjaro as the coach, and I the injured player. She loomed over me while I drifted in and out of sleep and made me feel like I was letting the team down. I felt considerable pressure to suit up, and show up, and climb her. Every morning when we awoke she nagged, "Today?" And every evening before we fell asleep she seemed to sigh with disappointment, "Perhaps tomorrow." Days and days went by. As I became weaker, she changed her tune to "The heck with you! I'll give someone else a chance to play," and the pressure was off a little.

Even though the urgency to climb Kilimanjaro had diminished, our symptoms hadn't. We felt more miserable and puny by the hour, so we finally took a taxi to St. Joseph's Hospital run by Tanzanian nurses known as the Sisters of Our Lady of Mount Kilimanjaro. The head nun-doctor tested our blood, found that the malaria had reached stage four, and admitted us. Scott, feeling slightly less horribly awful and without the dizziness that I felt, went to our hotel to fetch pillows, blankets, food, water, and such because most African clinics are run BYO, bring your own. It was just after he left that things took on a fairy-tale quality.

First the nurse came in and said her name was Happy. She asked me to give a urine sample, but I told her I had a bashful bladder. Then the doc came in and said she wanted to give me something for the pain, which would make me sleepy. But I told her not to because I was feeling dopey enough already. When Scott returned with our supplies he was really grumpy because the daladala bush taxi had broken down on the way back. Then we climbed into our hospital beds and waited for the quinine drip to do its magic. Aside from ringing in the ears, the quinine had no other side effects, but something in the room was making me awful sneezy. The next morning, Peter, a local Moshi man who had given us a lift to another clinic a few days before, came to visit us. As he walked in he took one look at me and exclaimed, "You're as white as snow!"

We checked out of the hospital after two days, mostly because Happy had somehow inserted the IV incorrectly and the vein in my right arm—from my wrist to my shoulder—was hard as a rock. We were pathetically frail with as much muscle mass as a newborn baby but still hopeful that we would regain enough strength to climb Kilimanjaro soon. Quinine tablets in hand, we made our way back to the Zebra Hotel where it occurred to me we had the same view from our room that Gregory Peck had while playing the Ernest Hemingway character in *The Snows of Kilimanjaro*.

"Remember?" I said to my husband as we lay in bed gazing at Kilimanjaro and willing the parasites to die. "As Harry Street lies delirious with infection on his cot under the acacia tree, he recalls all the great loves of his life."

"Yes, I do remember. But you don't look anything like Susan Hayward."

Recovery after our hospital stay was made tolerable by several mom-and-pop stores in the neighborhood run by Indians who sold Cadbury chocolate bars in boxes of thirty. We also had movies non-stop on the TV in our room. I think we saw all the Van Damme and Jackie Chan movies ever made.

It turned out that quinine had side effects other than the terrible ringing in my ears. At times my entire body would tremble. But maybe that was the malaria not the quinine. One night I felt so peculiar and the shaking was so horrible I thought I would surely be dead by morning. I even woke Scott up to tell him I loved him, but he was so out of it too I don't think he heard me. Finally, no alcohol was allowed with the malaria meds so, borrowing a line from W. C. Fields, we had to survive on nothing but food and water for days.

A weird side effect of the medicine (or the malaria, I could never tell which) is what it made us say awake or asleep. One night Scott heard me say in my sleep, "The can of whipped cream fell off the bed." We haven't had a can of whipped cream in our bedroom in years. The next day when he woke up, Scott announced, "Did you know that of the three squirrels in Cartoon Universe, one is a secret agent, one flies, and the other is a scuba diver in love with a sponge?"

It took three weeks before we felt better. During that time we hardly went out, but we did manage one cultural experience while recovering in Moshi. We went to Catholic Mass one Sunday for the children's service. There were thousands of adults and children singing their hearts out inside the cavernous church. Every pew was filled and the responses were given melodically and at great volume.

Communion was done the old fashioned way. The congregation proceeded single file up the aisle and knelt at the altar while waiting for the priest to deliver the host. With so many going up for communion, it took quite a while, and either I got distracted or flustered, but when the priest was finally standing over me with the host in his hand and said, "Body of Christ," in Swahili, I responded, "Body of Christ," in English, holding up the queue for a minute until, imitating my neighbor, I finally managed an "*Amem*," which I guess is Swahili for amen.

We were stared at quite a bit during the service, perhaps because we were *iloridaa enjakat*, but the handshake of peace was fun because practically everybody wanted to shake our hands and wish us peace. Or maybe they just wished we'd get out of those fart confining trousers

We never did "kill Kill," as they say about climbing Kilimanjaro. We could barely conquer the three flights of stairs to our hotel room much less attempt the tallest mountain in Africa. Malaria made us far too weak to have a successful climb. In the end we didn't feel too bad about not standing on the summit of Kilimanjaro. Most we met who made the climb came back with stories of puking, headaches, and altitude sickness. At least one person died.

We knew what it felt like to be at high altitude. In 1995 we trekked the Annapurna circuit in the Himalayas where the pass at 17,769 feet is only 1,500 feet lower than the summit of Kilimanjaro. While we did experience some altitude sickness, it was one of the greatest experiences of our lives and everyone we met on the way, or afterwards in Pokhara, said much the same. We never heard that said of the Kilimanjaro climb. All reported that it was definitely a challenge and an accomplishment, but no one we met seemed to have had a great experience. Because of the expense (over US$300 each day) most people try to climb the 19,341 feet in only five days. It's too high too fast, which is why all the puking, headaches, and altitude sickness occur. We climbed Annapurna in over fifteen days, which gave us adequate time to acclimatize.

That said, we still aren't ruling out Kilimanjaro for the future. It will just be the first thing we do in Africa before mosquitoes, tsetse flies, or mystery disease of the month has a chance to take hold. And we will take more than five days to summit.

Still, we would be leaving Africa without being able to say that we bagged Kilimanjaro. Instead, we spent day after day lying in our bed trying to feel better, eating Cadbury chocolate bars, watching movies, and occasionally making it to the coffee shop to hear stories from those who had made the summit the day before.

One day our movie channel stopped working. Scott reported it to the manager who said, "It will be off for one hour. The men are trying to make the satellite dish well in this moment."

Scott turned to me and said, "No Jackie Chan for an hour. How about I wash your hair?"

ZANZIBAR PIZZA

After a month living in Moshi, recovering from malaria, doing the daily crossword in the local newspaper, *The Nation*, and drinking filtered coffee at the Kilimanjaro trekkers meet-up spot The Coffee Shop, we took a bus to Dar es Salaam. From there we would catch a ferry to Zanzibar. Zanzibar, with its long strolling beaches, seemed a good place to regain some muscle mass after our bouts with malaria. It is also one of the best places on the east coast of Africa to take photos of light blue seas and small fishing dhows parked on fine white sand beaches.

Walking barefoot along the beach at sunset while taking photos that my friends say must have been Photoshopped would have to wait. First we joined an afternoon tour to a spice farm in the center of the island led by a man I will never forget. Alee had a very distinctive way of talking. He would draw out the last word of each sentence so that it was as long as all the words before it and while saying it, his tongue would flop out of his mouth. As we passed a yellow colonial house he said, "This was David Livingstone's house." But it would come out, "This was David Livingstone's howwwwwwwse" after a long intake of breath. "You can see that the color is yeeeeelloooooow." When we arrived at a nutmeg tree he said, "This is nut-maaaaaaaaaaaaag." Maybe it was mild heatstroke yet again, but it was the funniest delivery I'd ever heard. It was excruciating trying not to laugh. It was like when children try to behave during a church service but the urge to fidget and giggle is just too strong. And it wasn't just me. Those standing behind Alee were doubled over in silent laughter too. Soon we all had tears running down our cheeks and snot running down our chins as we held on to our stomachs trying to contain our laughter. Though the tour was thorough and informative, there is not a single fact I could give you today about Zanzibar spices. But to think of Alee makes me smile.

The sand is so firm at low tide on Zanzibar's eastern beaches that you can ride a bike for miles down the beach (or at least until the rapidly returning tide cuts you off) and take hundreds of perfect photos along the way. Everything begs for a photo. But it asks quietly. Apart from Stone Town, most of Zanzibar is very tranquil and quiet. It was like the Tsiribihina, only more tropical, lazier, more "mañana." The air, everything, was very still. Especially along the beaches. Even the waves sauntered onto shore. Raindrops whispered as they fell on our umbrella. Everyone and everything seemed to be moving in slow motion. Time dragged. The ocean there is a particularly hypnotic, sleep inducing blue-green color I haven't seen before or since. I never slept as much as I did in guesthouses along Zanzibar beaches. I love bed, but even I became tired of sleeping. All the relaxation zapped my energy. If there is such a thing as a place being too Zen, then Zanzibar takes the cake.

Occasionally slow moving Masai men walked the beach selling trinkets. "Where are your cows?" Scott asked a Masai selling bracelets.

"They are back on the mainland," said the Masai as he gazed in the direction of Dar es Salaam. "I am not happy without my cows. I come here to make money, then I go back and I can be with my cows." It made me sad to see a member of such a great tribe resorting to a part-time job in curio sales.

Stone Town is not so tranquil. It is the largest city on Zanzibar and home to a frenetic night market where you can buy all types of delicious and gut-gurgling treats such as Zanzibar pizza. This "pizza" consists of a kind of crepe swimming in palm oil and topped with a triangle of Laughing Cow cheese, a raw egg, mayonnaise, tomatoes, onions, pork (maybe it was pork), and something green I never could identify. All this is folded up in the crepe and grilled to become a great big Hot Pocket. Lines for Zanzibar pizza are three deep and eight wide, and believe it or not, it is delicious. After eating a Zanzibar pizza, people can be seen lining up for fresh coconut milk, as it is reputed to calm an upset stomach.

On a later trip, we discovered that Stone Town was also home to the Barack Obama Headquarters of Tanzania. The name was bigger than the office, for it consisted of a concrete planter around a tree. The planter was at seat height, and hand painted all around it in red, white, and blue was "OBAMA FOR PRESIDENT." A portrait of a smiling Barack Obama was nailed to the tree.

On the ferry from Zanzibar back to Dar es Salaam, people were so seasick or still suffering effects from the Night Market pizza that they were lying on the floor inside the cabin. When there was no more floor space, they had to go out on the deck where they were bombarded by waves. The rest of us watched *Rambo* on a small TV bolted to the ceiling. If the Zanzibar pizza didn't turn your stomach, the movie on the way back to the mainland would. I think they show movies like *Rambo* in order to change Zanzibar Zombies back into something resembling the stressed-out travelers they were before inhaling too much Zanzibar air.

AIN'T MISBEHAVIN'

"Let's see," Scott mused while studying a map. We've been to Zimbabwe and Zanzibar. Are there any other Z countries nearby?"

It would take us two days on a train to get from Dar es Salaam to Lusaka in Zambia. We were almost fully recovered from Malaria, but taking a train for two days instead of multiple buses or bush taxis for how ever many days sounded like a good idea in our weakened state. To be assured of a sleeper for the journey, we went to the train station the day before it was due to leave to book a compartment. Only, because Tanzania is a Muslim country, we learned that people of opposite sexes aren't allowed to share a sleeper, even with proof of marriage. When we asked the man at the ticket window why we would have to be in different compartments, he gave us a conspiratorial look and said, "So that there won't be any misbehaving." Scott told him we had been together many years and that we could probably go two nights without misbehaving, which made the ticket agent laugh, so as a concession, I guess, he put us in a four-berth compartment with two women from England. We didn't bother explaining that there's plenty of same-sex misbehaving going on in the world, not that there's anything wrong with that. Anyway, it's pointless to debate these things in a country that at the time was considering separating the sexes on all the city buses. This bus for men, that bus for women. I imagined conversations between husband and wife: "Muhammad, I'll meet you at the souk. Look for me at the goat market. And don't stop for tea this time!"

195

So Scott and I were able to be in the same compartment and the two English women were very nice. They never left the compartment together, which was disappointing because I had secretly been looking forward to misbehaving when they went to eat. The two British sisters only seemed to be interested in tea and Marmite. Or was it Vegemite? Whichever. It was some "-ite" food that only a Brit would love. Actually, I shouldn't say that. Maggie and Bill had shared their personal stash of Marmite with me while on the overland truck, and I began to crave the stuff and would spread it on toast whenever I could. It has the consistency of molasses but tastes like salty beer. Yummy.

Occasionally we walked the corridor to find other travelers to talk to. One of the things I most love about travel is the people you meet along the way. Two cars up, we met Lisa from New York who had lived in Zambia for a year while completing a documentary on the lives of African women. As part of her project she asked the same set of questions to each woman she encountered. Two of the questions have stuck in my mind. One was, "What do you fear most?" The number one answer was "God." To the question, "If you were an animal which would you be and why?" the most common answer was, "A sheep, because when you slit its throat it doesn't even move." I found it telling that the women she interviewed had the greatest respect for an animal that would suffer in silence.

In a compartment near the front of the long train, we met two women who worked on a project called Freeplay, which distributes windup radios to rural villages and classrooms in Africa. Through donations it hires teachers who broadcast their lessons over the radio. The little windup radio brings education and news to children who would otherwise have none.

Part of Africa's story is that there have long been an inexhaustible number of aid or charity organizations trying to make a difference. We were introduced to not one but two such organizations on the train to Lusaka. A Bridges to Prosperity engineer from America had just finished a project in Ethiopia and shared his enthusiasm with us for the non-profit foundation. Bridges to Prosperity doesn't find villages; villages must find them. The foundation will provide the expertise and materials, but the village initiates the project and agrees to provide all the labor. "It's really great," said the engineer with pride. "With a pedestrian bridge in place, children can continue crossing the river during the rainy season to get to school, and farmers can get their produce to market. And since they work on the bridge, they take ownership from the start." Then he shook his head and said with amusement, "It never fails, though. When we finish a project, they are very grateful, but it never seems to be enough. Even though there isn't a vehicle for a hundred miles, the villagers always say, "Why did you not build us a car bridge? This bridge is only for people.'"

Rounding out the sum total of Westerners on the train were two lads from Ireland who had previously transited Africa from London to Cape Town by way of Egypt and Sudan, which happened to be one of my dream trips. We swapped books and traded stories about traveling through Africa. Finally there was Raoul, a medical doctor from England who had been in East Africa volunteering his services and who seemed to be fascinated with our encounters with parasites. We learned from him too—mostly about his encounters with magic mushrooms back in England.

All over Africa we encountered NGOs or aid workers running rural development or education projects. Some ventures were far more beneficial than others. Many books have been written about the negative effects of aid, but we encountered a few non-profits like Freeplay and Bridges to Prosperity that seemed to make a lot of sense. They satisfy a need that *Africans* ask for and consider valuable. More commonly in the charity business, with the best of intentions, NGOs appear on the scene and start a project they deem necessary with zero input from Africans who live there. If Africans don't see the point of it, or didn't ask for it in the first place, infrastructure built for the project often goes derelict soon after the contract is over or the aid workers leave. That's not to say that every project brought to Africa without initiation or investment by Africans is unsuccessful. I've never seen a footbridge that wasn't being made use of or a well providing safe drinking water that wasn't being utilized whether it had been asked for or not.

FLAT DOGS

There is a special place in Zambia I will never tire of returning to as long as I live. A place that gets your heart pumping without having to bungee off a bridge or nearly drown to death on a white-water rafting trip down the Zambezi. A place where you can watch wild animals just be wild. A place called Flat Dogs. We learned about Flat Dogs from Suzanne. We were in the bar of a guesthouse in Lusaka and she unexpectedly walked in, saluting us immediately with an expedition gesture we had created in the crowded square in Marrakech so that we could spot one another. The expedition salute consisted of the right arm being flung straight up into the air while standing still at perfect attention. Scott and I returned the salute while the rest of the bar patrons looked on bemused. We shared a steak and caught up on all we had seen since leaving the truck in Ghana. While we had been drinking macchiatos in Ethiopia, Suzanne had become a dive master in Malawi.

"You guys *have* to go to Flat Dogs. I've just been and it's brilliant!" said Suzanne after ordering a round of beers for the three of us.

Flat Dogs, which is the local term for crocodile, is a place where you can pitch your tent on a small platform twelve feet up in a tree that overlooks the Luangwa River. Here you are able to watch fifty or more elephants cross the river each day as they walk from the South Luangwa National Park to the campsite on the opposite bank. They walk right by your tent or just below your platform. Most of the time you don't even hear them coming. You can't believe that anything that

SAFARI JEMA

big could be so quiet. Except when they are knocking trees over or emitting a low rumble in communication, they are completely silent.

Like so many worthwhile destinations in Africa, getting there is not easy. This time it appeared that it actually *would* be easy. All we had to do was go to the main bus station in Lusaka and buy a ticket on one of several new buses heading to Chipata. From there we would take a local bush taxi to Mfuwe, the town nearest Flat Dogs. Easy!

We secured our tickets to Chipata the day before it was scheduled to leave and were assured by the representative of the Zoom! Bus Company that we had assigned seats on the 11:00 a.m. bus.

Scott asked, "Will we have to wait until the bus is full before leaving?" This is almost always the case in Africa.

"No, the bus is scheduled to leave at 11:00 a.m., and it will leave at 11:00 a.m. whether or not the bus is full," the ticket seller said.

"Really? Because usually we have to wait until the whole bus is full before it leaves," I said, trying to get the rep to tell us what time it would *really* leave.

"You don't believe me? I tell you, the bus will leave at exactly 11:00 a.m.!" he replied huffily.

The next day we bid farewell to Suzanne once again and arrived at the bus station a half hour early so that we could be assured of having our assigned seats. Then at 11:00 a.m. we proceeded to wait for the bus to fill up.

As we waited Scott observed, "At least it's air conditioned. And it's brand new, so that means the tires must be new. There is a chance we won't need to stop a few times to change flats on the way."

And we waited. For three hours we waited. Until every last seat and lap was occupied. A few times Scott or I would leave our seats to walk around the bus station, which consisted of a dirt parking lot and a bunch of buses, and glare at the man who had sold us the tickets the day before. Circling back on one such walk, I noticed that the Zoom! Bus had a motto painted in enthusiastic script on the back of the bus.

I had to look at it twice before I realized what was wrong with it: "You Snooze, You Loose!"

Returning to the bus, I chuckled to Scott, "Their motto is, 'You Snooze, You Loose!' Shall we tell them it should be 'lose,' not 'loose'? Loose doesn't even rhyme with 'snooze.'"

It turned out "You snooze, you loose" was probably more accurate. By the time we finally left Lusaka, the bus driver turned into Speed Racer in order to make up for lost time. If you took a snooze, you might end up with your body parts loose all over the road. The bus repeatedly careened around bends. The rear tires shimmied across the tarmac. For the first time in my life, I was literally terrified and succumbed to whimpering while tucked into the crash position in my seat. We looked around the crowded bus and thought about all the children who might be ejected on the next curve. The mothers with babies on their laps appeared not to have a care in the world as they swayed violently to and fro in their seats.

Most travelers know that the riskiest thing you can do in the developing world is ride on public transport. So Scott, legs wide and crouched down for balance, made his way up the aisle to the driver. "We are all human beings on this bus, not cargo. Please slow down." The driver slowed to a semi-sane speed for about five minutes then reapplied his lead foot to the gas pedal and resumed his break (our) neck speed.

After seven hours of terror, we arrived in Chipata well past dark, completely drained from the repeated adrenalin spikes throughout the journey. We retrieved our packs from the bus luggage locker and quickly chose a taxi to drive us to a guesthouse. As I began to set up our tent in the garden, Scott went inside to pay for our accommodation at the bar. Back outside, he handed me a beer. We clinked bottles and took long swallows before Scott uttered the first words we had spoken to one another for the last several hours, "I guess it wasn't our day to die."

"Guess not," I said sitting down in front of the tent. "Today is over and tomorrow is bound to be better."

The next day *was* better. We still had a four-hour journey ahead of us to get to Flat Dogs, so we queued up at the transport hub early the next morning and eventually secured a ride in an airy van. It had so many gaps in its Swiss-cheese frame that even with the windows up and the hatch closed, we were completely covered in a fine brown talcum powder dust within minutes of departure. And we had the worst seats in the house, crammed in the very back, four across on two seats.

After showers to remove most of the travel grit, we pitched our tent twelve feet off the ground in the last available tree platform at Flat Dogs. While I arranged the sleeping mats in our tent and made it cozy, Scott scouted out the bar and restaurant. Shortly, from somewhere below the tent, Scott called to me in a shaky voice. I looked out to find two fear-stricken people crouched at the top of the wooden ladder that led to our tent. Then I saw Scott flat up against a tree facing a big mama elephant that had her ears fully flared out at him. We watched, frozen. Me in the tent, Scott against the tree, and the two strangers on the ladder, all of us were wondering what would happen next. Suddenly, after a brief sniff test of Scott, the elephant tossed her head, trumpeted, stomped her foot, then turned and walked silently away. "A mock charge," Scott uttered when he had the breath to speak. It took ten minutes to get the people off our ladder.

I could look out the fly of the tent pretty much any time of day or night and see an elephant around our tree. And people on our ladder. People who had been on their way to the bar or pool or just out for a walk ended up in our tree to escape elephants.

Many campers stay only one night at Flat Dogs. Our platform was the ultimate room with a view as far as I was concerned, so we stayed for four nights. Elephants peacefully munched beneath our tree every day and moved on. Usually. But elephants at Flat Dogs don't seem to like big overland trucks populated by twenty-somethings drinking their way through Africa, not that there's anything wrong with that. Every afternoon a trumpeting, head-tossing, foot-stomping herd would cross the river and run towards the scent of Tusker beer. Then, while the overlanders screamed, "Bloody hell!!" and dove either into or, more popularly, under their vehicle, elephants swept their trunks across the tables and made sure every last bit of tuna salad, sunscreen, and baked beans on toast was on the ground and thoroughly stomped on. They seemed especially fond of the crunch of expensive video cameras. Then the elephants would move away and silently appear at the swimming pool to enjoy a nice long cool chlorinated drink. That's when we got to see travelers in bikinis running around willy-nilly.

Flat Dogs is a sensory thrill. All day, we watched elephants move back and forth across the river. All night, we heard the bellowing of hippos or the tummy rumble of a nearby elephant. One morning while completely engrossed in a book by the river I failed to notice, until it was too late to make a mad dash for our platform or the bar, that an elephant was walking by not a few feet from me. Of all the times I held my breath at Flat Dogs, that one was the longest. Later that afternoon we arranged a game drive in South Luangwa National Park. A Land Cruiser picked us up in camp and drove us across the bridge into the park. We would see more elephants throughout Africa, but never eye to eye the way we did at Flat Dogs. To my disappointment, I have just learned that as of July 2011, camping is no longer permitted at Flat Dogs.

LION ZEN

"Here, kitty," I said, beckoning to the neurotic kitty at the Fawlty Towers backpackers in Livingstone near the Zambia-Zimbabwe border. While I stayed "home" in our tent pitched in the guesthouse garden reading and petting the communal cat, Scott did what most travelers do when they arrived in Livingstone. He rafted the Zambezi River. I'll take class-five kitty over class-five rapids any day. Besides, I had rafted the Zambezi once in 1995 and really, isn't once enough? I distinguished myself that year as the most verbose rafter: "*Oh my God. Oh. My. God. OhmyGodohmyGod,*" while begging our guide, Gift, "Pleeeeease don't let the raft turn over!" For pretty much the entire day I was bunched into the fetal position at the front of the raft pleading with my Maker to make it stop. Our raft seemed to teeter on the aft three feet while the rest of the boat pointed straight up to heaven. I hoped this unnatural angle at least helped my prayers get closer to their intended target. We did a watercraft wheelie the whole way down the Zambezi. Once was enough for me.

My choice for an adrenalin experience in Livingstone was to walk with lions.

The lions I walked with and petted were orphans taken in by a conservancy whose goal is to protect and rehabilitate them, breed them, and return them to the wild. Before we were introduced to the lions, we watched a video about the conservancy. After the video they handed out long sticks and led us over to where the lions sat panting in the shade of a mopane tree. They were bigger than I thought.

"Uh, do you have any bigger sticks?" I asked. "I don't see how this toothpi..., uh, stick, is going to dissuade a lion from, well, being a lion."

"It's more your tone and body language that will control the lion," said the guide. "If a lion gets cheeky with you, point your stick at him and say, 'NO' in a loud and firm voice. And don't ever assume a crouching position."

The first lion I approached fell at my feet and begged for a tummy rub. "How delightful!" I said as I assumed a crouching position. I have never felt so utterly content as when I sat stroking a lion. I don't know why, but it is pure bliss for me. The lions seemed to get something out of it too since they practically nodded off. I never once had to use my toothpick.

A few years earlier, we were in the bush in Zimbabwe camped on the property of a British family. One morning the owner came to our tent saying he had received a message that a black rhino had been spotted not far from his farm and did we want to see it? I passed on the offer. The day before he had generously offered to take us to see a pair of rare white rhino in the bush. Only he wasn't sure exactly where they were. It took about an hour, but we found them. We watched the pair from a distance. It was terribly exciting. Our host whispered, "Let's see if we can get closer." I was perfectly content to continue enjoying them from where we were behind a small bush. Our host, just an hour before, had told us a story about a local man who lost his arm to a lion he "knew." Shaking his head he said, "You see, people here sometimes get complacent. These are wild animals, and you must never forget that." Now he was suggesting we get close to a beast with an extremely large warning sign, a horn sticking out of his head, which should remind any sane person that complacency could get one killed.

"Well, what should we do if the rhino spots us?" I whispered back.

"We are downwind, and they appear to be asleep. And rhinos have very poor eyesight, so I don't think we need to worry. But if one of them starts to run at you, just hide behind a bush or tree. Their eyesight is so bad they won't see you." I looked around. The bush we were bunched behind was the only one around for seventy-five feet. We would be inching up on the rhinos in the open. So I made what I thought was a prudent decision at the time. I went last.

I didn't breathe as we neared the sleeping rhinos. Our host was very excited because he hadn't seen the white rhino for some time. We inched closer until we could see that indeed they were sleeping. This is thrilling, I thought. Risky but thrilling.

After squatting quietly for several minutes watching the rhinos dosing peacefully, our host, who had obviously completely forgotten any talk of the dangers of complacency, suddenly said, "Let me see if I can wake them," and he proceeded to vocalize and clap his hands. I immediately crouched into the position a hundred-yard-dash runner takes before a race and took a bead on a bush, *the* bush, which was now about fifty feet away. I ran back to the bush on tippy-toes as fast as I could with eyes, appropriately, as wide as those of prey. I looked back to see that the rhinos had woken up and were searching wildly around them for the source of what had disturbed their slumber.

All I can say is that rhinos must truly have colossally bad eyesight. Or these two were blind. They huffed a few times then suddenly charged off in the complete opposite direction of where we were. If we had been upwind, we might have been toast.

So the next day when our host asked if we wanted to go see a black rhino, I said thanks but no thanks.

Scott was not yet rhino weary, so off he went for more adventure, and I was left alone in the field contently reading in our tent. Then the best thing happened. I heard a rumble. I unzipped the tent to find a man and an elephant standing not four feet from me! The man was talking to the elephant in a gentle voice and feeding it some dry mashed grain by hand. I climbed out of the tent and asked how he had met the elephant. He told me it was orphaned as a baby and he had always taken care of it. "Would you like to feed her?" he said. "It's OK. You can touch her." Would I! I took a handful of grain and placed it deep inside the elephant's mouth, as the man had done. Then I touched her trunk, her ears, her body, and her tail. I even got to touch the bottom of her feet. I got to touch her all over. It was wonderful. Shortly the elephant began to move away, so I thanked the man and returned to the tent utterly content and glad I didn't go on another rhino hunt. About an hour later, Scott returned. They never did spot the black rhino.

Just before dusk, we were driven to the home of a farmer who had raised two orphaned lions since birth. They were too big to be allowed in the house any longer and were housed in a large enclosure in the yard. The owner let us in the enclosure so we could pet them. The lions had just eaten an impala leg, or something that looked like it might once have been an impala leg, and were now intently watching a pesky warthog that taunted them mercilessly from the safety of the other side of the fence. I walked over to one lion and gave him a good rub. He immediately rolled over to have me do his tummy. If I hadn't noticed the sharpness of the lion's claws, I would have been in that Tsiribihina River meditative state again. I was close to it. I got to touch an elephant and a lion, all in one day. It was the most blissful day of my life so far.

Aside from getting to walk with and touch lions, Livingstone has everything else a traveler could want in the way of outdoor recreation. You can canoe the Zambezi above the falls or raft or boogie board the rapids below the falls. You can fly an ultra-light or micro-light aircraft, bungee jump off a bridge, ride a zip line, take a helicopter ride, view game from atop an elephant. You name it, Livingstone has it. It is a budget-busting, adrenaline-pumping, booze-cruising stop on the Africa overland trail. My favorite part (after petting a lion, of course) was lying in our tent each night listening to the roar of Victoria Falls and the bellowing of the hippos from the nearby Zambezi River.

Scott had rafted the Zambezi and I had made like Joy Adamson, but to get our blood pumping in unison, we took an ultra-light flight over the falls. With Scott in one plane and me in another, we each felt like we were flying a butterfly with a lawn mower engine hung off its back. When we took off I almost tossed my cookies.

I mentioned to the pilot before takeoff that I had completed ground school and had one hour of flying under my belt, so he cheerfully let me take the wheel, a joystick that rose up between my legs. Cookies in my throat, I maneuvered the plane up, left, and right until we gained altitude. We floated over farms, the town, and then Victoria Falls. We could feel the power of the updraft as we flew over the massive volume of falling water. The engine of the ultra-light was so loud it was impossible to hear the falls. Without sound the water appeared to be dropping silently in slow motion over the ledge. From up river the white mist rising from the crashing water looked like smoke billowing upward from an enormous fire. It was a surreal experience. Of all the heart-pumping things one can do in Livingstone, I think flying an ultra-light over the falls offers the most bang for the buck.

THE MONEY SHOT

Flying an ultra-light over the Zambezi River may have gotten our hearts pumping, but now we were going to do something on the Zambezi that was reputed to be heart stopping—a four day canoe camping safari. During the day we would paddle amongst hippo and crocodile, and at night we would camp on the riverbank with Cape buffalo and elephant. Scott was very keen on canoeing the Zambezi, and he was extra pleased because he had booked it for a very good price.

I was nervous. I am more afraid of hippos than any other African animal, and I wasn't too excited about sleeping with Cape buffalo either. Because they are so territorial, hippo and Cape buffalo cause the most deaths to humans in Africa.

"C'mon Tris! It will be fun," Scott said trying to convince me. "You love the wildlife. It can't get more wild than this."

When we arrived in Kariba, we were told that the other people who had booked the trip cancelled at the last minute so it would just be Scott, me, and our guide, "Eddie." Eddie looked decidedly more frightened than I did. He also appeared to be about twelve years old.

I looked at Scott and said with my eyes, "There is no way in hell I am getting on the Zambezi with deadly hippos, crocs, and buffalo with a kid named Eddie." I don't know why his name bothered me so much but even "Edward" wouldn't have made him look any older or any more confident.

Scott turned to the booking agent and asked, "Do you have any other tours going tomorrow?"

Yes, they did have a canoe safari starting tomorrow, but it was a luxury tour staying each night at tented safari camps along the way and would cost considerably more than our camping safari.

"Would Eddie be leading the tour?" my husband asked quietly.

"Oh no," said the agent with understanding. "That tour is led by Maxwell, a very experienced guide."

We walked away to discuss bending the budget and going on the luxury safari. I reaffirmed my position aloud, "Scott, there is no way I'm going to put my life in the hands of a kid named Eddie who doesn't look as though he's ever even held a paddle before."

"Hmmm," Scott said, his sense of frugality trying to convince him that going on a camping safari with Eddie would be a good idea. "Well, I think I'll see if they will give us a discount on the other trip."

And that's what happened. There was only one couple booked on the luxury trip, so the agent decided it would be more fun for everyone if we made it a foursome, five with Maxwell.

Early the next morning, we met Maxwell and the Australian couple we would be canoeing with over the next four days. Maxwell gave us a spiel about what we could expect to see, smell, and taste on the Zambezi. Then he gave a "safety talk."

"Leave most of your gear here. You need very little on the river, just a small duffle bag with a few changes of clothes will do. Do not bring any food, especially citrus fruit. Elephants are crazy about oranges." He paused for emphasis before continuing. "Never stand up in your canoe. If you see a hippo, don't panic. Paddle single file behind my canoe. When we stop for lunch or a pee break, do not wander far from the canoe—there are elephants and Cape buffalo that come to the river each day to drink. If a hippo or elephant charges you, don't worry. I have a weapon in my canoe that will stop them."

"Maxwell, have you ever had to fire your weapon?" I asked.

"Only once," he answered with a frown. "I had a guest one trip who insisted on bringing a very large hard-sided suitcase with him.

He was traveling alone and kept to himself. Each time we stopped for lunch or a break he disappeared into the bush with the suitcase. One day as I prepared lunch, the man came running out of the bush hysterical and without his suitcase. Behind him I could see a big bull elephant hot on his heels. I ran to the canoe for my gun and took aim on the elephant." Maxwell paused. "I have never killed an animal, and I did not want to kill this elephant. But the elephant was very angry, and he kept coming behind the man. I made a quick decision to fire my gun into the air hoping to startle the elephant. It worked. He stopped charging then stomped the ground and tossed his head before running away."

"How frightening! Why was the elephant chasing the man?" I asked.

"Elephants love oranges. It turned out that the man's suitcase was filled with nothing but oranges. He would take the suitcase with him into the bush, find an elephant and toss oranges to it until we were ready to leave. That day he tossed oranges until his suitcase was empty. Only, the elephant wanted more. I was so angry at this man who almost made me shoot an elephant!"

Before we left I discarded my citrus-scented shampoo.

The lodges we stayed at each night were simple yet beautiful. Genteel Zambian hosts at each tented safari camp excelled at the art of conversation and made us feel comfortable and catered to. At the end of each day they greeted us on shore with welcoming smiles and our favorite cocktail. We had more cocktails at the bar as we watched the sun go down before dining together at a meticulously set table. We listened to exciting stories about adventurers in Africa as we settled into comfortable chairs around a campfire after dinner. All night long we heard the rumble of elephants nearby. Little did I know I would soon be telling an exciting Zambezi story of my own around the campfire.

The Zambezi is the fourth longest river in Africa. Through six countries it provides food, transportation, and recreation to locals and visitors. Acacia trees and dense brush overhang the Zambezi's banks like an unkempt mustache. You can hear the animals crashing through the vegetation to get to the river long before you can see them. The main river is wide with many narrow channels to paddle in and out of while looking for wildlife. But you never have to search for long. Opportunities to get close to wildlife are a guarantee. It isn't uncommon to see herds of more than one hundred elephants along the riverbank. Cape buffalo, baboons, crocodiles, and many bird species are also in abundance. But the most prevalent animal in the Zambezi by far is the hippo.

Canoeing the Zambezi is not for the faint of heart. Each day we had to weave our canoes among pods of territorial hippos. Maxwell took the lead and when we came upon a group of hippos blocking our path he would stand up in his canoe and hold his oar high over his head "to look big and dominant," he said. Though Maxwell was little more than five feet tall, to our amazement this usually worked and the hippos would scurry out of the water. Usually. One day however, as we canoed through a very narrow side channel, Maxwell spotted a lone hippo some distance ahead asleep in the water. He turned around and said softly, "I think if we paddle quietly he will not wake up. Just follow me and try not to make any noise."

We went single file, Maxwell in the lead, the couple from Australia following, and Scott and me bringing up the rear. As I watched Maxwell slide past the hippo, the hippo continued to sleep. As I watched the Aussies glide past, the hippo didn't move. As Scott and I neared the hippo, it suddenly woke up with a start and sprang up in the shallow water with a look that said, "What the hell! Where did you come from?" We panicked and began flailing our paddles with such desperation that our canoe T-boned the bank opposite the hippo. Not more than ten feet from us, the hippo went into territorial mode. First it took a big dump, splattering its poo over the water and bank with a frantic and repetitive wag of his tail. Then it took a bead on us.

We corrected our course and paddled with all our might away from the hippo. I saw Maxwell ahead stand up in his canoe and raise his oar high over his head. The Aussie couple was watching us with eyes wide and mouths agape. I noticed a look of horror on the face of the Aussie man and, oddly, a look of opportunity on the face of the Aussie woman. I watched things unfold in slow motion as the woman, not taking her eyes off us for a second, reached for her fancy long-lens camera and began to take shot after shot of us and what was going on behind us.

Then Maxwell and the Aussie couple suddenly began paddling quickly down the river. Without saying a word, Scott and I continued paddling as if we were in a race for a gold medal. We were too terrified to speak. Soon we were even with the Aussies and in another minute we had passed Maxwell. I thanked God that Scott had been on an outrigger team when we lived in Hawaii; he really knew how to dig an oar into the water. We didn't stop paddling until we could see the lodge ahead of us. Completely spent, I put the paddle down and let Scott guide us in to shore.

The lodge host must have sensed by my expression and limp arms that something memorable had happened on the river, because as soon as our canoe hit the bank, she was there by my side wrapping my hand around a double gin and tonic.

"That was bloody terrifying!" said the Aussie man as he walked to the bar. His wife, who it turned out was a professional film (not digital) photographer, remained on the bank snapping photos, one after another. She shot photos of the lodge, of the reeds, of the sunset, of the gin and tonic, until she slowly advanced the camera one last time with a sick look on her face.

"That hippo," she said to us. "It was right behind you. It had its mouth wide open as it chased you down the river. I thought it would take half your canoe in its mouth." She sighed. "I thought I had a money shot." With trepidation she opened the back of her camera to confirm her fears. The film was intact, its little tail barely out of it canister. The entire day, it had never wound on. She hadn't gotten a single photo.

"I know you are disappointed, but we could have been killed!" I said.

Oddly, for the rest of the trip she barely spoke to us. Somehow it was our fault that she had missed her award-winning photo.

It's All About the Booty

As we waited at the crowded border crossing for the car ferry that would take us across the river to Botswana from Zambia, I saw the most original hairstyles I had seen in all of Africa. One woman had a hairdo that looked like a lion's mane. Another had broad streaks of yellow, orange, and purple through her hair. Even the little girls had creative hairdos. I thought it was odd that I never again saw such avant-garde hair styling anywhere else in Africa. Apparently hairstyle innovation starts and stops at the Zambia-Botswana border.

We camped in the wild in the Okavango Delta. To get to our camp we were slowly propelled by long oar in a *mekoro* (dugout canoe) through tall reeds in narrow meandering channels that were only a few feet wide and a few feet deep. There are camps rimming the delta that can be driven to, but most people experience the world's largest delta by dugout canoe. Mekoros are like fingerprints: each one is unique. We were told that when a local boy is young, he carves his name on a tree that will someday become his mekoro. When he reaches maturity, he cuts it down and begins digging out the inside of the tree until it is shaped like a canoe. One tree. One canoe.

The warm morning sun hit my arms then gradually lit up the surrounding reeds turning them from light green to the red, yellow, and golden hues that you see on autumn leaves. By 8:00 a.m. the entire Okavango glowed. From the air it might have looked as if a red-orange blanket covered the earth—all but the waterways, which appeared black, even up close. We camped on a small island abundant with brush and trees. During the day our mekoro driver stood on the tapered stern at the back and pushed the canoe along with a twelve-foot pole, guiding us from lagoon to lagoon. In the late afternoon we were content to sit in the shade of a large tree and watch the colors of the reeds change again. Just before sunset one evening our driver spotted an elephant, and we watched it lumber across a patch of land to the water's edge to drink. The sun was setting, the moon was rising, and an elephant was doing everyday elephant things right near camp. Life was good.

I fell asleep that night listening to hippos call in the distance. I was thoroughly in the "commune with nature" groove—until a hippo's loud munching just outside our tent at three in the morning woke us out of a sound sleep. Scott immediately thought that taking a photo of the hippo was the best idea ever. For some inane reason I thought it was a great idea too and that our tent would protect us should the hippo disagree. It is true that most African animals seem to view a tent as something impenetrable without realizing there are easy pickings inside, so I guess I was relying on that assumption when I handed Scott the camera. Our primary camera was broken, so we had to rely on a small spare the size of a deck of cards that people who owned expensive camera bodies and several large lenses derogatorily referred to as a "snappy cam." The camera was set to "automatic," but there was a dial that could be spun to customize the shutter speed and adjust for low light. We rarely used it and couldn't remember how to set the camera for night photography. As the munching grew louder, we anxiously tried to find the right setting in the dark.

"I want to get a clear shot," Scott whispered, while slowly unzipping the screen of our tent so that there would be nothing between the hippo and us.

Both of us had our hands on the camera pushing buttons and trying to turn the flash off so we wouldn't startle the hippo.

"Hurry!" I urged at a whisper. The hippo was perfectly framed between two trees just outside our tent. "Try the museum setting."

Suddenly the flash exploded, illuminating the inside of our tent. The hippo froze in place with about a bushel of grass hanging out of its enormous mouth. The munching, and our breathing, had stopped at the same instant. We scooted quickly and quietly to the back of our tent. watching the hippo through the open fly. If he was startled and blinded by the flash, he could inadvertently run right through our tent and smash us flat in the process. If he was startled and angry, he could *deliberately* run right through our tent and smash us flat in the process. We waited to see which smash-flat scenario would happen. After two full minutes, the hippo suddenly turned in the opposite direction from the tent and ran into the bush.

"That was great!" Scott whispered. "Push the review button. Let's see the photo!"

It is a wonderful, perfect, museum-quality photo of a tree trunk.

In the morning a German woman who had been sleeping in the next tent scolded us. "I heard you taking photos of that hippo last night. Do you think you are funny? That is very dangerous! Please do not do that again." I kept waiting for her to swear at us in German the way my mom did when I was a kid and I wondered if she ever had an urge to pack up and go to Timbuktu. Despite our improper wildlife photo-taking etiquette, I don't think she ever swore at us in German, or in English for that matter. Though we probably deserved it. We were just lucky the hippo had read the manual that explained a tent is part of the landscape, like a rock.

It seemed a peaceful sleep was not something we would ever get to enjoy in the Okavango because the next night a rowdy group from Spain spectacularly extinguished the tranquility of nature's sounds with their singing. Even the most boisterous of bellowing hippos couldn't be heard over the din. And it wasn't a lyrical Spanish ballad sung with the accompaniment of a well-tuned guitar. The Spaniards spent half the night teaching their mekoro polers, in unison and at great volume, the lyrics to *The Macarena*. It was very disturbing to see

Africans doing the very uncool moves of the Macarena the next morning. I was tempted to teach them something else very un-African, like Groucho Marx's walk maybe, but I was afraid it would be integrated into the Macarena and what a travesty that would be to the memory of one of my comedic heroes. I waited to see if the German woman would swear at the Spaniards, but for some reason, she gave them a pass. Sleep deprivation aside, I was mostly upset because the exuberant singing chased the animals away. Man-made noise is an anomaly in the Okavango because most of the time it is a place of tranquility interspersed with only the sounds of nature.

I was happy about our decision to travel by mekoro to a bush camp deep within the delta to experience quiet Africa from a mekoro, but it didn't feel like a complete experience. To get a broader sense of the landscape and movement of animals in the Okavango, one must fly over it. From high above the delta, we picked out one game trail from thousands and traced it with our eyes to a herd of elephants making their way single file through the reeds to a group of trees. We tracked zebras heading to a pool for a drink and watched a pod of hippos in repose in a lagoon. We tried to count the giraffe and impala that were migrating through the flooded plain, but there were too many. From the air we could see large clear ponds and countless channels that crisscross the delta. Like constellations on a map of the night sky, the channels radiated out in all directions linking lagoons to islands. To get the big picture of the Okavango, a bird's-eye view is best.

The annual flooding of the Kalahari is what brings the vast concentration of wildlife to the Okavango Delta and the delta is what brings most tourists to Botswana. But there is more to Botswana than the flora, fauna, and Macarena of the Okavango. Botswana is rich in tribal culture. Two tribes, the Herrera and the Himba, have many divergent customs including manner of dress, yet a Himba chief will sometimes take a Herrera woman as one of his wives.

The Herrera woman is usually quite stocky, and she dresses in an old-fashioned colonial manner. Her costume consists of a long apron over a heavy, neck-to-ankle dress, and on her head sits a substantial hat that resembles a set of cow horns. This unique headdress is how they came to be known as "the cow tribe."

The Himba women, on the other hand, are very tall and shapely. They cover their bodies in rancid fat and red ochre powder from head to toe. They glow like an African sunset. They adorn themselves with shell, pearl, and copper necklaces, and their hair is decorated with thick globs of buttery ochre and headdresses made of animal skins. They wear nothing other than a short flap of leather around their waists that hangs down to cover the rear end. Though they are topless, they take great care to cover their tushies in layers of soft leather because, in Africa, it's all about the booty. Breasts are for food production.

The Himba children are among the happiest I have known in Africa.

Swaziland Maidens

It took a few days to get to Swaziland from Botswana by bush taxis, but once we crossed the border we no longer had to rely solely on public transport to get from A to B. Swaziland is relatively small, and it's commonplace for people to take on hitchhikers.

Outside a shopping center in Mbabane one day, a math and science teacher offered us a ride back to our guesthouse. Within minutes of settling in the back seat we learned that in addition to being an educator in Swaziland, he also happened to be a refugee from Rwanda. It is a universal truth, but especially in Africa, that everyone has a story. While he drove, he told us that he witnessed the Rwanda massacres that began around Easter Sunday in 1994. He described how he had lost his two sisters and a brother in the killing spree. He barely escaped with his wife and three children first to Uganda, then Tanzania where there were no jobs, then to Swaziland where he had been for the last seven years. His account of the violence became more vivid as he spoke. By the end of his story his body language, shoulders up around his ears, eyes wide, hands gripping the wheel, was such that he was back in Rwanda reliving the horror all over again—and we were sick to our stomachs.

A few years prior we had seen the movie *Hotel Rwanda*, which depicts the collective madness that is the Rwanda massacres. From what we heard that day from an eyewitness, nothing in the movie is an exaggeration.

What does one say to a refuge? What do you say to someone who may never again see their homeland or what is left of their family and friends there? "I'm sorry," and an embrace seemed so inadequate, but it was all we could come up with as we parted. "Safari jema," he said, wishing *us* a good journey.

The timing of our visit to Swaziland was nearly perfect. We had heard it might be possible to meet the king of Swaziland. Unfortunately he was up to his eyeballs ruling his kingdom when we arrived. We missed, by one day, the Celebration of the Reed Dance where maidens from all over Swaziland present themselves to the king in commemoration of their chastity. Why they do this while topless is a subject of debate for others. Scott expressed his regret at missing this great cultural experience, "Thirty thousand topless maidens! And it was *free!*"

Each year the forty-year-old king usually picks out a maiden as a new bride, adding to the thirteen or more wives he already has. But he is a very altruistic king. A few years ago he gave one of the maidens to his friend. He also presents each wife with her own home. A local warned that we be careful when discussing the king, because it's likely that the person we are speaking to is related to him.

The Reed Dance was historically held for the king's mother, who rules alongside him. For more than a week, tens of thousands of maidens travel to the queen mother's home, present her with cut reeds, and dance for her. I thought the queen mother of Swaziland had the best title of queen mothers the world over. They call her, *"Ndlovukati,"* which means, "The She Elephant."

I imagine the Reed Dance Festival inspired much discussion from activists around the world who feel it is wrong for one of the richest monarchs on earth to test maidens for virginity and parade them around topless while his country, with one of the lowest life-expectancy rates in the world, continues to live in poverty. We read an article about the Zulu Reed Dance of South Africa in the local paper and in it King Goodwill Zwelithini was given a chance to answer his critics: "It is here where we can feel our umbilical cord" (is that what you call it King

Goody!) "connect so effectively with our ancestors. It is an occasion when people, friends, and I the King, renew that bond and the vibrancy of our togetherness! It is precisely why I revived this ceremony 21 years ago—" (Goodwill has been king since he was fourteen years old) "to fulfill an important responsibility which is inherent in my duties!"

"Some king," I said with distaste as I folded the paper.

"But Iris," Scott said. "Don't forget, he was only a teenager when he became king." From the look in his eyes I could tell that Scott had transported himself back to the age of pubescence, perhaps remembering his Boy Scout paper drive days when copies of *Playboy Magazine* were sometimes discovered in stacks of the local newspapers being donated.

Scott had a sudden look of renewed appreciation for the king of Swaziland. "I mean, what boy of fourteen who suddenly finds himself head of a kingdom wouldn't choose a topless maiden parade each year over a social welfare program or public works project? Think of all the things a boy of fourteen would wish for as king! I bet there is even a skateboard park or two in town."

"Yeah," I responded. "But I bet he doesn't test the skateboards to see if they've been ridden before."

GAME RANGER TRAINING

On the way to breakfast one morning in a Johannesburg guest-house, Scott picked up a tattered issue of the *South Africa Getaway Magazine* off a nearby table. *Getaway Magazine* is filled with articles on safari and leisure trips in Southern Africa. Thumbing quickly past the pretty pictures of luxurious safari camps, he went to the very back of the magazine, "to the interesting part," he always called it, and found a miniscule three-line ad offering a two-week Field Guide Association game ranger training course in Klaserie near Timbavati and Kruger.

"Tris, look at this. It sounds wonderful!" said Scott as he wrote down the phone number. "Two weeks in the bush where we will see animals every day and learn all about what it takes to be a game ranger."

"We can't be game rangers," I said. "To be a game ranger you have to know how to repair a Land Rover, how to fire a gun, and how to mix a perfect gin and tonic. You have to look good in a pair of short shorts and have a sexy South African accent."

"I don't mean we would actually become game rangers," Scott replied, looking at me as if I wasn't getting it. "We love being in the African bush, right? We love going on game drives and being sur-rounded by animals, right? We are even closet birders for God sakes. Doing this course would only enhance our experience in Africa. At the very least we would get to camp out in the bush for two weeks."

I handed him the phone.

We joined our instructor John near Durban, along with two South African men who would be our classmates. The two students were obviously serious about being game rangers. They looked pretty good in their short shorts.

John turned out to be a very interesting man. He grew up along the Zambezi and came to know all about the plants and animals along the river at an early age. His playmates were mostly black Africans. As an adult he was a soldier in a mixed race unit where he fought terrorism in Zimbabwe for a few years before returning to his passion of living among animals. He studied to become a game ranger and soon became a respected trainer of future game rangers throughout South Africa. He cared deeply about the land, and the animals, and what the future would hold for Africa as a result of deforestation and population pressures. Most game rangers are conservationists at heart. If you love nature you know that every living thing shares this one planet and that we had better take care of it. John spoke at length about the consequences of poaching and snaring of animals, yet he understood that there are locals who took game in order to survive. We felt lucky to have him as our instructor.

When we arrived at Klaserie, we were told to choose one of three spacious tents. The tents were set well apart, around seventy-five paces from each other. The only other structures were a canteen tent, a canvas cubicle around a long-drop latrine, and a small open-air wooden enclosure where we could bathe under a plastic sun shower. As far as the eye could see was nothing but wild African bush.

Fifteen minutes after we arrived, we stood breathless and listened to the first of many lion roars that we would hear each night and morning while on the course. Though a terrifying sound at first, a lion's roar is something we became used to and even looked forward to. We missed it when they were farther away or came a little later in the evening than usual.

As John walked with us to our tents, he gave us a spiel on what to expect over the next two weeks.

"Each morning you will take turns getting up before dawn to start the campfire and get the breakfast started. You are in an area populated with lots of wild animals. Lion, elephant, hyena, and leopard are all around us so *before* you unzip your tent fly, shine your torch all around to make sure you will be walking to the cook tent unaccompanied. Try not to have to use the loo during the night if you can help it, because that's when leopards are most active and they just might tear your head off. After breakfast we have class under that tree," he pointed to an easel, a whiteboard, and four chairs sitting under an enormous shade tree. "After class we will either do a game walk, or you can study or rest. After lunch we have another class and a game walk. At the end of two weeks you will be tested on what I have taught you and hopefully receive your Level One Game Ranger Certification."

"Oh, you picked a good one!" John said with a smile as we arrived at the tent we had chosen. Our heavy-duty canvas tent contained two cots and a small nightstand. There were large mesh windows on the sides and a screen door at the front.

"Why is this tent special?" I asked.

"The last man who slept in this tent woke up to find an adult male lion looking in that window." He pointed to the window nearest the cot I had chosen. "He didn't remember how he ended up under the cot, but that's where he was when he woke up in the morning. Also," he said indicating we should follow him outside, "a scorpion lives under this tent." He carefully lifted up the front half of the tent to show us the scorpion. "Very deadly. But it's a quick death."

"Uh huh," I said looking around my feet. "John, I noticed there are a few spiders inside the tent that jump. Are any of *them* venomous?"

"I'd have to see one. If you can catch one, bring it to me and I'll have a look."

After John left to check on our two classmates, we moved the cots to the center of the tent as far away from the windows as possible.

"I don't know about you, but my plan is to leave my boots on for the next two weeks," I said while searching for a spider to show John. I trapped one in a drinking glass and slid a small notepad over the top to keep it from jumping out. "I can see we aren't going to get much sleep out here," I said, noting lumpy areas under the tent floor. "I'm going to take this spider to show John."

I found John sitting near a fire pit enjoying a nice hot cup of tea. "John, I have one of those spiders here. Can you tell me if it's venomous?" I held the glass up to John, then slowly slid the notebook from the top so he could get a good look at the spider.

"Oh yes, very venomous," John said briskly before taking another sip of tea. Only I didn't register his sarcasm. I yelped and my hand jerked, and the spider jumped into John's lap. As he leapt up out of his chair, he spilled hot tea all over his bare legs.

"John! You should never tease a woman about spiders!" I said.

From then on John was more careful about what he said to me about spiders. And I wasn't allowed to ask him questions while he was drinking tea.

I was right about one thing. We hardly got any sleep those two weeks. All day we were kept busy with classes and game walks. We practiced drawing the intestinal tracts of ruminant mammals and of Land Rovers. We took turns leading the group back to camp after John had led us hours away from anything familiar. Each morning we looked for signs of animal activity around the fire pit while John said, "tell the story." After examining the spoor we had to take a stab at explaining what chased what around camp. We found lion prints once and hyena prints every day. One morning when it was my turn to be leopard bait and walk to the canteen before dawn to get the coffee on, a hyena and I startled one another in the cook tent. Fortunately he quickly ran off. I will never be cut out to be a game ranger because those 150 paces from our tent to the canteen were sheer terror for me. It was worse than being chased by a charging hippo. Also, because we stayed awake all night listening to sounds of lions calling to one another or a leopard "coughing" in the distance, we were consumed by a sleep-deprived giddiness during the day. When we took a break on our cots in the afternoon to nap or study, we would look at our drawings or notes and begin to guffaw like idiots.

Some nights, as we lay in our tent listening to the sounds of Africa, we would tape-record some of the more interesting noises. One night around two in the morning I heard a leopard calling. He was very close and getting closer. The sound was chilling. Of all the African cats, leopards have the most horrifying call. It sounds like the cough of a heavy smoker who is a serial killer. It is so focused, as if the leopard is saying, "I don't care if you can hear me, I'm coming. I will not stop until I separate your head from your neck." To listen to a leopard on the hunt is to experience a wide-awake nightmare.

My heart in my throat and barely breathing, I lay perfectly still as the leopard neared. I wanted to reach over and turn on the tape recorder but was too frightened to move. I wondered if Scott was sleeping through it, but I could not even turn my head to check. Suddenly the coughing stopped. Then there was a terrible commotion of wild leaping and running and crashing through bushes. Something bounced off the side of our tent and the leopard snarled *right there*. Then silence.

I lay in the cot for what seemed an eternity, afraid to move in case the leopard was still nearby. Then Scott turned his head to look at me, so I whispered, "Did you hear that?"

"Yes," he answered softly. "Now *that* was scary." He too wasn't moving a muscle. "But what is that whooshing noise?"

"What whooshing noise?" I whispered. "I don't hear that."

"Oh my God," Scott said after a brief pause. "It's my own circulation. I can hear the blood rushing though my head!"

One day at the end of a long game walk during which we had a contest to see who could spit dried impala dung pellets the farthest, John suddenly turned to us and said, "Follow me closely single file and don't make a sound."

I quickly fell in right behind John as he led us towards a bushy tree thick with vegetation spread wide around its base. He motioned that we should proceed slowly and silently. We crept forward on John's heels until we were standing before an opening in the bushes surrounding the tree. Within the bushes was a tamped down shallow depression the size of a kiddie pool. Suddenly John straightened up and said with regret, "Oh that's a pity. They aren't here."

"Who's not here?" I asked.

"There are usually a pride of lions resting here during the day," replied John.

"What! What would we have done if they had been here?" I asked.

"Enjoyed them!" he answered.

The day wasn't a total bust since I did win the dung-spitting contest.

We learned an incredible amount of information about the African bush and conservation over those two weeks. We visited a ranger office where hundreds of recovered snares were draped over logs. They had either been found in the bush or removed from the leg of an unfortunate animal. We saw where tusks had been cut from an elephant skull. Poaching is rampant. Being an anti-poaching ranger is one of the most dangerous jobs one can have in the South African park system. Poachers can be desperate folk who trap game for one of two powerful motivators: hunger or greed.

We learned what caliber weapon would drop an elephant or Cape buffalo in its tracks, and I noticed that John had one with him whenever we went on our walks. One day when we had been out on one of our game walks for over an hour, John turned to me and said, "Teresa, why don't you lead us back to camp?"

"Oh, is it my turn?" I asked.

John nodded without giving me any indication which direction I should go.

"Oh. Well. Ahem." I turned in a slow circle wishing I had been paying more attention to where we were going instead of staring at the ground looking for caterpillars. The caterpillars in South Africa demand attention. They are incredibly big and hairy. The first time I saw one I thought Andy Rooney had lost one of his eyebrows.

As I turned, I saw a termite mound. I remembered that a termite mound could give you a compass heading because they lean primarily in one direction. But I couldn't remember if they lean north, south, east, or west. "Hmm," I said, trying to get a hint from the supposed gentlemen who were my classmates. It was a hazy day, so I didn't even have the sun to give me a hint.

I chose a direction and began striding confidently left.

After ten minutes I stopped by a tree that had moss growing on its side. But does moss grow on the north or south? I couldn't remember. I begged Scott with my eyes to point the way home. I got nothing. "Hmm," I said, index finger to temple, studying the tree. If I could read the tree I was sure I could solve the mysteries of life. "Aha!" I snapped my fingers and began walking briskly to the left again as if I had just been given directions from the tree moss.

This went on for some time until I had confidently led us in a complete square. John, thoroughly exasperated, called a halt and said, "You are utterly lost!" He took the lead and cut a diagonal to my square (I think), and thirty-five minutes later we were back at camp.

It was difficult at times being the only woman in the group, mostly because South African men are unyieldingly polite. When dinner was ready the men refused to dish up until I had served myself first. "Ladies first," they would say each mealtime. It didn't matter if I was away in the shower or negotiating the long drop latrine, they would wait (impatiently) until I served myself. One evening Scott said, "I'm sure Tris won't mind if we go ahead," and he picked up a spoon and prepared to dish himself a healthy serving of potatoes. John quickly reprimanded him, "Serving yourself ahead of a woman is not an option."

In all other areas I was treated no differently than the men. In fact the only time John seemed to resent my presence was when he had to wait for me to dish up my food. It was infuriating. I pleaded with him to go ahead without me, but he refused. Even when it was my turn to prepare the meal, I had to serve myself before the men. "The cook goes last where we live,"

I said. "I really wish you wouldn't wait for me." I thought it strange. The men weren't particularly gentlemanly any other time during the course (especially during orienteering). But they thought nothing of making me cut short a shower or a poo to rush to the canteen and fill my plate.

After fourteen days, Scott, I, and the two other students sat under the tree taking the Field Guide Association of Southern Africa Examination. We would have two hours to complete the exam. If we passed we would earn Level I certification and be qualified to move to the next level to become a guide. I took it as a good omen that a small scops owl sat in the tree watching us take our test.

Scott received the highest score, and I trailed him in second place by two points. The two South African men came in third and fourth. We were shocked. Everyone was shocked. But we really had studied very hard in our tent during siesta/giggle time, and the exam didn't cover orienteering, thank God. The two South African men would have scored higher if the classes and tests were given in their first language, Afrikaans.

I know my limitations. While I mix a mean gin and tonic, I'll probably never be a field guide. I'll always be more interested in looking for Andy Rooney caterpillars than leading a group back to home base after a walking safari. And those short shorts? They look OK on me—but not great.

Go eBay!

I'll admit it. Our time in Africa wasn't all about roughing it. A year before we even knew we were going to Africa, Scott, on a whim, bought a week at a luxury private game reserve in South Africa on eBay. After we completed the field guide course, we contacted the owner of the reserve and the booking was made with the stipulation that we would somehow get ourselves to Insinkwe, the village nearest the game reserve.

The first leg of the journey was easy. We traveled on a comfortable Greyhound bus from Durban to Empangeni, the city closest to the game reserve. From there we would need to get ourselves about sixty miles up the road to Insinkwe where someone from the lodge would meet us. It seemed straightforward and (compared to the previous nine months) relatively easy.

We arrived in Empangeni at noon, glad that we would have plenty of daylight hours left to find our way to Insinkwe. We walked into a shop next to the bus terminal and asked where the bush taxi stand was located.

"You mean the black taxis?" answered the woman running the store.

Puzzled that there was a distinction I said, "Well, we need to get to Insinkwe and we would like to go by bush taxi."

"Not in South Africa," she said with conviction. "You must be careful. Something very bad could happen to you if you are not careful. You should take the proper white taxi."

We told her that we had been traveling throughout Africa for nine months, mostly by bush taxi and had never had a problem or felt threatened.

"Well, you can't do that in South Africa," she repeated.

We walked outside not sure what to do next. "I don't believe it," I said to Scott shaking my head. "Let's just find the bush taxi stand and check the vibe there."

We began walking to the main road. Almost immediately a police car pulled up next to us. The officer approached us briskly while asking bluntly in the South African way, "What are you doing? Where are you going?"

"To Insinkwe," we answered.

He looked at us like we were insane. "You can't just walk around with your bags like that here. You'll be mugged or worse. Empangeni has the highest crime rate in Africa right now. Every day there is carjacking, mugging, robbery—we've got our hands full. My wife and daughter were carjacked yesterday."

As he spoke I began to notice police sirens screaming in the distance.

"Well, what do you suggest?" Scott asked, frowning.

"You should rent a car or take a proper taxi. There is a taxi stand around the corner. But you can't walk there. It's not safe. I will fetch a taxi for you." He drove off after telling us to stay put. Two minutes later a taxi pulled up, and the driver said he would be taking us to Insinkwe.

I started to get in the taxi when Scott stopped me with, "Tris, wait." And I remembered the promise we had made to one another a few years prior to ask the price of something *before* buying. I backed out of the taxi and asked the driver, "How much?"

After a short pause he answered without blinking, "One hundred U.S. dollars."

Scott stared at him in disbelief. "What do you think this is, Manhattan?" Then he added more politely, "That's not in our budget, but thank you for stopping."

"Maybe it was a mistake to send him away but I'm glad we asked the price first," Scott said as the taxi drove away. "I would have felt like a chump paying a hundred dollars for a short taxi ride." He paused then added, "Remember that steak in Rome?"

I thought about the evening that ultimately inspired our "ask first" policy, the night we ate at a local restaurant in Rome. The restaurant was crowded with Italian couples and families and the aromas emanating from the kitchen made our mouths water. There wasn't a tourist in sight, and none of the waiters spoke English. Although it was an Argentinean-style restaurant featuring copious portions of meat, we both felt like eating pasta and pointed to the noodles we recognized on the menu (fettuccini) and a carafe of red wine at the table of a couple seated next to us. The meal was delicious. But as we ate we couldn't help notice how delectable the meat looked when it arrived on big platters to almost every table around us. We resolved to return to the restaurant for a steak dinner the next night.

The following evening the restaurant was even more crowded. After a half hour we were seated and presented menus.

The only items we could actually recognize on the menu were fettuccini (the pasta we had eaten the previous night), and *insalata* (salad). The rest of the menu was confusing. Nothing looked familiar, and the prices, in euros, seemed far too reasonable. We knew what we wanted, but we didn't know which line on the menu to point to. So when the waiter arrived, we simply pointed at the steak for two we saw a couple enjoying at a nearby table. The waiter responded in rapid Italian, which seemed to end in a question so we pointed to a carafe of red wine. "*Si,*" he said, then, shaking his head, "No." He took out a small pad of paper and wrote some numbers on it and a question mark. We had no idea what he wanted, so again we pointed to the wine at the table next to us and to the steak at another table and put up two fingers as in, steak for two. "And insalata!" I said showing off my Italian by adding a salad for us to share as well.

The waiter looked dismayed. He fired some more rapid Italian at us then shook his head again and retreated to the kitchen.

It was quite some time before the steak arrived. When it did it made our jaws drop. Its mass practically covered the entire table.

I had the presence of mind to say, "No insalata!" before the waiter left. Scott said, "I wonder what this is going to cost us."

It took us over an hour to eat most of the steak. When the bill arrived everything became clear. Steak was to be ordered by the kilo. When we had held up two fingers, we had inadvertently asked for two kilos of steak. That's nearly five pounds of meat. And the cheap prices on the menu? It turned out that was the price *per quarter* kilo. The steak alone set us back over $120.

"When are we going to learn to nail down a price before ordering? Didn't we learn our lesson that time in France?" Scott said staring at the bill for the steak in disbelief and referring to another one of life's "teaching moments," the ones we seem to forget as soon as we are taught them. We are usually on to daydreaming about something else almost immediately instead of remembering to relive the pain of a teaching moment. Years earlier our inability to remember to ask first came back to bite us while bicycling through rolling fields in the hot and dry Champagne region of France. We had run out of water and there was not a town in sight. We were starting to get seriously dehydrated when we came upon a stone house that had a sign hanging from the eave, "Bar." It was the worst time of day to be stopping since it was mid-afternoon, when all shops are closed until the evening and proprietors are home relaxing with their families. Fortunately the door was open. The bar was dark and incredibly cool. We thought if we couldn't find water we could at least wait inside until the heat of the day subsided. Soon a man came in and spoke to us in French. After determining we were tourists, he switched to fluent English. We asked for some water. "Certainly," he said filling two large glasses with water. "Would you like ice?" he asked.

"Ice? Well sure!" Scott said pushing our empty glasses toward him.

"Would you mind filling our water bottles as well?" Scott asked, grinning at me with a look that said he thought he was the cleaver one.

"Of course! Shall I put ice in your water bottles? Would you care for a cold Coca-Cola?" said the barman with a smile.

"Why not!" Scott answered, not in any rush to rejoin the oppressive heat outside.

I leaned over to Scott and whispered, "What a nice man!"

And we sat on bar stools chatting with the nice man and re-hydrating for some time.

Finally when we couldn't linger any longer, it came time for us to pay our bill and say adieu.

The nice man not only charged us for each drop of water and each cube of ice, the Coke alone was *twelve dollars*. More than being irritated about being overcharged, it just felt lousy that we had been too lazy to ask "How much?"

We stood at the curbside in Empangeni and tried to justify our decision to dismiss the overpriced taxi. "Maybe it *was* a mistake to let that taxi drive away, but I'm with you. A hundred dollars is a ridiculous price to get us to Insinkwe. Though our timing might not be perfect, maybe we are finally learning. Besides," I added with a frown, "this whole situation just feels weird. Let's take our time and figure out what to do next."

It felt very strange to suddenly have such hassle and expense trying to get transport, when all over Africa we had managed it with relative ease. It had been time consuming and uncomfortable, yes, but no one ever told us we needed to hire a "white taxi" and we never once felt threatened.

It made us angry. We are both a little stubborn and wanted to try finding the bush taxi stand again. But the sirens hadn't stopped, so we agreed to take a time-out and think about our options. We went to a small eatery nearby and sat down at an outside table. Exasperated with the situation, but wanting to move on to Insinkwe before dark, Scott looked at me and said, "Would you stay here with the bags? I will walk to this "proper" taxi stand and try to negotiate a more reasonable fare to Insinkwe." He left his wallet and our passports with me and set off down the street.

I sat sipping a Coke (fifty cents—I asked first) and watched a black man trimming a low hedge. "Excuse me," I said to him as he neared my table. "Could you please tell me where the bush taxi stand is located?"

He would barely make eye contact with me. "It's down that road, one *kilomet* (kilometer)," he said indicating the direction of the main road. "But you cannot take the bush taxi. It is not safe for white people," he added before returning to his clipping. I sat back flabbergasted. Then I started to worry about what might have happened to Scott who had been gone almost twenty minutes.

A group of white South Africans seated a few tables away began to question me about our plans and proceeded to relate story after story of the recent crime wave in their city. Soon Scott arrived back at the café and said with frustration, "I never found the 'proper' taxi stand. But I did encounter a bush taxi. I asked the driver about taking us to Insinkwe. He said, 'That's not possible.'"

The group at the other table overheard Scott's report. One of the men, Hank, said, "I don't want you and your wife to be a headline in tomorrow's paper. Please allow me to drive you to Insinkwe."

We looked at one another and decided to give in to the situation. "Thank you very much," said Scott. "I guess we have either been very fortunate traveling safely through Africa so far, or South Africa is very different from the rest of Africa," acknowledging that while he was grateful for the lift, he was still upset by the reality of life in Empangeni. "I guess we will have to be more careful from now on."

During the drive our Good Samaritan told us more violent crime stories. Soon he began initiating his sentences with "I'm not racist or anything but…" and he would go on to say completely racist things. South Africa, at least Empangeni, has a long way to go to rebuild its future and heal the troubles of its past.

When we arrived at the Insinkwe Bush Camp where we would spend the night, we had a beer with Hank while he told us more horror stories. He wouldn't take any money for the ride.

After he left, Scott looked at me, tired and saddened by the day's events. "I'm glad we didn't *start* our trans-Africa journey in South Africa. A day like today might have soured us or made us afraid to take bush taxis with the locals, and that has been the best part of the entire journey."

The next day we entered another world, another South Africa, when a ranger picked us up and drove us to the private game reserve that was to be our home for the next five days. We were cocooned in the secure dreamland that is a luxury safari lodge.

We were given our own chef and our own game ranger and our room was like a set from *Out of Africa*, only it had a big bathtub in the middle of the suite. I have to admit, my first impulse was to do laundry in it. The king-size bed was romantically draped with mosquito netting (why *does* that always look so romantic?) and there was a view of the hills, wildlife, and swimming pool from a writing desk under a window. It felt weird to be catered to after so many months of "the bush" and treated as if we'd spent lots of money to be there. I think they would have been surprised to know how little we paid for it on eBay.

We were nearing the end of our journey. Cape Town was calling. Staying at the lodge was a good way to begin the transition back to the developed world. No mosquitoes (the net is there purely for romance), good food, liberal amounts of gin, and lots of game drives. But I had to admit, my favorite part of staying at the luxury safari camp was the nice long soak in the Maytag.

SORRY, BOSS

The shift from luxury game lodge to a big African city was unpleasant to say the least. The eight-hour, music blaring, air conditioning on overdrive bus ride from Durban to Johannesburg had been horrible, and our connecting bus to Cape Town wasn't due to leave for another eight hours. We were both sleep deprived and grumpy—not a mood we wanted to be in as we neared the end of our journey. I was unhappy about leaving Africa but mostly perturbed that we had ended up in Johannesburg, my least favorite place in Africa. Fear chokes much of the city. Crime is rampant. It's like Empangeni but on a much larger scale. Scott and I had one of the few arguments we had on the entire trip over my insistence that we try to avoid Johannesburg completely. We came to a compromise when Scott said, "All we have to do is change buses there. We won't leave the bus station."

We had previously spent a few disheartening days in Johannesburg in 1999. Our taxi driver from the airport said we shouldn't go out even in broad daylight or we would be robbed. Of the five people staying at the guesthouse, four had been mugged. And we were staying in what was considered a nice district, Observatory. Shards of glass lined the tops of brick walls around each house, and a guard stood outside the gates to the driveways. Living in a city like that just isn't living to me. Most upsetting were the racist overtones that were sometimes still present long after apartheid had ended. It isn't like this everywhere in South Africa to be sure. But it was only there that I had heard whites make comments about blacks without even realizing just how offensive they were. A smiling white South African once said to me with pride,

"How do you like our blacks?" as if black people were a couch or lamp to be admired because they were such useful possessions. Another time as I made my way to a toilet at the South Africa-Botswana Border, I was stopped by a white woman who gestured to another building and said, "Don't you want to use the white toilet?" to which I replied, "Lady, I don't care what color the toilet is, I need to pee." She was not pleased. As I entered the toilet block, sure enough, there was a sign that read BLACK TOILET. As far as I could tell, it was no different from the other building, save the signage.

I realize that my indifference as to what color a person's skin is might have something to do with my upbringing. I was raised in the fairly liberal and culturally diverse San Francisco Bay Area. Also, after my parents became empty nesters, Mom offered our bedrooms to foreign students attending the nearby University of Santa Clara or San Jose State. Over the years, more than twenty students from Africa, the Middle East, and Europe stayed in our old rooms. They also became members of our family. They called my mom, "Mom" and my dad, "Dad" and there were usually no fewer than twenty-two of us around the table at Christmas, Easter, and Thanksgiving. They even came to enjoy corned beef and cabbage on St. Patrick's Day. So I could understand why someone who did not have the advantage of such colorblind parents might be fearful of those who didn't look like themselves, but whenever I encountered it, I became uncomfortable to say the least. That is why I sat there in the bus station grumpy about being in Jo'burg. I wrote letters home to family to pass the time.

After the letters were written, I asked the Greyhound clerk if there was a mail drop in the bus station. She said the only place to mail letters was the post office outside, and she gave me directions. "Be careful," she added. I took only the letters with me and walked out of the station. It was around two in the afternoon on a bright sunny day, and there were hundreds of people browsing the makeshift marketplace that edged sidewalks around the entire block. I walked along slowly looking at the tennis shoes, belts, blouses, and trousers for sale in the small booths while keeping my eye out for the post office. I circled the entire block but never found it, so I returned to the bus station.

"Couldn't you mail them?" Scott asked seeing the letters still in my hand.

"I never spotted it," I said sitting down. "Let's mail them from Cape Town."

Scott took the letters saying, "I need to stretch my legs anyway. I'll try to find it."

"Give me your wallet. It's very congested out there, lots of people standing around." I almost asked him to give me the money belt, which was inside his trousers, and anything else of value, but the waiting room was crowded with people, so I said nothing.

Not more than ten minutes went by before Scott was standing before me completely disheveled, crumpled letters in his hand, trousers sliced wide open along his leg.

"I was mugged," he said miserably.

My initial reaction was appalling. Without thinking, instead of hugging him, or crying, or showing outrage or fear, I put my hands on his chest and pushed him, like Elaine pushed Jerry on *Seinfeld* while saying, "Get, out!" except I shouted, "No!" I instantly felt horrible. But I understood why I did it. The adventure of the last ten months hadn't been a walk in the park. It was challenging to say the least and lots of bad things *could* have happened but hadn't.

Even before we left California, several of our friends expressed concern when we told them that we were about to transit Africa. We were asked, "Is that safe?" more times than I can remember. One friend even said, "I don't understand why you like going to a continent where everyone is killing one another." That he was incapable of seeing Africa in any other way than violent depressed me, but I knew from previous experience that I would be safer in rural Africa (risk of being eaten by a lion or flattened by an elephant aside) than in most any major city the world over. We had just spent more than three hundred days in Africa without witnessing violence of any kind. Yes, in Empangeni we heard about it, but we never actually saw a single person become violent towards another. And yes, maybe we had just been incredibly lucky. That the mugging had to happen when we were only twenty-four hours from the finish line of our journey was disheartening to say the least. So when Scott announced that he had been mugged, I didn't want to push him. I wanted to push the event out of our African experience.

Thankfully, because Scott had heard me say more than once during our journey, "I love Africa so much, I hope nothing bad happens to us" and because he knows me so well, he understood my reaction. Still, it is not the first thing you would want your wife to do just after you have been mugged.

I took a step back and really looked at him. I had never seen Scott look so dejected. I put my arms around him and said what I should have in the first place, "I am *so sorry* that happened to you. Are you OK?"

"I'm OK. They wanted what I had in the money belt, not to hurt me necessarily."

"They?" As I inspected his leg for blood where his trousers had been cut open, he told me how it happened. Almost as soon as he had stepped out of the bus station, four men jumped on top of him and brought him to the ground. He struggled until one of the men held a knife to his throat. Using a second knife they ripped the seams from his shirt pocket and threw the letters on the ground. Then they sliced open his trousers from waist to knee, cut the money belt away and ran off with our passports, credit card, fifty British pounds, our health cards, and a cell phone. The whole while it was going on, hundreds of people watched but no one did a thing to help him. One lady sitting at her table selling vegetables not a few feet from him looked Scott in the eye, *as he was being mugged*, and said, "Sorry, Boss."

SORRY, BOSS

We were shattered. We gathered our packs and made our way to the security office. We reported the mugging to a woman who barely made eye contact with us and seemed bored by the story. Nothing was written down and no one was sent out to interview any of the many witnesses. "Shouldn't you try to find these guys?" I asked. "They might be eyeing their next victim as we speak." She looked up and shrugged. While we waited an hour for police to show up, I spent most of my time on the phone trying to get someone in South Africa to connect me with Citibank in America so I could cancel our credit card. Of the five or six people I spoke to in South Africa on the phone, and the three people in the security office, no one asked if my husband had been hurt in the mugging or offered a single word of concern. More profoundly, no one expressed surprise that it happened. When I was finally connected to Citibank in the U.S. and repeated my story for the seventh time (in the same bland manner each time for I too had become numb) the Citibank agent exclaimed, "How awful! Is your husband OK? Is he hurt? Are you OK?" I burst into tears. I couldn't handle her outpouring of sincere compassion after the cold non-caring attitudes of the people we had spoken to up to that point in Johannesburg.

I went back to the security office to wait with Scott for the police. Soon an old Zulu woman entered in obvious distress. She approached the staff while wringing her hands and wiping away tears and spoke to them in Zulu. When she finished speaking, the staff waved her away dismissively. The old lady sat down on a bench in the office crying. I asked the security officer what had happened to her. "She was mugged. Someone took her little purse and she has no way to get home now," said the officer dully.

I lost it. The old woman could have sat there all night and no one would have helped her. Shocked at the lack of simple human compassion, I rummaged in my jean pockets and came up with a total of ten Rand, about US$1.25 at the time, and handed it to her. I looked at the

247

security guard with frustration, worn-out not only from our long bus journey and the mugging but from the callousness of Johannesburg. "You must help each other. You must start caring what happens to people. You must care!" I said with futility.

When the police arrived, they said we had to file the report at the police station downtown and put us in the back of a small paddy wagon, which was like a cage on wheels, and drove us into the city. On the way, the vehicle stopped several times while the officers observed loitering hoodlums, some dealing drugs as we watched. There were hundreds of young men standing idly in the streets all the way to the station. I could see why it would be impractical to confront all of them, but that is also part of the problem. In Johannesburg the criminals outnumber the police to such an extent that a lot of crime goes unpunished.

As the vehicle drove away after each stop, we received some funny looks from the men and boys who had been reprimanded by the police. I could see they were puzzled as to why a middle-aged white couple was in the back of a paddy wagon.

When we arrived at the station, there were a few men hanging around out front who stopped whatever they were doing and stared at us as we were let out the back of the vehicle. To lighten our moods I explained, "We were arrested for over-packing."

Inside the station there was a guardian angel in the form of Captain Stephan Weinstern. He asked with concern if Scott was all right, invited us to be seated, and gave us both something to drink. He waited while we filed the report, then took us in his own vehicle to a hotel "in an area that is safe," he said, while telling us stories of crime in Jo'burg that made me shudder.

Poor Scott. He looked so fallen. I think it was the first time in his life he was put in a seriously vulnerable position. Scott is a strong guy. That four men could take him down so quickly gave him pause, and having knife at his throat made him realize how fragile life can be.

At the hotel we showered, "to get the crime slime off," and realizing we hadn't had anything to eat all day, we walked downstairs to the hotel restaurant. I told our tale to the waitress and she responded flatly, "My uncle was robbed and burned alive. You have to be careful here." I told our tale to everyone we met, and they always had a story about what had happened to them or someone they knew. But they told it in such a matter-of-fact manner, as if it was to be expected and accepted.

I felt as if we were suddenly in some sort of twilight zone where zombies had replaced human beings. Doors had bars on them. Buildings had armed guards. I couldn't wrap my head around it. Why do people put up with living like this? Rural Mali is more civilized than Jo'burg.

We spent the rest of the evening deciding what to do. Fortunately we are both dual citizens. Our Irish passports had been stolen, but we still had our U.S. passports, so there was no reason to hang around Johannesburg waiting for replacements.

I felt that if we could just leave Johannesburg as soon as possible we would be able to recapture the Africa we had come to know over the previous ten months. Scott suggested we go back to Livingstone or Victoria Falls for a few days before going to Cape Town. Get right back on the horse so to speak.

"You are amazing," I said with admiration.

"Iris, it wasn't a hate crime. It was four desperate men, probably illegal immigrants from Zimbabwe or Mozambique. I'm definitely going to be more careful about how I carry valuables, especially when we are in cities from now on, but this isn't going to color my entire view of South Africa."

"Well, I really don't feel like going back to the Johannesburg bus station, and I don't think you do either. I know it goes against the grain since we have endeavored to do this journey overland as much as possible, but I suggest we fly to Cape Town tomorrow morning instead of spending twenty-four hours on a bus getting there."

I had a hard time closing my eyes that night. Even though Scott insisted he was not physically hurt, I kept thinking, what if he had struggled? What if they had stabbed him? I couldn't sleep until I encased Scott in a protective blanket by draping the left half of my body over his. For weeks after, I would barely let him out of my sight.

Since the mugging I had been telling everyone I met about it in an effort to get him or her to notice, I guess, that it seemed they were accepting crime and fear as a way of life, so when we arrived at the Kenyan Airways counter the next morning, I said to the agent, "My husband was jumped by four men and mugged at knifepoint yesterday." He looked up at me and said, "Welcome to South Africa."

SAFARI JEMA—CAPE TOWN (EXCUSE ME!) SOUTH AFRICA

After ten months, seventeen countries, and more bush taxis than I could count, we arrived in Cape Town, South Africa. Our journey through Africa was coming to an end. We were back in the first world of laundry machines, shopping malls, sidewalks, crosswalks, and streetlights.

It was strange being around so much in the way of Western conveniences and quantities again. Sometimes it was downright uncomfortable. After an almost steady diet of bland, unprocessed foods over ten months, the land of plenty had a price. We hit the First World Guaranteed to Bloat You Diet of rib eye, ice cream, hotdogs, and McDonald's so hard when we first arrived in Cape Town that the first page of our passports could contain the accurate observation and advice, "Looks gassy. Do not pull finger." I had serious thoughts about using my bloated condition to effect, particularly when it came to Cat Stevens music. I was sick of it. His music was everywhere. It drifted out of open car windows and it was piped into elevators. It permeated the mall at the Waterfront.

"If I hear 'Hey! Ride on the Peace Train' one more time, I vow to eat another rib eye and aim my musical end towards the DJ!" I told my husband, giving him fair warning.

There are advantages to the First World of course. I used a hairdryer for the first time in ten months—with far less dramatic effect than I thought. After I'd spent ten minutes making my hair fluffy and full of body like the woman in the Herbal Essence commercials, Scott came in and said, "I would have thought the first thing you would have wanted to do after ten months is use your hair dryer."

Doing laundry in a Laundromat instead of a sink (or bathtub) was kind of fun. And not having to roll my pant legs up before taking them down when squatting to use the toilet or more commonly, hole in the ground, was pretty good too. (Practical note: Travel the Third World before your knees give out. It would be quite impossible otherwise.)

And remember when that monkey jumped on our breakfast table in Ethiopia making my husband bite down hard on his fork while yelling, "Ya! Ya!" like John Wayne? Well, Scott was able to get his chipped front tooth fixed by a dentist in Cape Town, and it looks a beauty! But that was only the beginning of his dental woes. An X-ray taken by the dentist revealed an impacted wisdom tooth which prompted Scott to say, "No wonder my jaw has been aching," and me to say, "No wonder you've been so grumpy." The doctor, looking over the X-rays said, "Oh, this is bad. There is only one oral surgeon here in Cape Town that can do a complicated extraction such as the one you need, and he is on holiday for a month." So he gave Scott antibiotics and painkillers, enough to hold him until we would be back in America.

First World dentistry and reliable transportation aside, we agreed that we still preferred the African bush to the big developed cities. We were especially glad to be away from the civic disengagement that hung like a cloud over Johannesburg. Cape Town was the perfect antidote. It is a visually stunning city and a major tourist destination with plenty to keep us occupied during our last few days in Africa. We took the cable car up Table Mountain and, after a picnic at the top, spent hours hiking all the way down. Each evening (despite the side effects) we enjoyed the fine dining at the Waterfront, where beef was definitely beef. The area surrounding the Waterfront was so touristy and commercial I could have been in San Francisco or Sydney.

But all I had to do was listen to locals around me, and we were back in the Africa of my mind's eye because in addition to Afrikaans and English, the local language is Zulu, which has all the tongue click-ing. For example, "Kwa Zulu natal" is "click Zulu natal." I loved how it sounded but it was impossible for me to imitate. A man on a ferry tried to teach me a few Zulu words as we approached Robben Island where Nelson Mandela spent twenty-seven years in a tiny cell. As we toured the island and learned more about Mandela from guides who had also been political prisoners there, we came away with enormous respect for this remarkable man who lived his life with a mantra of patience and integrity and unburdened by bitterness. As everyone knows, Mandela went on to become the first president of post-apartheid South Africa.

We had been lucky to be in Cape Town several years earlier dur-ing the Rugby World Cup finals in 1995, a year after Mandela's elec-tion. The collective joy felt in Cape Town and all through southern Africa after South Africa claimed victory over New Zealand in the final match brought almost everyone to an apex of cooperation and kumbaya. There was more than just dancing in the street. Blacks and whites celebrated together and hugged one another in open joy. And oh, the singing! It was the kind of singing that you feel deep in your chest rather than hear with your ears. The World Cup win by the Springboks represented a united South Africa for the very first time in their history. There was a sense of renewal and hope, that things would be forever better thereafter in South Africa. We felt privileged to witness the start of a "new" country. Ten years later, we had to look hard for this sense of hope for the future, especially in places like Empangeni or Johannesburg.

At night we lay in bed and talked about our journey from Casablanca to Cape Town. We had a *safari jema*, a good journey. We thought about the people on the expedition and the Mechanic and felt sad that we had not made it all the way together. But traveling independently had given us so many more opportunities to meet local people in each of the countries we visited. We felt we better under-stood what it means to be nationally or tribally unique yet altogether

"African." Customs, cultures, architecture, and food changed as we moved from country to country, but there was a common thread of joy, hope, struggle, children, and music—always music—that ran through the continent with us. We felt grateful that we had the opportunity to learn more about a continent and her people, but we again came away with a feeling that Africa might never get the break she deserves. Many people are working hard to come up with ways to extend life expectancy, increase birth weights, and decrease death due to malaria and other diseases, but no one is smart enough, or rich enough, or powerful enough to take away the drought, or famine, or monsoon, or civil wars that continue to devastate millions and reverse any gains.

As always, the best part of Africa for me is her children. I remembered the time I sat in on a class in a rural schoolroom and learned all about goats. Everything there is to know about goats, those kids know. After class, I took a lot of photos, and when I showed the children their images on my digital camera, they fell on the ground laughing. Then we were all laughing. I held the camera up for another photo and they suddenly pulled straight faces, very serious. Again I showed them the photo and they fell on the ground laughing. I could never get a photo of them rolling on the ground laughing because as soon as I held up the camera, they pulled a passport-photo face.

I guess I have to keep my favorite memories of Africa, the images of kids laughing the hardest a kid can laugh, in my memory, not on my memory card.

FEELING GRATEFUL

Hurry-hurry has no blessings, so we came home slowly, by sea. We knew we needed more than a mere twelve hours on a plane to begin to wean ourselves from Africa, and we also hoped two weeks on a ship with a bunch of Westerners would ease us somewhat into the life that would await us back home.

The ship was far nicer than we anticipated. It felt strange at first to be surrounded by so much unnecessary decadence. We were astounded how quickly we became used to it! Each day during the fourteen-day crossing, we ate more, socialized more, and felt less and less out of place. Everything on the ship was first class. Well, except for the initial check in.

On sail away day, we walked to the ship wearing our backpacks. Some of our apparel had been with us for almost a year, so our clothes were clean but definitely faded around the edges. At the pier we were directed to a discolored tent in a very plain embarkation area. A member of the cruise staff approached us and said, "OK, you guys. Put your bags on the conveyer belt and wait here." Scott and I stood looking at each other thinking something just didn't seem right. Noticing our hesitation the man turned back and said slowly in an uh-oh voice, "Um...you *are* crew, aren't you?" When we laughed and said, "No. We're passengers!" groveling commenced at an astonishing speed.

"Merde!" swore the French staff member under his breath. "Permit me to take your bags! Right this way, madam..." From "you guys" to "madam" in less than thirty seconds. He led us to a spotless ivory colored check-in pavilion decked out in flowers, white tablecloths, champagne, and more groveling.

The best part of coming home by ship was that we didn't experience any jet lag. Also, since almost everyone on the ship spoke English, we got used to talking to other people again and gave the charade playing a rest. (Though I did have to perform charades with our Filipino cabin steward to get him to understand that the contraband gin in our fridge was for medicinal purposes and that it should under no circumstances be removed.) I would come home by ship again in a heartbeat. But I must first find a way to fit cruise attire into a backpack. I had the least belongings of any female, including the four-year-old little girl on board.

When we arrived home, the first question everyone asked was, "What's it like to be home again after being in Africa for so long?" It's a mixed bag. On the one hand it's really great seeing family and friends again. The neighborhood welcome-home dinners, catching up on news, and showing the tiny scar on the bottom of my foot were all great. On the other hand, reality sure does bite.

Imagine a year of unopened mail. For the most part, there were no really big surprises. It seems that I prepared and prepaid so completely before we left that we could have stayed in Africa forever and no one in the financial world would have noticed. However, there was one unexpected piece of news at the bottom of a mountain of mail. It was only three little initials, but it was enough to give me a blood pressure surge. IRS.

We paid our taxes before we left, five months before they were due, and our accountant filed our tax return on time in our absence. No problem. Except for one thing. Our signatures were missing.

The letter from the IRS went something like this: "Even though we received your return and cashed your income tax check, you didn't include a form authorizing your tax preparer to sign your return for you, so we do not consider your return officially filed." It went on to say that we owed a pretty substantial penalty.

I won't quote Scott's reaction. Your eyes might explode. But my husband is a clever guy. He called the IRS agent, explained that since we were out of the country for eleven months, would they consider waiving the fee in light of the fact that they received our tax return and cashed our income tax check.

"If you provide proof that you were in Africa, we may consider waiving the penalty," said the IRS agent with no conviction whatsoever. First we considered inviting him over to look at my foot. But I didn't feel like putting my size nines on display for a total stranger. Insect egg infestation is a very personal thing.

"Our passports were stolen in the mugging so we can't provide that as proof," said Scott. Then he smiled at me with that creative glint in his eye. "Why not send them a copy of your journal as proof? It's got names. It's got dates. It has savannah smear and elephant smoosh. It's even got labels off libations found only in Africa pasted in on blank pages! Not to mention the Cadbury chocolate wrappers and hospital receipts."

It worked. By return mail we had our refund check and "Wow!" handwritten on an attached sticky note.

As far as glitches go, I think it could have been worse. In fact, the emotion I most often feel since being back is grateful. I seem to be grateful for everything. I recommend a trip to rural Africa for anyone with a case of "poor me." I guarantee it will change your perspective. Many people in the developed world live bounteous lives without really appreciating it. If everyone knew how *most* of the world lives, I think there would be a whole lot more appreciation for what we do have. Sometimes we need to be reminded of the difference between want and need. We hear people say, "I *need* that gizmo," or, "I have that gizmo but I *need* a new one." I can relate. Or could. Before I went to Africa I really needed, uh, wanted, a Mercedes Gullwing, my dream car. After my time in Africa the words want, need, option, and choice have taken on new meaning. So often having and making choices every day seems to be viewed as an entitlement in America. Not happy? Switch jobs. Need a break? Vegas, here we come. Hungry? Use the ATM card and grab some takeout. Most have abundance of choice here in Silicon Valley. Whims are usually fulfilled in pretty short order.

In most of rural Africa, luxuries, narcissism, and idle consumerism are inconceivable concepts. There are no "spa days" or "time off just for *me* days." There is no such thing as urban ennui. Try to explain to a rural African that a leaner body, whiter teeth, greater status, more attention (from people they don't even know!), or more *things* are relentless pursuits for many in the developed world, and they will think you are joking. The unending cycle of mere existence occupies most of the waking hours for the majority of Africans. This isn't to say that most rural Africans don't desire things. But the things they most want usually aren't for sale. They want their children to be healthy and to attend school. They want clean water to drink and to be free from disease and famine.

It's not uncommon to come back from Africa with strong impulses to help her in some way, and I wasn't immune to the urge. After ten months it was clear to me that the best thing I could do for Africa would be to help her children, especially her girls, receive an education. If girls in developing nations are able to attend school, all sorts of good things start to happen. They become more aware of their rights and make better life choices. They delay marriage and delay starting a family, and when they do have children, their babies are healthier. More and more charitable organizations and NGOs such as UNICEF, Oxfam, Room to Read, and The Campaign for Female Education recognize that providing for a girl's education is a productive and efficient way to make positive changes in the lives of *all* Africans. Investing in the education of a girl in a developing nation is the single best investment you can make there. When you pay the school fees for a girl in Africa, you contribute to the development of a whole continent in the process.

As I dove headfirst back into life in California, the number of choices I could make in a day overwhelmed me. And because we arrived during the Christmas shopping season, we were bombarded by consumerism at its peak. Seeing the stacks of useless never-to-decompose imports crowding the aisles and shelves during a trip to Costco, I actually became nauseated.

Still I was glad to be home. I had missed my family like crazy. Whenever I wanted to remember the "realness" of Africa, I merely needed to gaze at the six-foot tall giraffe named Cuthbert that sits in our entryway, or visit my mom. In fact, the best part of being home was getting to have a nice long cuddle with my ninety-year-old mom after so many months away. It was even better than camping at Flat Dogs. And it turned out that serendipity extends beyond African borders. We were lucky to come home in time to have a good many cuddles with my mom before she died just a few months after our return. Unbelievably, the day Mom entered hospice was the same day my eldest brother Mike was given the news that he had terminal cancer with six months left to live. We are indescribably grateful for the time we had with both he and my mom before they died.

So that's what it was like "being" home. Mentally "staying" home is still difficult. While my backyard is not as exotic as Timbuktu or the Ngorongoro Crater, the raptors (hawks) overhead are diving at the prolific game (squirrel) population, the sun is shining, and sundowners are but a few hours away, so if I squint really hard I can imagine I am in one of the more developed African countries that we visited such as... No, I can't squint that hard.

Friends called to say they heard more from us when we were in Africa than they do now. It's just that compared to rafting the Zambezi, or getting chased by an elephant, or petting a lion, nothing much newsworthy happens. Mostly we preoccupied ourselves adjusting (poorly) to being back home. For me adjusting consisted of thinking about Africa and thinking about being back in Africa every day. I tried to get back in the swing of things by remembering how much I wanted a Mercedes Gullwing before the trip, but even that didn't work. I didn't want it anymore.

We gave a slide show presentation about our ten months in Africa for Scott's mom and the residents of the senior living apartments where she lived. It went better than I expected. Everyone enjoyed it, and Scott's mom was surprised by the number of people who came to talk to her about "her kids who went to Africa" and how "delightful" (me) and "informative" (Scott) our presentation was. When I demonstrated for the crowd how we did laundry bent over a bucket while squatting on the ground, the wince was audible. Anyway, no one fell asleep or had to go to the john during our presentation.

In the weeks and months after we arrived home, we were asked many questions about our journey. We never tired of talking about Africa and, as anyone who has completed a journey of the heart knows, we endeavored to hang on to the travel glow for as long as possible. In addition to the presentation to Scott's mom and her senior friends, we gave slide show presentations entitled "Casablanca to Cape Town— Ten Months Overland through Africa" at REI outdoor recreation outfitters around the Bay Area and to family and friends at home. We were even asked to give a talk to APTA, The Association for Promotion of Tourism to Africa, which included agents from the high-end safari specialists, Abercrombie & Kent. Since clients who book with Abercrombie & Kent usually aren't the market that rides around in bush taxis or sleeps on the ground, they had requested us purely for entertainment value. After the presentation, one travel agent came up to me and said, "Dear, you and your husband certainly are adventurous and fun loving. But I suggest you don't talk about crowded transportation, disease, bugs, and malaria. It will make people not want to go to Africa."

I looked at her and knew that unless she had the opportunity to someday take a full-to-capacity bush taxi from Gambia to Senegal and a sweet little boy tells her he loves her while discarding pits all over her lap, she wouldn't understand. I said it anyway, "But that's what makes it so real."

EPILOGUE

Since writing this book we have spent another 300 nights under canvas in Africa. We traveled overland from Cairo across Sudan and down the Rift Valley to Nairobi and transited Lake Tanganyika on the oldest continuously operating passenger ferry in the world. A year ago, in Zambia, we volunteered for a month as construction managers for Bridges to Prosperity, the non-profit we first learned about during that two-day train ride from Dar es Salaam to Lusaka. Camping on the grounds of the school, working on the bridge, and enjoying countless classrooms in the sand with children from surrounding villages turned out to be our most rewarding African experience to date and we consider the people of Kamunjoma our second family.

In 2013 we picked up the thread of our dream once again. Just weeks after publications of this book we purchased a 1973 Series III Land Rover in Cape Town. For fifteen months we traveled through South and East Africa and points beyond.

Best of all, I'm happy to report that serendipity is alive and well. Today a man who grew up in what is my home today stopped by to share some memories of the house and neighborhood. He didn't remember me, but I grew up near this neighborhood too and played in his yard as a kid. We spent an hour talking about our childhoods — the ocelot that lived in the big pink house on the corner, playing in the giant orange tumbler in the front yard, having dirt clod fights, and building forts on vacant lots. In my kitchen he spied the many photos of Africa I have attached to our fridge and said with a smile, "Oh, I see you have the Mal de Afrique (the Africa bug) too", and promptly invited us to stay at his home on Lamu, an island off the Swahili Coast of Kenya.

Stay tuned! There are sure to be many more African adventures to come.

ACKNOWLEDGEMENTS

From the time he read the first e-mail sent from sub-Saharan Africa, to the last sent ten months later in Cape Town, South Africa, my neighbor and role model Ed Hodges encouraged me to write a book about the journey.

A big thanks goes to my friends and family. Your patience and support when it comes to our travel addiction can't be measured. For all the times we have said, "We would love to come, if we are in town!" we ask forgiveness. We are indebted that you keep asking anyway.

To my wonderful neighbors, Keith, Julie, Ramona, Carol, Betty, Judy, Sabrina, Dave, Elizabeth, Clay, Lisa, Ron, Cat, Ai, and all the rest, we are grateful to live among such generous and caring beings. The phrase, "You can count on me!" was invented in College Park. Thanks for the support. And to my wonderful brothers Joe and Sean, thanks for all the love and support that you give me everyday.

To Ross and Marilyn Jackson, and especially to my mother-in-law Jane who said, "You should write a book about this!"—thanks for the encouragement.

I am indebted to Larry Habeggar who helped me realize the thread that runs through all my stories.

Special thanks go to our dear friend Dr. Barbara Newman and to our exceptional physician Dr. Creger who both try to keep us healthy while we are on the road and, in the case of Dr. Ceger, bombards us wisely with lab tests once we return home. We like it that you admire what we do even though you think we are crazy to do it.

Most thanks go to Scott, the man who puts the "lust" in wanderlust. I can't wait for our next adventure!

Finally, to you the Reader—the greatest gift you can give an author is a positive review. I am truly honored that you took the time to read Safari Jema. I hope you enjoyed taking the adventure with us and look forward to reading your feedback on Amazon or at the bookstore where you purchased Safari Jema. Thank you!

ABOUT THE AUTHOR

Teresa O'Kane lives and writes from around the world and from her home in San Jose, California. She has restored old homes, owned and managed a small business, sailed a catamaran to Hawaii, lived in Africa, and travelled the seven continents all with her lover and husband (same person) Scott. She earned her degree in Economics from the University of Hawaii, which is where she learned to see the humor in life and commerce and that experiences, not things, have the greatest value. Safari Jema is her first book. Watch for the second book in the series due out in 2015, Dream Safari, Around Africa in a Forty Year Old Land Rover.

teresaokane@gmail.com

You can read more travel stories and follow my next adventure on my website teresaokane.blogspot.com and at facebook.com/safarijema and

twitter.com/trisokane

APPENDIX

How Can I Do This and, What Was That You Said About Dual Citizenship?

You may be wondering by now how we manage to travel for such long periods and how you might do the same. If you think we get so much time off because we are sitting around on lots of disposable income or that we are trust fund babies, you would be wrong. What makes it possible that we can, and do, travel the world is that we have the will to do it. Most people don't have the desire to pitch their own tent in Africa and sleep on the ground, or take a sixteen-hour hot, sticky, crowded bus ride, or sit on a sack of potatoes all day in an open truck on a rutted, dusty road just to get to a new destination, but we do. We have a strong desire to do that.

We wouldn't be able to travel for such extended periods if we didn't lease out our house in our absence. We lease our home fully furnished, with linens, utensils, pots and pans, wine glasses, and cookbooks in place. Our personal items go into boxes and into a small study off our bedroom that we exclude from the lease. Everything else stays in the house. We've never paid for a commercial storage unit during our absence. They are far too costly, and moving belongings back and forth is too time-consuming. We recognize that it's just furniture, just stuff, and spend the time instead planning our trip and visiting with friends and family who we will miss while we are away.

It usually takes some time to find the right tenant. Our house is pretty nice, and we care what happens to it. If we take the time to find the right family to live in our home while we are gone, we find that they usually treat it as their own. The main thing is, you don't need to sell your home to do this! Some people think this is their only option, and they come back after a year with nowhere to live. In some cities the income you receive from renting your house can even cover your mortgage expense plus a portion of your travel costs. I know not everyone lives in a good rental market, but you can lease your house for *something* and still travel the world, if you are willing to do it on a budget.

If you don't yet own your own home, you have to be committed to squirrel away every dime of disposable income. Think about downsizing your apartment or moving in with family or friends for a time to save money. Most of the Europeans we know who travel for a year or more take this tack to achieve their goals.

You might worry that your bills won't get paid on time if you are gone for months on end. In this day of e-mail, Internet cafés, and online banking, it's simple to keep track of your financial life back home. You can check your bank and credit card balances or pay bills online almost weekly, if you want to. And with Skype, you can call almost anywhere in the world from Internet cafés if you prefer person-to-person contact.

Even before the Internet, when we did our first long trip, I was able to arrange directly with my bank for the bills to be paid automatically from our checking account each month. The few bills we had were paid on time, and I never had to worry.

When we had pets, we had to find a home for them while we were gone. My parents (when they were alive and healthy) took them in and cared for them with as much love as we would. I know not everyone is lucky to have such a supportive family, but you would be surprised who will offer to help you if you just ask and if you are open to the possibilities.

We weren't fortunate enough to have them, but if we had children we would have taken them around the world with us. There is no better education than showing your children other cultures and how the rest of the world lives. We've encountered many families with children of all ages doing extended travel, even in the most difficult places. We met families on safari in Africa and a single parent trekking with children in the Himalayas. What could be better than home schooling from the top of the Acropolis or from a canoe in the Okavango?

The main thing is to put yourself in the mindset that you can do it. Start by selling things you don't use or need. Cancel magazines you never read. Get your energy bill down by installing efficient bulbs or appliances. It saves you money, and it helps the environment. We drive older model cars that we paid cash for. No, they are not flash. But I wouldn't trade a night at Flat Dogs for a new BMW. Experiences, not things, are what make us happy.

When we are home and have a project, we work long hours. We stay focused on why we are working, and it gets us through even the toughest days. We set up our lives so that we can take on projects that have a start and end date. When the project is done, we are done and it's time to go traveling.

You may be saying, "I've got a job, I can't leave it for more than two or three weeks a year." That's true. But you could fly to lots of places in the world for a few weeks each year and still travel on a budget. You just need to engage your imagination. I know of some teacher couples that can and do travel for two months every year. There are some companies that offer sabbaticals. There are job-sharing opportunities that could be negotiated. If you want to do this, you have to be creative, you need to plan your life out, not just let it happen. Scott often asks friends after they start a new job, "How much vacation time did you get?" They sometimes don't even know! Most workers in Europe, Australia, and New Zealand wouldn't dream of starting a new job without negotiating sufficient holidays. Make it a priority to make time for yourself and your family to see the world and pursue what interests you.

I'm always amused when someone says with a tone of smug victim, "Gee, we'd sure like to do that, but we're not as lucky as you. We have never taken more than two weeks off." That they say this after complaining about the mortgage on their newer and bigger house from the seat of a thousand-dollar recliner or brand new leather upholstered car always makes me think, "Hey! No complaining from the yacht!" If you commit to scaling down and simplifying, and being satisfied with less, you will wonder why you ever had all that stuff you thought you couldn't live without in the first place.

Changing your goals to include travel is mostly a case of long-term thinking and knowing what is really important to you, then taking the steps to make it happen. During the 2009 economic downturn, many of our friends took a good look at what they needed, versus what they wanted, and made some pretty big changes in their lives. Do any of us really need the latest import from China cluttering up our yards, or rooms, or closets, or driveways, or God forbid, costly storage lockers? We find, and you might too, that the fewer things we feel we *must* have in life and the more simply we live, the more control we have over our destinies and the happier we are. Besides, the more you travel, the less you seem to need or want.

A belief among some economists these days is that we need to spend our way out of recessions. If you believe that too, why not spend your dollars on experiences instead of things? Travel, even in your own country, gives one a chance try new customs and cuisines and to see firsthand that there are lots of different ways to live. With that you gain more understanding of our world and that can be a force for change.

One aspect that made our trip uniquely easier and a little less expensive, at least at border crossings, was that we were able to travel under Irish Passports. I can hear you now, "Wait. Aren't you Americans?

How did you get Irish passports?" Like many things in my life, it all started over a craving for bacon and a desire to make my dad happy.

About ten years ago, my father phoned me and said, "Tris, I'd really like it if you would come to the Irish breakfast with me." San Jose, California, and Dublin, Ireland, are "sister" cities, and all people of Irish decent in San Jose are encouraged to attend a breakfast at a local hotel once a year to honor this family tie. I didn't know then the amount of money we would save as we traveled around Africa just because I attended an Irish Breakfast that morning.

"Um, OK, Dad," I responded. Though I wasn't sure I would be able to endure a room full of Irishmen at eight in the morning, I never could say no to his enthusiasm. "Will there be bacon?" I added hopefully.

As soon as we arrived, the Irish consul general approached me and said, "Have you got ye Irish passport yet, Lass?"

"I can't get an Irish passport. I wasn't born in Ireland. Besides, I haven't had my coffee yet," I said trying to continue my forward motion toward the massive copper-colored coffee urn across the room.

"That doesn't matter!" he said ignoring my need for caffeine. "Were either of your grandparents born in Ireland?"

I began to feel like I was being rushed by a Gaelic fraternity. "Oh, yes. Both my grandparents on my father's side were born in Ireland."

"Well then! Your father is an Irish citizen. And through him you can claim citizenship of your own. Are you married?" I nodded. "Through you, your husband can obtain citizenship as well."

"Are you asking me…to pledge?" I asked as I finally reached the coffee bar.

He took out his card and said, "Look. Here is the number of the Irish Consulate in San Francisco. Call on Monday morning and ask them to send you an application for citizenship."

On Monday I phoned the consulate as instructed and two days later I received an application in the mail to become an Irish citizen.

The application was about sixteen pages long and required, among other things, that I obtain original birth, marriage, and death certificates of my grandparents from Ireland. In my grandmother's case I had to track down her records on the wee island of Inis Meain (or Inish Man) in the Aran Isles. The Aran Isles, located at the extreme west of Ireland, was once poetically described as the "three stepping stones out of Europe."

When I submitted my passport application, a woman at the consulate said, "We are swamped with requests for citizenship. Even Marlon Brando has applied!" It was eighteen months before I actually had my Irish passport in hand, but it is one of the best things I've ever done for myself. We saved hundreds of dollars in visa fees in Africa by using our Irish passports. Not only that, the documents I received from Ireland pertaining to my grandparents were fascinating, heartwarming, priceless. I never met any of my grandparents, so being able to read and hold a copy of their birth and marriage certificates made me feel close to them. With a little piece of her history in hand, I was inspired to learn how my grandmother lived in the Aran Islands.

After I obtained my passport, Scott and I took a trip to Ireland with the intention of getting to know the land of my ancestors while circling the country on our bicycles. However we didn't take into account the many peninsulas, short steep hills, and strong winds along the route, and after three weeks on our bikes, we had barely taken a nibble out of Ireland. In twenty-one days cycling the coastal route, we managed to ride only from Cork to Galway. It would have been only a two-day ride if we took the direct route right across the country. Our intent had been to cycle the entire country on the coastal route, but given the many long fingers of land jutting into the ocean, it would have taken months. Vowing to come back and complete the circuit some day, we moved on to the main reason we had come to Ireland in the first place. We had some roots to dig up. From Doolin, south of Galway, we took a boat to Inis Meain to see if we could find my grandmother's house.

Ireland and the United States have a special relationship. It's quite common for Irish descendents to return to the "old country" to trace their roots. Upon arrival in Ireland, Americans are usually greeted with a smile and, "You'll be wanting to know where your uncle (father, grandfather, etc.) lived, isn't that right now?"

It was that way for us upon arrival in Inis Meain. We were on the island less than an hour before everyone knew who we were and where we were from. The proprietress at our guesthouse suggested we visit the pub, the only pub in town, to see if any of the old regulars remembered my grandmother or great-grandmother.

We found three ancient Irishmen sitting together at the bar. When we introduced ourselves and said why we were there, one of the men said he remembered my great-grandmother sitting on her stoop taking snuff. A memorable image to be sure, and I was content if that was all I would come away with. But the more Guinness we bought him, the more he remembered. By the time we left the pub, I had a sense of what kind of woman my great grandmother was—or how the Irishman remembered her anyway.

We walked the cliff path, passing countless low rock walls built along narrow winding paths that crisscross the island. We ended at a high rocky outcrop reputed to be a spot favored by the author John Millington Synge. He wrote that the Aran Islands were the last outpost of ancient Europe, a place where traditional Irish culture still exists. And it does. As we looked down at all the short stone fences spread out over the quiet island below us, we felt we had taken a step back in time.

It was nearing dusk, so we began strolling back to the pub. Walking towards us up the path was an old man dressed in quintessential Irish fashion in wool suit and hat, hunched over a shillelagh. Periodically he lifted his head to check our progress. When we met, he stopped directly in front of me, leaned on his cane and began to sing a song in Gaelic. Then with a broad smile and a twinkle in his eyes he said,

"Now, that's a song about your great uncles who were the finest stone fence builders in all of Ireland. We still sing about them in the pub today." I got all choked up.

The next day the postmistress of the island took us to the gravesite of one of my great uncles and showed us the spot where my grandmother's house had stood. Now it is a pile of stones and grass. Before we left the island, she presented us with a tape recording in Gaelic, with translation in English, of the song about my great uncles.

"These are my people!" I said to Scott, feeling more Irish by the minute. Something about that visit to the Aran Islands tapped into an emotional, nostalgic side of my being. I gazed at the Irish coastline with tears in my eyes and said, "I have a sudden craving for snuff."

The advantages to dual citizenship are many. First, we paid a lot less in visa fees when presenting our Irish passports. In some cases, countries base their fee for entry on arbitrary reasoning. When a country has friendly relations with another, the fee is conventional. Countries such as Great Britain and the United States, however, are sometimes charged fees that seem almost usurious. Some of the more disgruntled former British colonies in Africa charge British tourists the highest visa fees on the world chart. It's the same with the United States. When the United States began limiting the number of Brazilian visa applications that would be processed, the visa fee for a U.S. citizen wishing to travel to Brazil rose to $130. The next highest visa fee for entry to Brazil, $65, is charged to Canadians. Most other countries, including Ireland, pay only $20. We were once at a border, I think it was Pakistan, with several British citizens who complained that the exorbitant visa fee they had just been required to pay exactly matched the cricket score that the Brits had run up in a recent game against Pakistan, "even after Britain was assured victory!" chastised the border official. Irish were allowed in for free.

Apart from the money we saved, it came in very handy after Scott was mugged in South Africa and our Irish passports were stolen, because we were able to continue traveling on our U.S. passports. And whenever we arrive in Europe, we just hold up our Irish passport and breeze through the European Union line instead of the lengthy "all others" line. Sad to say, it also has come in handy when we are feeling attacked just for being Americans. Of course, we look and sound American. But debating America foreign policy is simply not that rewarding overseas and the less we have to do it, the happier we are. So when we stand at a hotel desk or border crossing after one or another American president raises the ire of the rest of the world with an unpopular new policy and we present our Irish passports instead of the U.S. ones, the desk clerk or border official goes from glowering at us to welcoming us with open arms.

It's discouraging that some people feel that way about America. Though when they finish their rant they usually always add, "We like the American people. We just don't like your government." I love my country, so of course hearing things like that gives me angst. During a trip before we had our Irish passports, we were almost not allowed into Zambia "because of the policies of your government!" It took some cajoling but we managed to turn "No entries until you change your policies!" into a hundred-dollar visa fee, and ultimately to a more normal ten-dollar fee and we were admitted. We allowed the border official, whose tone had softened during our exchange, the last word with the predictable, "We like the American people. We just don't like your *government.*"

It goes both ways, though. You never know when someone will come up and hug you just for being an American. The Kurds in Turkey wanted to shake our hands when they found out we were Americans because the United States sometimes protects and supports Kurds. And in Madagascar people said, "Thank you! Your government gave our country $20 million for new road construction!" We had no idea we were so generous. When Ghanaians learned we were from America they said, "Your former president George (H. W.) Bush is a good man!

He ended the war in Liberia." Sometimes I learn more about what my government has done when I am outside my own country.

We don't have exchanges like this when we use our Irish passports. Wherever we go, (except maybe for some countries in the EU) people seem to love the Irish. Or at least, they don't have anything against them.

In 1995, during a four-month trip across Europe and the Middle East to Nepal, before we had Irish passports, Iran was on the itinerary. We tried to get visas before we left California, but it proved difficult due to iffy U.S.-Iranian relations at the time (so what else is new?) We tried several times while in transit to obtain a visa, and at one point Iranian officials indicated they would be willing to issue us visas as long as we agreed to pay three hundred dollars each for them. As expensive as that seemed, paying the fee and going through Iran would have saved us the cost of flying over Iran to Pakistan. It would also have saved us the cost of accommodation for a week while we waited for our group to catch up. But before we were able to obtain the visa, politics and world events denied us our chance. Right about the time we were applying, the United States imposed a trade embargo on Iran. The United States successfully blocked a Russian agreement with Iran to finish construction of two nuclear reactors south of Teheran. The next time we contacted the Iranian embassy, they said they would not issue visas to us under any circumstances. If we had Irish passports at the time, they would have said, "Welcome! Come on in!" In the end we were glad that we had to cool our heels in Quetta for a week while waiting for our group, because that's when we had the opportunity to have tea with Muhammad and his family.

Aside from Irish, the best passport to carry for travel seems to be Danish. We traveled for a time with a group of five young Danish women who rarely ever had to pay a visa fee. They also carried student cards (my husband called it the good-looking Dane card), which they flashed at museums, archeological sites, and parks to get in free.

We have saved probably close to a thousand dollars by presenting our Irish passports at border crossings. Be clear, though, I'm not unpatriotic. I'm frugal! Scott has managed to infect me with thriftiness second to none, except Scott of course.

The only hard part about being an Irish citizen is that everyone wants to discuss Ireland's latest rugby, cricket, or football scores with us. They can't fathom how we can be so uninformed about Irish sports, and that can be a sticky wicket.